Bar Harbor Babylon

MURDER, MISFORTUNE, and SCANDAL on MOUNT DESERT ISLAND

DAN and LESLIE LANDRIGAN

Down East Books
Camden, Maine

Down East Books

An imprint of The Rowman & Littlefield Publishing Group, Inc.
4501 Forbes Blvd., Ste. 200
Lanham, MD 20706
www.rowman.com

Distributed by NATIONAL BOOK NETWORK

Maps by Melissa Baker

British Library Cataloguing in Publication Information available

Library of Congress Cataloging-in-Publication Data

Names: Landrigan, Dan, author. | Landrigan, Leslie, author.
Title: Bar Harbor Babylon : murder, misfortune, and scandal on Mount Desert Island / Dan and Leslie Landrigan.
Description: Camden, Maine : Down East Books, 2019. | Includes bibliographical references and index.
Identifiers: LCCN 2018051996 (print) | LCCN 2018059539 (ebook) | ISBN 9781608939022 (Electronic) | ISBN 9781608939015 (cloth : alk. paper) | ISBN 9781608939022 (e-book)
Subjects: LCSH: Mount Desert Island (Me.)—History—Anecdotes. | Mount Desert Island (Me.) —Social life and customs—Anecdotes. | Scandals—Maine—Mount Desert Island—Anecdotes.
Classification: LCC F27.M9 (ebook) | LCC F27.M9 L27 2019 (print) | DDC 974.1/45—dc23
LC record available at https://lccn.loc.gov/2018051996

♾️™ The paper used in this publication meets the minimum requirements of American National Standard for Information Sciences—Permanence of Paper for Printed Library Materials, ANSI/ NISO Z39.48-1992.

Printed in the United States of America

CONTENTS

CONTENTS

Crimes and Misdemeanors

Oddities, Misfits, and Miscellaneous Downfalls

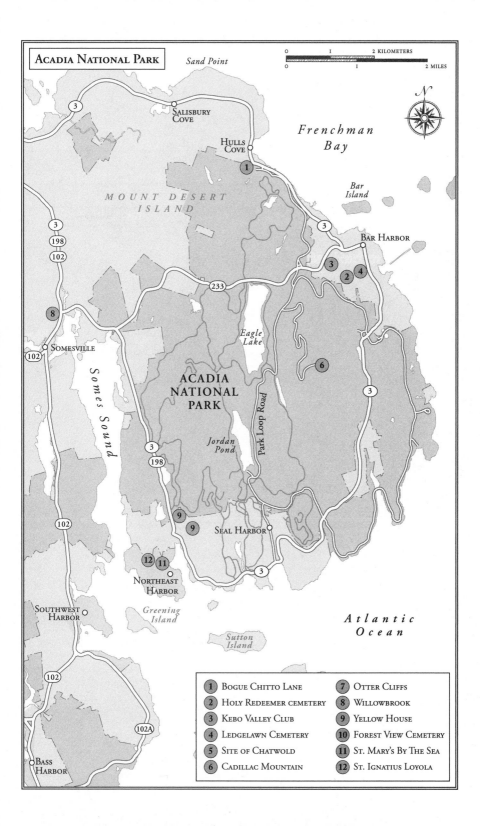

ACADIA NATIONAL PARK

Sand Point

0   1   2 KILOMETERS
0   1   2 MILES

N

Salisbury Cove

Hulls Cove

Frenchman Bay

Bar Island

MOUNT DESERT ISLAND

Bar Harbor

233

Eagle Lake

Somesville

Somes Sound

ACADIA NATIONAL PARK

Park Loop Road

Jordan Pond

Seal Harbor

Northeast Harbor

Southwest Harbor

Greening Island

Sutton Island

Atlantic Ocean

Bass Harbor

1   Bogue Chitto Lane   7   Otter Cliffs
2   Holy Redeemer cemetery   8   Willowbrook
3   Kebo Valley Club   9   Yellow House
4   Ledgelawn Cemetery   10   Forest View Cemetery
5   Site of Chatwold   11   St. Mary's By The Sea
6   Cadillac Mountain   12   St. Ignatius Loyola

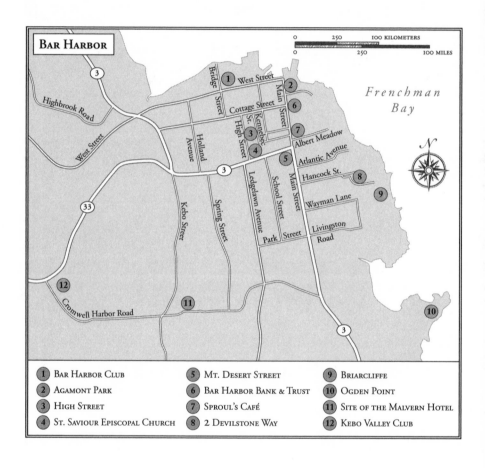

BAR HARBOR

0   250   100 KILOMETERS
0   250   100 MILES

Frenchman Bay

3

Highbrook Road

West Street

Bridge Street

West Street

1 West Street

Cottage Street

Main Street

2

6

St. Kennebec

High Street

Holland Avenue

3

4

7

Albert Meadow

5 Atlantic Avenue

Hancock St.

8

9

3

Ledgelawn Avenue

School Street

Main Street

Wayman Lane

33

Kebo Street

Spring Street

Park Street

Livingston Road

12

11

Cromwell Harbor Road

3

10

1 Bar Harbor Club	**5** Mt. Desert Street	**9** Briarcliffe
2 Agamont Park	**6** Bar Harbor Bank & Trust	**10** Ogden Point
3 High Street	**7** Sproul's Café	**11** Site of the Malvern Hotel
4 St. Saviour Episcopal Church	**8** 2 Devilstone Way	**12** Kebo Valley Club

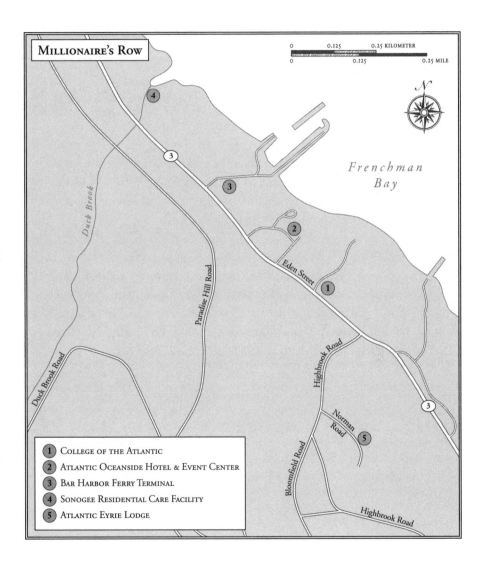

MILLIONAIRE'S ROW

0   0.125   0.25 KILOMETER
0   0.125   0.25 MILE

*Frenchman
Bay*

Duck Brook

Paradise Hill Road

Eden Street

Duck Brook Road

Highbrook Road

Norman
Road

Bloomfield Road

Highbrook Road

1. COLLEGE OF THE ATLANTIC
2. ATLANTIC OCEANSIDE HOTEL & EVENT CENTER
3. BAR HARBOR FERRY TERMINAL
4. SONOGEE RESIDENTIAL CARE FACILITY
5. ATLANTIC EYRIE LODGE

INTRODUCTION

For nearly a century, a stream of wealthy summer visitors turned Mount Desert Island into a Petri dish for scandal and intrigue.

Artists were among the first tourists to come. Hudson River School painters like Frederic Church and Thomas Cole captured in oil the grandeur of the mountains next to the sea. Their paintings, sold in city galleries, inspired people to come see for themselves the beauty of Mount Desert Island. And the trouble began.

Camps gave way to hotels, and hotels begat cottages, and cottages grew into miniature palaces as the influx of summer visitors grew ever richer and more ostentatious until, inevitably, the resort's status faded.

Creating a comprehensive catalog of the scandals that touched the island would fill ten books. In *Bar Harbor Babylon* we offer a sampling of the tales of excess, political shenanigans, marital intrigue, and outright criminal antics that fascinated tourists and locals alike over the years.

In its heyday, the visitors to Mount Desert Island enjoyed the salacious details of high-society scandals almost as much as the fresh air and beautiful vistas of the region. We hope you will find them entertaining, as well.

It's a Rich Man's World

The Man Who Stole Cadillac Mountain

IF GEORGE DORR IS THE FATHER OF ACADIA NATIONAL PARK, JOHN Stewart Kennedy is its rich uncle—and one of the black sheep of the founding fathers of Acadia. As Mount Desert's opulent Cottage Age was beginning to crumble, Dorr was casting about for donors to preserve the island's natural beauty. Kennedy avidly supported the effort. More importantly, with his millions, he could help pay for it. When Dorr needed a check written for some piece of land or other, Kennedy proved a soft touch. A philanthropist who funded many charities in his home city of New York, his largesse also extended to his summer community—or at least one of them—at Bar Harbor. When Kennedy died, he left an estate worth $67 million. Of that, $25 million went to charity and $35 million to his widow.

Kennedy bought the summit of what we now call Cadillac Mountain for Dorr. And when Dorr needed money to acquire Pickett Mountain and part of Champlain Mountain, Kennedy again agreed to fund the purchase. Before it could be bought, however, Kennedy took ill in 1909. On his deathbed he whispered to his wife: "Remember . . . that I promised Mr. Dorr . . . to help him get that land." And so Mr. Dorr got his land.

Kennedy made his generosity seem gracious and effortless. But perhaps it's easier to give away money when you stole it in the first place.

Though some of Kennedy's wealth was the product of hard work, his biographers explain that his big score came from swindling his richest and most trusting clients.

Early biographies of Kennedy, probably influenced by his family, tend to put his business practices in a positive light. The *National Cyclopaedia of American Biography*, a collection of biographical articles based on questionnaires sent to relatives, notes: "He "won an enviable reputation for clean and safe methods and a dignified and exalted standard of business ethics." Unfortunately, it's a bit of stretch. Kennedy made his money as a banker, but he was not known for his business ethics.

The Man Who Got the Money

Kennedy was a Scot, born into a family of modest means in 1830 and raised in Glasgow, a booming Industrial Age city. He had little formal education by today's standards, but for the times his public schooling put him well above most children his age.

He started his working life at thirteen as a shipping clerk. He then got a job as a manufacturer's representative, selling to railroads for the Glasgow branch of a London iron firm. Like most ambitious businessmen of his day, he set his sights on America. So, at the age of twenty, the company sent him to New York.

In New York, John Stewart Kennedy found a banking firm that took him on. He was ready when opportunity knocked in the form of a deep recession caused by the Panic of 1873.

In September of 1873 the bank Cooke & Co. failed. Founded by financier Jay Cooke, the firm had been built on Cooke's deals with Treasury Secretary Salmon Chase. Cooke sold war bonds to support the Union Army during the Civil War and pocketed enormous profits for himself.

Convinced of his financial genius and backed by wealthy investors, Cooke plunged into railroad stocks. His goal was to build a second intercontinental railroad to the Pacific Northwest through the Midwest. Cooke, however, was not as smart as he thought. Along the way he managed to bring down a government in Canada with his shady practices. And when he discovered that he was overextended—to put it mildly—in his railroad investments, he shuttered his bank and declared its insolvency.

The fallout was enormous. A panic on Wall Street ensued. The stock market closed for two days, and America's giant banks took a hard look at their books and discovered (surprise) that they, too, were overinvested in valueless railroads. One by one they toppled. As the financial crisis worsened, America sank into a long depression. Commercial activity slowed, building construction stopped, and companies cut workers' wages. Labor unrest spread, and in 1877, one hundred people were killed during riots and police violence in a nationwide railroad strike.

Cooke's railroads went bankrupt. Most of the partners in his firm escaped serious losses, having moved their money elsewhere because they knew of the impending failure. The naive investors, however, were not so lucky. Far away in Holland, Cooke's major Dutch investors had millions invested in his railroads. They began looking for a man they could trust to help steer them out of the mess. They turned to John Stewart Kennedy.

On the surface, Kennedy seemed like the perfect man for the job. He was an anchor of calm experience in a storm of business collapses, labor strikes, violence, and depression. He'd cut his teeth selling steel to the railroads, and he knew the pennies and nickels of the business, not just the Wall Streeter's view.

The Dutch syndicate was baffled to find its investment insolvent. Eight years earlier in 1865, the Dutch investors had pulled the St. Paul and Pacific Railroad from bankruptcy. They held majority ownership with bonds that had a face value of $28 million. The railroad had five hundred miles of track and millions of acres of land pledged to it. And no word of financial trouble had been communicated to its investors. Was it possible the management had plundered the railroad so savagely that it was broke and insolvent again after just a few years?

It was possible.

From Bad to Worse

In 1875, the bankruptcy court appointed a steamboat operator named J. P. Farley to run the railroad while it sorted out the remains of the company. Kennedy, speaking for the Dutch investors, had given Farley his blessing. He and Farley had worked together finding railroad investments in the 1860s, and Kennedy knew him well.

While the public perceived the railroad as a boondoggle, a group of four men knew otherwise. The St. Paul and Pacific had valuable land grants and access to the growing cities of the Pacific Northwest, which were in dire need of better railroads. If someone actually built the railroad, rather than simply robbing it of its wealth, a formidable business was possible.

Led by James J. Hill, known as the "Empire Builder," the four men wanted to buy the railroad. But first they had to get it away from the Dutch. What ensued was a three-way tug-of-war. The Dutch owned the railroad and wanted their $28 million. Hill had the experience and political connections to make the railroad go, but he didn't have $28 million to buy it. And Farley wanted to run the railroad for himself.

John Stewart Kennedy faced an interesting temptation. He could make all efforts to recover money for his Dutch clients. Or, if he could dupe the Dutch into thinking the railroad was worthless, he might turn the railroad into his own personal gravy train. Michael Malone, in his book *James J. Hill: Empire Builder of the Northwest*, summarizes the dilemma: "As for Kennedy, even by the easy moral standards of the Gilded Age, he obviously had a glaring conflict of interest on his hands." But not for long.

Kennedy cast his lot with Hill and his partners. He persuaded the Dutch investors that their best chance to get anything for their bonds was to sell out to Hill and his group. They proposed buying the bonds for as little as thirteen cents on the dollar. The Dutch investors went for it hook, line, and sinker. Their $28 million in bonds netted them just $4.3 million.

Quick as a wink, Hill, now owner of the bonds, foreclosed on the railroad. Now he owned a railroad worth tens of millions of dollars free and clear. Kennedy, for lying to the Dutch, demanded payment of $100,000. Hill and his partners agreed to pay him $80,000 in cash. But Hill's real payment to Kennedy for clearing out his Dutch clients was a one-fifth share of the new railroad.

"Contemporary wisdom had it that the Dutch got bilked," Malone concludes, which "surely is at least half-truth."

The little swindle didn't go without a hitch, however. Hill, Kennedy, and their associates found themselves in hot water with two injured parties. A small group of bondholders hadn't gone along with the Dutch. They sued the Hill-Kennedy group, charging fraud. Eventually they forced Hill to pay full face value for their bonds.

A bigger problem, however, was J. P. Farley, the ferry operator who had taken charge of operations at the railroad. Hill and Kennedy moved to cut him out of any share of the railroad, and he made trouble. Farley sued, claiming Kennedy's one-fifth share of the railroad was supposed to be his.

The old steamboat operator told an ugly tale. He, Hill, and their associates had agreed that Farley would slow construction of the railroad and run it so badly the Dutch would have to sell on the cheap. And prior to the sale, Kennedy had denied having any interest in the railroad. Farley accused Kennedy of hiding from the Dutch the fact that he owned a share of the railroad and would profit from making the sale as cheap as possible.

In their book, *The Man Who Found the Money: John Stewart Kennedy and the Financing of the Western Railroad*, Saul Engelbourg and Leonard Bushkoff concluded that Kennedy was at least "disingenuous" in his statements.

However, they note, whatever deal was struck between Kennedy and the Hill associates before the sale was masterfully hidden. All parties "preferred to avoid leaving a paper trail that might prove potentially embarrassing."

Though he fought his claims all the way to the US Supreme Court, Farley simply couldn't prove his case. He might have proven Kennedy a liar, but he couldn't prove that Hill had ever promised him a stake in the railroad. Farley was out of the money, while Kennedy and Hill and the other associates became millionaires ten times over as the railroad grew.

George Stephen, one of Hill's partners in the railroad, would later state matters succinctly in a letter: "When I first knew Kennedy he considered himself a very rich man having by 20 years of hard work accumulated $500,000. He was agent for the Dutch bondholders. . . . Kennedy was very useful to me. To reward him I gave him one-fifth interest . . . and that is how he became the Scotch millionaire."

And that is how Cadillac Mountain came to be part of the national park. Kennedy retired from business in 1883 at the ripe old age of fifty-three. Though not stingy, Kennedy was not lavish in his spending in his early life, having only one home in New York. That changed in 1892, when John Stewart Kennedy began living large. Really large. He first tried to acquire a manor house in Scotland, but the sale ended up in court, and Kennedy walked away. After that, he built a mansion befitting a Gilded Age robber baron on Bar Harbor's Shore Path. He called it Kenarden.

Kenarden belonged to the second wave of cottages built in Bar Harbor. And in contrast to the earliest cottage builder's love of simplicity, the second wave was marked by ostentation. Marble halls, elevators, indoor pools, and enormous size were the vogue.

It took one hundred fifty men to build Kenarden, one of the most beautiful estates in Bar Harbor. It was situated on twenty-three acres of lawns, gardens, and woods. The seventy-two-room main house had eight master bedrooms, five master baths, and thirteen rooms for the servants alone. The house was lit by 650 light bulbs, requiring its own power plant. Newspapers said it looked like a "fairy palace" when lit up at night.

Scattered around the grounds were a gate house, property manager's house, garage, stable, greenhouse, laundry, and tool house.

Famed landscape designer Beatrix Farrand designed the exquisite Italian Garden. Emma Kennedy, in the style of the English nobility, opened the garden to the public one day a month.

Kennedy's lavish lifestyle extended well beyond Mount Desert. When trout season opened, John Stewart Kennedy was always at the South Side Sportsman's Club of Long Island. He also opened the salmon season in Canada, often at the Restigouche Salmon Club, of which he was president.

Winters found him on Jekyll Island off Georgia, where he built a mansion on the grounds of the Millionaire's Club, arguably the most elite country club in America. The club didn't allow just any rich socialite to join, admitting only one hundred members. Kennedy rubbed elbows with Marshall Field, William Rockefeller, William K. Vanderbilt, and

J. P. Morgan. How influential was the Millionaire's Club? In 1910 a secret ten-day meeting was held at the club to establish the Federal Reserve System.

Back on Mount Desert, Kennedy made few waves, though he was known for his eccentricities. Despite his embrace of Wall Street speculation, he waged a personal crusade against gambling. In Maine, he insisted that all gambling and card playing be done out of sight in the clubs or hotels.

He was well-known for his afternoon naps, which he defended fiercely. One afternoon a carriage driver refused to shuttle J. P. Morgan— the world's most powerful financier— to Kenarden. Morgan had to call first and obtain permission to disturb Kennedy's siesta.

The Fabulous McLeans and Their Hoodoo Diamond

THE MCLEANS' HALF-CENTURY IN BAR HARBOR BEGAN WITH BRIGHT promise but ended in tragedy and madness.

Beginning in 1890 and continuing for more than fifty years, members of the McLean family were fixtures of the summer season at Bar Harbor. First, John McLean brought his young son Ned to summers on the island. Then Ned and his wife, Evalyn Walsh McLean, maintained the tradition of visiting Mount Desert.

Evalyn's father bought the couple Briarcliffe (or Briar Cliffe) in 1909, a summer cottage on the Shore Path, where they hosted lively parties for decades. That first year was a happy time for the couple. Perhaps the happiest they ever knew, for their lives over the next thirty years would slowly, steadily decline into madness, scandal, and ruin. The couple's demise coincided almost perfectly with their ownership of the world-famous Hope Diamond, known to the superstitious as the Hoodoo Diamond.

When the Walshes bought the 45.52-carat diamond, it already had a reputation as a stone that carried a curse. In light of what happened to the McLeans, you could believe it easily enough. Over the next thirty years, the fabulous Ned McLeans would suffer one tragedy after another as they lived life at a blistering pace, hobnobbing with heads of state, partying around the clock in Washington, D.C., and traveling the world.

Evalyn Walsh McLean said she didn't believe her family's misfortune stemmed from the diamond's curse. In her memoir, *Father Struck It Rich*, she suggested something else put a curse on her family: money.

Evalyn Walsh: Rags to Riches

Evalyn Walsh McLean was the daughter of Irish immigrant Thomas Walsh, a carpenter, and Carrie Bell Reed, a schoolteacher. As a child, Evalyn and her younger brother, Vinson, moved around western mining towns while her father prospected for gold. In 1896, when Evalyn was ten years old, her father came into her bedroom and said, "Daughter, I've struck it rich." He had discovered the Camp Bird gold mine in Ouray, Colorado, one of the richest ever found.

Thomas Walsh moved the family to Washington, DC, where the fashionable wealthy were settling around the turn of the century. When Evalyn told her father that walking to school was "trying for my dignity," he gave her a blue carriage with a pair of matched horses and a coachman in silk hat and gloves. In 1902, he spent $1 million building a sixty-room mansion on Massachusetts Avenue, where the family ate off gold plates. He encouraged Evalyn's compulsive spending on clothing. She wore the latest Paris fashions, and if she wasn't wearing jewelry, she said, her family assumed she wasn't feeling well and called a doctor.

She was feisty, reckless, kindhearted, impetuous, a gambler, a showoff. "It's only when the thing I buy creates a show for those around me that I get my money's worth," she wrote. "I cannot remember when I did not hunger after thrills. That is the key to all my recklessness, I fancy. For some thrills I have paid terrific prices, but we live just once, and of all the things in this world, I hate boredom most."

Her brother, Vinson, shared her reckless streak. He died when the Mercedes he was driving ran off the road in Newport, Rhode Island, in 1905. Evalyn was seriously injured in the crash. She was given morphine while she recovered and became addicted to it. Eventually her doctors withheld the drug, and she lost her craving for it—but not permanently.

Ned Meets Evalyn

Evalyn met Ned McLean at dancing class when she was eleven and he was eight. He fell in love with her at first sight. As he grew into a young man, Ned asked her to marry him dozens of times, but she refused because of his drinking. At times he drank so heavily he had to make a sling from a handkerchief to steady his drinking hand. Finally, though, she acquiesced when he promised to give up alcohol.

Ned was handsome and shy, from a long line of military heroes. Evalyn always admired his pedigree, if she didn't always admire him. He was the only child of John Roll McLean, who inherited the *Cincinnati Enquirer* and the *Washington Post* from his father and owned a share of the Cincinnati Red Stockings. The elder McLean and US Senator Stephen Benton Elkins built the Great Falls and Old Dominion Railroad in Virginia, and the town that grew up around it was named McLean.

Ned's mother, the former Emily Truxtun Beale, was the daughter of Edward F. "Ned" Beale, a towering figure in nineteenth-century America. Beale was a military general, an explorer, the first man to bring gold back from California, a diplomat, a rancher, and a friend to Kit Carson, Buffalo Bill Cody, and Ulysses S. Grant. In 1872, he bought the Decatur House, right across from the White House. Ned's uncle, Truxtun Beale, was a diplomat who married Secretary of State James G. Blaine's daughter.

Ned's aunt Mary married the last Czarist Russian ambassador to the United States, George Bakhmeteff. That relationship prompted Ned and Evalyn to visit Russia, where Evalyn charmed their Russian hosts. Cole Porter immortalized her in a song, *Anything Goes*: "When Missus Ned McLean (God bless her) / Can get Russian reds to "yes" her / Then I suppose / Anything goes."

Evalyn eventually realized the Beale genes she so admired had weakened by the time they got to her husband. "The great traditions of the Beales were funneled into Ned—and there, somehow, smothered," she wrote. But that insight came after many years of marriage.

She would have preferred a society wedding, and Ned's mother wanted to hold it in Bar Harbor. Ned, however, persuaded her to elope. They were married in Colorado on July 22, 1908. "A queer, queer fellow was this Ned McLean, that I had married," she wrote. She described him as "unearned wealth in undisciplined hands," a case of the pot calling the kettle black.

The Wedding of the Decade

Ned and Evalyn's marriage started out with a bang. The newspaper society pages fawned over the couple and their carefree, extravagant lifestyle. Ned and Evalyn's lives, it seemed, could have been the model for *The Great Gatsby*, opulent, pointless excess papering over a hollow existence.

Their parents gave them $200,000 for a three-month honeymoon in Europe and the Middle East. Typical of Ned and Evalyn, they blew through all of their money by the time they reached Paris and couldn't pay their hotel bill.

They set up housekeeping in Friendship, a sprawling mansion built for Ned's father near the National Cathedral in Washington, DC. There they threw extravagant parties for which they became famous.

"Everybody who was anybody went to their luncheons," reported the *Boston Globe*. "There one saw Senators, judges, diplomats, Cabinet members, generals and admirals—famous personalities of every kind."

At one New Year's party, forty cases of champagne were consumed before dinner. Two thousand Washington socialites attended another. Idaho Senator William Edgar Borah once looked around Evalyn's sumptuous ballroom and remarked, "This is what brings on revolutions."

A single ostentatious mansion wasn't enough for the Ned McLeans, so Evalyn's father bought Briarcliffe for them. It was a large old-fashioned shingle-style cottage. They talked of tearing it down, but in the end they added a bowling alley wing, a ballroom with murals of the Bay of Naples, a nursery suite, and a wing for Evalyn's mother.

The house had originally been designed by William Ralph Emerson for J. Montgomery Sears, owner of America's Cup challenger *Puritan*. John D. Rockefeller Jr. rented it before the McLeans bought it, and his son Nelson was born in the cottage.

A Diamond Is Forever

The McLeans first laid eyes on the Hope Diamond while vacationing in Paris in 1910. The jeweler Pierre Cartier came to their hotel room and showed them the gem. By then, the curse of the fabulous blue jewel was well known. It was associated with murders, financial failures, and the guillotine, having been in Marie Antoinette's possession.

The jeweler undoubtedly knew the McLeans by their free-spending reputation. But at first, Evalyn didn't care for the bauble. It wasn't the curse that troubled her, or even the exorbitant price. It was the setting that put her off. Months later, Cartier came to Washington with the diamond, which he had reset, and tried once more to lure Evalyn with it. He let her keep it over the weekend. She put it on her dresser. "For hours that jewel stared at me," she wrote. "At some point during that night I began to want the thing."

Ned made the deal for the Hoodoo Diamond in the offices of the *Washington Post* in January 1911. It cost $154,000, according to Evalyn. Today the gem's value is estimated at $200 million. It's called the most expensive object that can be held in one hand.

Evalyn didn't think the Hope Diamond would bring her bad luck, but she confessed to a certain wariness. And the purchase had an out. If the McLeans felt the diamond caused them misfortune, they had a right to return it. "Do I believe a lot of silly superstitions, legends of the diamond?" she wrote. "I must confess I know better and yet, knowing better, I believe. By that I mean I never let my friends or children touch it."

When she bought the diamond, Evalyn called her mother-in-law to tell her about it. Mrs. John McLean was with Mrs. Robert Goelet and nearly fainted when Evalyn told her the news.

"It is a cursed stone," she said. Both ladies tried to talk Evalyn out of keeping the jewel, even driving over to her house to do it in person.

Within a year both Mrs. John McLean and Mrs. Goelet were dead. In September 1912, Evalyn and Ned got word that his mother had a bad head cold and rushed to her side in Bar Harbor. She died despite extraordinary efforts to bring her vacationing doctor to her bedside all the way from North Carolina.

Evalyn had the diamond blessed in a church, but even that effort seemed overshadowed by doom. As the minister consecrated it, lightning flashed, and a huge tree across the street suddenly crashed to the ground.

That year was especially difficult for Evalyn. She had been overcome with grief over the recent death of her father and relapsed into morphine addiction. Through her drug-and-alcohol haze, she often didn't recognize guests at the parties she continued to host. Rather than send her away,

Ned fashioned a sanitarium on the top floor of Friendship, where Evalyn could recover. She roamed her mansions convinced reptilian monsters were crawling all over the rooms.

Suffer the Little Children

In 1909, the McLeans had their first son, Vinson Walsh McLean. Danger followed him from the start. He was called the "hundred-million-dollar baby," which exaggerated somewhat his financial prospects. He slept in a golden crib, a gift from King Leopold of Belgium.

Their second son, John "Jock" McLean, would be born seven years later, followed by Edward Beale McLean Jr., and their only daughter, Evalyn Washington McLean.

In 1910, Briarcliffe was burgled. Police suspected it might have been part of a kidnapping plot against the baby. The kidnap fears intensified as the publicity over the Hope Diamond raised the McLeans' profile. The child was watched around the clock by nurses and bodyguards. In 1918, all the McLeans' efforts to protect Vinson came to naught. The nine-year-old boy evaded his minders, ran into the street, and was struck and killed by a car. Later the McLeans' great-grandson said Vinson had been carrying the diamond in his pocket, though that contradicts Evalyn's claim that she never let her children touch it.

The death of young Vinson was probably the greatest tragedy to befall the McLean children, but it was not the only one. In the summer of 1922, John McLean was fishing on a boat off Bar Harbor. He caught an enormous cod that pulled him into the ocean, and he nearly drowned.

Years later, the curse of the McLeans would claim another victim. In 1941, the McLeans' daughter Evalyn wore the Hope Diamond at her wedding to US Senator Robert Rice Reynolds. Reynolds, a North Carolinian who'd already been married four times, was known as "Buncombe Bob." He was fifty-seven; she was nineteen. He was a bitter isolationist, an apologist for Nazi Germany, and co-owner of a fascist anti-Semitic newspaper, *The Defender*. Six years into their marriage, she committed suicide by taking an overdose of sleeping pills.

Yet, for all the misery associated with the Hope Diamond, it seems Evalyn Walsh McLean's real curse was her husband.

A Powerbroker Unspools

When he was just twenty-two years old, Ned McLean was named managing editor of the *Washington Post*. Evalyn later said he was neither an editor nor even a cub reporter. He was just a rich man's son.

Over the next seventeen years, Ned McLean turned the *Post* into a reactionary, juvenile newspaper viewed with disdain by most journalists. He had little interest in politics, except for his friend President Warren G. Harding. He was more interested in hunting, baseball, golf, and horse racing. He bought Belmont Plantation in Loudoun County, Virginia, built a stable, and filled it with thoroughbred race horses.

McLean was a difficult man: charming, suspicious, changeable, a falling-down drunk, a plausible liar, a wanton womanizer. Evalyn claimed she was the only person who exercised any control over him, but she accurately predicted his disastrous end in dissipation. Even his pets were dissipated. He had a pet seal that he fed whiskey every day. Once, in Palm Beach, McLean shared his whiskey with a trained bear and took it to a whorehouse. The bear badly mauled two women.

A *Washington Post* reporter once woke up on a transatlantic ocean liner. Ned had drugged and kidnapped him because he wanted company on the trip. In bars, he liked to knock hats off men's heads, then stamp on them while his bodyguards stood by, waiting to reimburse the victims.

At one point, Evalyn thought Ned's friend Warren G. Harding would be a good influence on him. She was wrong about that. Ned turned out to be a bad influence on Harding. They were drinking buddies who led the Secret Service on chases in Ned's convertibles. Together they applauded the showgirls at the Gayety Burlesque from a concealed box. Ned especially annoyed Florence Harding when he urinated into the fireplace in the East Room of the White House.

Harding frequented the Love Nest, a house owned by the McLeans that was convenient to the White House on H Street. It was connected to the McLean mansion next door. Ned and Evalyn rented it to Attorney General Harry Daugherty and his gofer Jess Smith. There was a butler and a cook and a weekly delivery of confiscated liquor. A poker game was usually in progress, and Ned brought call girls and prostitutes from New York City.

One night, Ned invited several chorus girls from New York to dinner at the Love Nest after a show. Harding was there, along with Jess Smith and Harry Daugherty. By 3 a.m., the partygoers were wildly drunk. Someone suggested they clear the table so the girls could dance on it. The guests started throwing things from the table. A water bottle hit one of the women in the head, knocking her unconscious.

Smith called Gaston Means, an FBI agent, and told him to come to the Love Nest, where there'd been some trouble. Means later wrote there were half-drunken women sprawled on sofas and chairs "with terror painted on their faces." No one had called a doctor. President Harding was leaning on the mantel with his bodyguards beside him. Means took the unconscious girl to his car and drove her to a nearby hospital. She died a few days later, but the scandal was hushed up. The *Washington Post*, of course, never reported it.

By then, the bickering between Evalyn and Ned had become the stuff of Washington society columns.

Teapot Dome Blows Up

In August 1923, President Warren G. Harding died suddenly of a cerebral hemorrhage. Distraught by the loss of Ned's good friend, the McLeans left Washington for Bar Harbor. While they were out of town, they lent the use of their mansion Friendship to Harding's widow, Florence.

Safely out of the White House, Florence launched a futile effort to protect her husband's reputation. At Friendship she sorted through Harding's papers, burning hundreds of the most damaging documents in the fireplace. It was all for naught. Long-suppressed stories of Harding's extramarital affairs emerged in the press.

And then the Teapot Dome scandal broke.

The scandal was named for the California wilderness called Teapot Dome, where the US government had set aside oil reserves for use by the US Navy. Ned McLean's friend Albert Fall, secretary of the Interior, had taken a large bribe in return for leasing the lands without asking for bids.

Ned McLean was implicated in the scandal as a minor accessory after the fact. The US Senate was investigating Fall when he asked Ned to say he had loaned him $100,000.

Oil man Ed Doheny had actually loaned Fall the money, but he didn't want it known. Doheny was in the process of raising $20 million to consolidate his oil holdings. He knew the revelation that he had bribed Fall would scuttle his plans, so he asked Fall to ask Ned McLean to lie, and he did.

Evalyn had harangued Ned not to perjure himself before the Senate. Senator Tom Walsh of Montana, who was leading the investigation, suspected Ned couldn't have loaned Fall the money. He had heard through the Washington grapevine that Ned was broke.

Ned finally confessed he hadn't lent Albert Fall the money. Fall went to prison, and Ned became a laughingstock.

The End of the Fabulous Ned McLeans

The *Washington Post* continued its slide. Evalyn, by 1925, was drinking heavily, and her fortune was slipping away from her. Ned was drunk all the time and carrying on an expensive affair with another woman. When he needed money he just came to the newspaper and took cash—$90,000 of it in one year alone.

In 1929, Ned left Evalyn for Rose Douras, sister of film star Marion Davies, who was coincidentally mistress to another newspaper mogul: William Randolph Hearst.

In October 1931, Evalyn sued Ned for divorce on the grounds of infidelity. He countersued in Mexico, then lied that he was already married. Finally, he took up residence in Riga, Latvia, and filed for divorce again. It was granted in 1932.

Evalyn didn't believe her Hoodoo Diamond caused her marital misfortunes, but it played a big part in the next chapter of her life. This one involved an actual kidnapping.

On March 1, 1932, Charles and Anne Lindbergh's twenty-month-old son was taken from their home in Hopewell, New Jersey. Evalyn remembered the threats to kidnap Vinson and felt the Lindberghs' anguish.

As the FBI searched frantically for the baby, Evalyn contacted Gaston Means, the rogue FBI agent who had helped cover up the death of the chorus girl at the Love Nest. Evalyn asked Means if he knew where the baby was. He said he could find out but that he'd need $100,000 for ransom and $4,000 for personal expenses.

Evalyn hocked the Hope Diamond to raise the money. For more than six weeks, Means strung Evalyn along. He told her he was negotiating with the kidnapper, who he called The Fox. Finally Means asked for another $35,000, and Evalyn realized she was being swindled. Evalyn contacted FBI director J. Edgar Hoover (who would later be godfather to her granddaughter).

The Lindbergh baby was found dead. Bruno Hauptmann was convicted and executed for the crime, though many doubt that he did it. Means, meanwhile, was arrested and later convicted of fraud. He died at the federal penitentiary in Leavenworth after serving six years of a fifteen-year sentence.

The *Washington Post* finally succumbed to Ned's mismanagement. In 1933, the newspaper was sold at auction to Eugene Meyer, who called it "mentally, morally, physically and in every other way bankrupt."

That year, Evalyn McLean had her philandering ex-husband declared insane and committed him to a sanitarium in Towson, Maryland.

Ned McLean spent the last eight years of his life in the insane asylum, denying his identity. Once, he danced the hokey-pokey with fellow inmate Zelda Fitzgerald. He died there of a heart attack in 1941, cutting Evalyn out of his will. He left more than $300,000 to Rose Douras.

Evalyn's free spending caught up with her as well. By 1935, the former Love Nest and the Walsh mansion on Massachusetts Avenue were leased to the government for office space.

Evalyn never recovered from the death of her daughter. She died on April 26, 1947, of pneumonia. She was said to be wearing the Hope Diamond when life left her, as the plaster fell from the walls of her home.

Later that year the Hope Diamond was sold to jeweler Harry Winston to pay Evalyn McLean's estate taxes. Winston donated the gem to the Smithsonian Institute, where it has been on display since 1958 at the National Museum of Natural History in Washington, DC.

Joseph Pulitzer and His Tower of Silence

THE MEDIA TITAN JOSEPH PULITZER BOUGHT HIMSELF ONE OF THE ALL-time great mansions in Bar Harbor in 1894: Chatwold. He immediately set about renovating the stucco and half-timbered cottage with its twenty-seven rooms and seven bathrooms.

The Pulitzer family filled the baronial interior with European antiques and entertained in grand style. Greenhouses were expanded so the family could have fresh fruit and flowers, including a gardenia on every breakfast tray. Dinners were served under the John Singer Sargent portrait of Kate Davis Pulitzer, which was shipped to Bar Harbor every summer. If the dinner guests questioned or disagreed about a fact, the waiters would bring the appropriate reference book to the table. No food was to be served until the matter was settled.

Toward the end of his life, Pulitzer would create the prize for journalism excellence that bears his name. But the Pulitzer Prize could not cover up the reality: His fortune was built on the back-breaking labor of newsboys as young as five years old, many of them homeless.

Assembling an Empire
What was perhaps most shameful about the way Pulitzer treated his ragamuffin vendors was that he himself had arrived poor and alone in the United States. Born in 1847, he had grown up in Hungary, the son of a well-to-do businessman who could afford to have his children privately tutored. But his business went bankrupt after he died. Young

Joseph came to America when a military recruiter paid for his passage so he could fight for the Union in the Civil War. He joined the Lincoln Cavalry, a regiment that had many German immigrants.

When the war was over, Pulitzer bounced around for a little while without much success. Flat broke, he went to New York City, where he slept in wagons parked on side streets. Finally, he hopped a freight train to St. Louis, where he eventually got a job as a reporter for the German-language newspaper the *Westliche Post*.

From then on, he rose rapidly. He worked hard, and eventually became managing editor and part owner of the *Westliche Post*. In 1879, at age thirty-two, he bought the *St. Louis Post* and the *St. Louis Dispatch*, combining them into the *St. Louis Post-Dispatch*. The newspaper took the side of the common man against corruption, greed, and exploitation.

By then he had married the well-born Katherine "Kate" Davis, a relative of Jefferson Davis. They had seven children, of whom five lived to adulthood.

By 1883 Joseph Pulitzer was wealthy enough to buy the money-losing *New York World* from financier Jay Gould. He built the newspaper into the country's largest, increasing the circulation from fifteen thousand to six hundred thousand. He did it by introducing color comic strips, human interest stories, and exposés written by investigative reporter Nellie Bly. He covered sports, women's fashion, and scandal, topping them off with eye-catching headlines. He railed against corrupt government officials and rich tax evaders.

The *World* featured large photographs of gruesome crime scenes and sensational headlines. A story about a deadly heat wave in New York bore the heading, "How Babies Are Baked." When in 1898 the USS *Maine* sank in Havana Harbor, Pulitzer published false stories about a plot to sink the ship, pushing the United States into war with Spain.

He would eventually be indicted for libeling another regular at Bar Harbor, J. P. Morgan, and President Theodore Roosevelt, but the indictment was dismissed. Another Bar Harbor neighbor, James G. Blaine, would come under relentless attack by the *World*.

An Empire Built on the Backs of Children

In 1884, the newsboys of New York staged their first of several strikes.

Pulitzer, like other newspaper owners, relied on an army of poor children to distribute their newspapers on the street. Census enumerator James B. McCabe Jr. described them in 1872:

> *"There are 10,000 children living on the streets of New York," he wrote. "The newsboys constitute an important division of this army of homeless children. You see them everywhere. . . . They rend the air and deafen you with their shrill cries. They surround you on the sidewalk and almost force you to buy their papers. They are ragged and dirty. Some have no coats, no shoes and no hat.*

Pulitzer, on the other hand, lived large. He owned a mansion in New York City and a yacht rivaling J. P. Morgan's *Corsair*. He hobnobbed with Rockefellers and Vanderbilts at his winter retreat on Jekyll Island.

But all was not a bed of roses in the life of Joseph Pulitzer. A workaholic, he had begun to suffer health problems: blindness, depression, and an acute sensitivity to noise. He refused to attend other peoples' dinner parties unless he was promised to be seated between two soft-spoken women. He hired the architectural firm of McKim, Mead & White to design a soundproof wing at Chatwold. The result was a four-story stone tower with a heated pool in the basement. His bedroom was at the top of the tower, with a floor on ball bearings, steel wool–insulated walls, and triple-glazed windows.

His family called it the Tower of Silence.

A Madman Hides in Maine

The Tower also had offices and bedrooms for Pulitzer's six secretaries, who traveled with him. During his illness he ran his newspapers from afar, using a secret code to direct everything from advertising typefaces to editors' vacations. Later another tower was added to the main building, and the servants' wing was nearly tripled.

William Randolph Hearst, a mining heir and California newspaper owner, took note of Pulitzer's success. In 1895, Hearst bought the *New York Morning Journal* and set into motion the greatest newspaper circulation battle in American history.

By 1896, Hearst's *New York Morning Journal* was going head-to-head with Pulitzer's *World*. The two newspapers increased their staff and raided each other's best reporters. When Cubans rebelled against the Spanish, the two newspapers showed no restraint in stoking their readers' wrath toward the colonial rulers. They exaggerated atrocities, altered facts, and made up news. When the USS *Maine* blew up, both newspapers urged war—it was good for business.

The war lasted from April 1898 to December that year. The demand for war news increased circulation so much that publishers could raise the price of newspapers sold to the newsboys from fifty cents to sixty cents a hundred. The cost increase was offset by a rise in sales.

After the war was over, circulation fell, and most publishers lowered the cost of their newspapers to fifty cents per hundred.

Pulitzer and Hearst had both lost money in their bitter circulation battle. In 1897 alone, Pulitzer lost an estimated $8 million, while Hearst was losing $100,000 a year. At the end of the Spanish-American War, they decided to recoup their costs by keeping the price of the newspaper to the vendors—the poor newsboys—at sixty cents.

In 1899, the newsboys went on strike again.

The Newsboys Strike

On July 21, 1899, the *New York Tribune* reported the newsboys were outraged by the news barons' refusal to lower their prices. They were only able to earn about twenty-five cents a day; the higher price meant they were earning even less.

Dozens of boys announced they wouldn't buy the *World* or the *Morning Journal*. One of their leaders, Jack Sullivan, was reported to have told a group of newsboys, "If you sees any one sellin' the Woild or Joinal, swat 'em. Tear 'em up, trow 'em in de river—any ole ting."

On July 23, Pulitzer and Hearst sent out their delivery wagons to Park Row in New York, the main distribution point for the newspapers.

The boys stoned them and tore up the newspapers. They fanned out and called any newsboy selling the *World* or *Journal* a "scab" and tore up his newspapers.

They also created an arbitration committee to meet with Pulitzer and Hearst. Kid Blink, a small newsboy blind in one eye, was on the committee. They met with Hearst in his office and asked him to lower the price of newspapers. Hearst told him he'd give them an answer early the next week. Then he and Pulitzer hired club-wielding strikebreakers to sell the newspapers.

The newsies held a public meeting in lower Manhattan. Kid Blink spoke to the crowd: "I'm trying to figure it out how ten cents on a hundred papers can mean more to a millionaire than it does to newsboys, and I can't see it."

The newsboys held parades to draw attention to their cause. Public sympathy for them grew. The news dealers stepped in and agreed to support the newsboys by refusing to carry the *Journal* or the *World*. Those who didn't paid a price: The boys tore up newsstands that dared to sell either paper. Advertisers stopped placing ads in the *World* and the *Journal*.

The strike grew to include five thousand newsboys and spread to Providence, Rhode Island; Fall River, Massachusetts; Rochester and Troy, New York; and New Haven, Connecticut.

Beating the Bosses

As sales of the *World* and the *Journal* dropped by two-thirds, rival newspapers gleefully reported on the newsboys' success.

Cosseted in his tower of silence, one of Joseph Pulitzer's secretaries read him a memo from the managing editor of the *World*:

> *The newsboys' strike has grown into a menacing affair. Practically all the boys in New York and adjacent towns have quit selling. . . . The advertisers have abandoned the papers. . . . It is really a very extraordinary demonstration.*

Two weeks after the strike started, Pulitzer and Hearst knew they were beaten—by children. The two media moguls kept the price of their newspapers the same but agreed to buy back unsold newspapers. The newsies, now guaranteed a profit, accepted the deal. On August 2, 1899, they began selling the *World* and the *Journal* again.

Whitewashing the Pulitzer Name

Joseph Pulitzer moved away from yellow journalism after the war. In 1902, he was struck by the idea of a school of journalism at Columbia University. He dictated the plan to his secretaries in his library at Chatwold. The Columbia University School of Journalism opened in 1912, and five years later the first Pulitzer Prize for journalistic excellence was administered. Some viewed the prize as a make-good for his long lapse into sensationalism.

Pulitzer rarely returned to the New York office of the *World*. In 1904, he turned over the editorship to Frank I. Cobb, and in 1907 his son, Joseph Pulitzer II, took over business operations.

Joseph Pulitzer died in 1911 aboard his soundproof yacht the *Liberty* while sailing to his winter retreat on Jekyll Island.

His wife, children, and grandchildren continued to enjoy summers at Chatwold, sailing, dancing, hiking, and riding horseback. Meanwhile a photographer named Lewis Wickes Hine was taking pictures of ragged small children selling newspapers on the streets of St. Louis, New York, Hartford, and Washington, DC. "The object of employing children is not to train them, but to get high profits from their work," Hine said.

Joseph Pulitzer II inherited Chatwold in 1924. Changes such as the national income tax forced him to economize. He downsized from the three-hundred-foot *Liberty* to a more practical seventy-five-foot schooner.

He also cut back on the gardenias. They were only for Mrs. Pulitzer and special guests. "The children won't really miss them," he said.

The Stotesburys Send the
Better People Packing

NED STOTESBURY AND HIS WIFE EVA BREEZED INTO BAR HARBOR IN 1925 with a strong scent of new money and fresh scandal. The Stotesburys were well known to Bar Harbor summer society for years, but they finally plunged in and bought a cottage in 1925 from one of their Philadelphia friends.

They arrived among the final wave of wealthy socialites to settle in the resort town. Ned Stotesbury had amassed $100 million through very questionable business dealings. And his wife was hell-bent on spending it all before he died. She almost succeeded.

Even more scandalous than the stories about how Ned Stotesbury acquired his wealth, however, was the strong suspicion that his son-in-law was involved in the death of a New York City showgirl.

Ned Makes a Fortune
Edward T. Stotesbury was a Philadelphia Quaker born in 1849. He graduated from Union College and started his career as a clerk at the Philadelphia investment bank of Drexel & Co., later an affiliate of J. P. Morgan & Co. He was always punctual and rarely absent, attributing his success to keeping his mouth shut and his ears open.

His critics would say he kept his hand open as well. He was a director of United Gas Improvement Company, which bought Philadelphia's municipal gas works for a song in 1905. The sale was notorious as the "gas steal." Philadelphia's city council had approved the sale even as a raucous crowd of citizens protested. The deal was sealed with shouts of "Thieves, thieves!" thundering through City Hall.

UGI went on to control nearly all the street lighting companies in the United States. The company was accused of violating US antitrust laws in 1922. Stotesbury escaped indictment by a grand jury, but the arrangement stunk. Newspapers speculated that the antitrust suit was later dropped because of Stotesbury's friendship with Attorney General Harry Daugherty. President Calvin Coolidge later sacked Daugherty because of suspicions about his corrupt dealings.

When the US Senate looked into the case, witnesses said Daugherty had insisted that only low-level managers of UGI be indicted, leaving his friend Ned Stotesbury safely out of the soup.

Stotesbury also served as chairman of the board of the Philadelphia Rapid Transit Co., which was accused of bribery, fraud, stock watering, and payment of excessive dividends. Train riders paid the price for Stotesbury's involvement with the transit company. When Stotesbury became chairman, he raised fares by $2 million a year.

Family Matters

As a young man Ned Stotesbury was less lucky in love than in business. He married Frances Berman Butcher in 1873. Eight years later she died in childbirth with their third daughter, Frances. Their first daughter, Helen, lived less than three weeks, but their second, Edith, survived to adulthood.

Edith had an uneventful marriage to Sydney Emlen Hutchinson. Frances, on the other hand, would find herself in the middle of a murder mystery—more about that in a moment. She married John Kearsley Mitchell III, president of the Philadelphia Rubber Works, which would be sold in 1929 to B. F. Goodrich. He was a relative of S. Weir Mitchell, a physician and writer who had presided over Bar Harbor society in an earlier era. Despite that connection, James Kearsley Mitchell would not add luster to the Stotesbury reputation.

After his wife died, Ned Stotesbury remained a widower for three decades. He met Eva Roberts Cromwell while on a cruise, and soon after that she too was widowed. They married in 1912. President William Howard Taft attended their wedding.

Thus, Ned Stotesbury became the stepfather of Oliver Eaton Cromwell, James H. R. Cromwell, and Louise Cromwell Brooks. His stepchildren would have colorful lives of their own.

Louise divorced her husband in 1919 and claimed that two prominent generals were fighting over her. She married General Douglas MacArthur, claiming General John J. Pershing wanted to marry her instead. She said Pershing sent MacArthur to the Philippines to get him out of the way, a story Pershing dismissed as "damn poppycock."

James married Doris Duke, known as the richest girl in the world, and became an ardent New Deal supporter. Ned Stotesbury was decidedly not a fan of Franklin D. Roosevelt. One day in 1936 Ned Stotesbury said to his stepson, "It's a good thing you married the richest girl in the world because you will get very little from me. I made my fortune and I am going to squander it myself; not your friend Roosevelt."

Stotesbury was as good as his word. He and Eva had been spending at an astounding rate. In Philadelphia they built a 147-room mansion called Whitemarsh Hall. It was nicknamed "America's Versailles." Henry Ford visited the Stotesburys at Whitemarsh and was said to have commented, "It was a great experience to see how the rich live." But the Stotesburys were not satisfied to be a one-mansion family.

Wingwood House

In 1925, Ned and Eva bought Wingwood House on Eden Street in Bar Harbor from a fellow Philadelphian. More than ten years earlier, Ned had bought a major portion of Bar Island, which is connected to Bar Harbor at low tide but is actually part of the town of Gouldsboro. He commissioned Frederick Law Olmsted to develop an island cottage there. But the plan was never completed.

Under Eva's direction, however, the Stotesburys would finally become major figures in Bar Harbor summer society. Wingwood was expanded and transformed into one of the most spectacular of the Bar Harbor cottages.

It had fifty-six electric wall heaters, five furnaces, fifty-two tele-phones, and twenty-eight bathrooms, some with gold fixtures. Eva bought not one but two twelve-hundred-piece sets of dinnerware. Teas in the summer drew hundreds of guests.

Wingwood wasn't the only thing Eva and Ned Stotesbury spent money on. She hired a full-time fashion designer and once spent $500,000 on an alligator safari to harvest alligator skin for matching luggage.

Around that time, there was another drain on the Stotesbury bank accounts. Rumors flew that Stotesbury spent as much as $1 million of his money to hide his name, and his son-in-law John Kearsley Mitchell's name, from news stories of Dot King's alarming death. But it didn't work; a murdered showgirl was too good a story to cover up.

Connecting the Dots

At first glance there was nothing to connect Mitchell to the Dot King murder. Mitchell, a prosperous financier, lived in one of the finest homes on the Philadelphia Main Line, Red Rose, with his wife, Frances.

The Mitchells, like Frances's father Ned, were regulars on the Maine coast during the summer season, well known on Mount Desert and Isles-boro, where they owned a home at Dark Harbor. The Mitchells' first child was born in Bar Harbor.

On March 15, 1923, Dot King was discovered by her maid, murdered in bed. At the time there was no obvious link to Mitchell.

Dot King had been born Anna Marie Keenan and claimed "artist model and actress" as her profession. She was known better as the "Broad-way Butterfly," the "Dashing Dot" who epitomized the Jazz Age flapper.

An empty bottle of chloroform that killed Dot was found on the floor of her West Side apartment in New York City. Her apartment had been ransacked, and several thousand dollars' worth of jewels and an ermine coat were missing. But police also found a mysterious pair of yellow silk pajamas at the crime scene—far too big to be Dot's.

Her murder was catnip for a scandal-craving country. "Dorothy King was enamored of the sparkle of wine. She knew not when to say 'no' and when the fumes of alcohol stole away her senses she had a predilection for kicking the glass out of taxicab doors," the *New York Daily News* reported. "She was not averse to 'smoking hop' and often she was found at the 'layout' of a man friend in his apartment on West Fifty-fourth Street."

Investigators revealed that in 1922, a gray-haired businessman had introduced himself to her as John Marshall. Newspaper reporters quickly learned the man identified as "Mr. Marshall" and his secretary, "Mr. Wilson," were the last people to see her alive on the night she died. An autopsy put her death at about 7 a.m. The district attorney wanted to talk to this mysterious Mr. Marshall.

But Mr. Marshall's identity was not a mystery for long. For nine days District Attorney Ferdinand Pecora kept "Mr. Marshall's" identity under wraps, whipping newspaper reporters into a frenzy of speculation. They pounced on every juicy tidbit about Mr. Marshall and Dot King.

"Mr. Marshall's little flyer into romance cost him precisely $10,000 in cash, in addition to gifts, according to information in Mr. Pecora's possession," the *Boston Globe* reported. "He met Miss Keenan a year ago—the circumstances are not explained—and since then he has visited her ten times, he told Mr. Pecora. It cost him just $1000 a visit."

Newspapers reported Mr. Marshall was quite madly infatuated with the woman he called "My Dotty" and her hair of "spun gold." She called him her angel and "Sir John." And she gave him one more pet name that would last far longer than their affair: "Sugar Daddy."

Sugar Daddy Revealed

On March 24 the sensational news broke that "Mr. Marshall" was actually the very married John Kearsley Mitchell, described as "capitalist, clubman and son-in-law of E.T. Stotesbury of J. P. Morgan & Co."

A tawdry story emerged. Dot King had given up on acting and modeling and had been set up in an apartment. There she was regularly visited by Mitchell, under the name Mr. Marshall, and "Mr. Wilson," who turned out to be John H. Jackson, Mitchell's lawyer.

On their visits, the two men were wary of discovery. Jackson would make sure the lobby of the apartment building was clear and then accompany Mitchell up to Dot's apartment. After a drink, Jackson would leave.

Mitchell came forward and told his story to District Attorney Ferdinand Pecora the day after the murder hit the newspaper. He admitted to keeping Dot as a mistress. He admitted that he and Jackson had gone to her apartment the night she died. The yellow silk pajamas were, in fact, his. He gave her a $1,000 Liberty Bond, several hundred dollars in cash, and a valuable jade bracelet on March 11, four days before she died.

But, Mitchell insisted, he had left at 2 a.m. the morning Dot died, and she was very much alive. Mitchell said he telephoned Dot's apartment the next day. The phone was answered by a stranger who said, simply, "Dorothy is dead." Mitchell said he hung up the phone and told his lawyer to hire a private detective, who called the medical examiner's office. Then he asked the district attorney to keep his name out of the press for the sake of his family.

Car Chases and Crash Landings

When the news leaked that Ned Stotesbury's son-in-law was the mysterious Mr. Marshall, Mitchell quickly found out what it meant to be page-one news. A pack of reporters set out to find him. When they spotted him exiting a building, he refused to stop. Instead he led reporters on a high-speed chase through Manhattan. Two taxicabs, one carrying Mitchell and his lawyer and the second carrying reporters, sped through the city to the subway entrance at Times Square.

Mitchell and his lawyer rushed down the subway steps. "Two detectives braced themselves against a revolving door at the subway entrance, but a husky reporter sent them sprawling, and his fellows bounded over their bodies," the newspaper reported.

Mitchell and his lawyer doubled back to the street, clambered into another taxicab and were off. So were the reporters. The two cabs, "disregarding amazed traffic cops, cleared a path down Seventh Ave., swung over to Fifth, thence onto 35th St."

The reporters' taxicab crashed into Mitchell's cab in a traffic jam. There was a "lurid exchange of compliments" and the battered cars sped on. Again, Mitchell and his lawyer dove into the Times Square subway, the reporters close on their heels. The pair were finally cornered in a couple of phone booths and coaxed to make a statement.

"We can't," they puffed, "Our counsel has told us not to." Asked where they planned to go, the lawyer said, "We don't know. It looks as if we're going to spend the night in taxicabs."

Fallout at Home

Reporters hounded the Stotesbury family as well as John Kearsley Mitchell. They reached Mitchell's wife, Frances, who was in Palm Beach with their children, Frances, twelve, and Jack, ten. She professed complete surprise that her husband was the mysterious "Mr. Marshall."

"Why, we are the best of chums, my husband and I, and I know he could not have been unfaithful to me," she said. "What if he did dine with a woman or two, in the company of friends? Is there anything wrong in that?" She refused to believe he had given any woman money or presents without her knowledge, she said. Then she broke down sobbing into the telephone.

Ned Stotesbury also stood by his son-in-law, telling the Associated Press his confidence in Mitchell was unshaken. "We are pained and mortified," he said, "but we still believe in Mr. Mitchell, who always has been all that was right, and we are not inclined to believe newspaper reports of his digression now."

Hordes of reporters stalked Mitchell. They thought he might meet his wife arriving from Palm Beach at Washington's Union Station before going on to Philadelphia. He managed to elude reporters before boarding Ned Stotesbury's private railroad car. They finally caught a glimpse of him smoking a cigar with his father-in-law on the platform in Philadelphia.

The papers had a field day, reporting, "The ultra-blueblood society of old Rittenhouse Square was shocked into silence today. . . . With one exception none would discuss openly the news that J. Kearsley Mitchell, wealthy club member and son-in-law of E. T. Stotesbury, multimillionaire banker, was the "Jack Marshall," "Angel," and "$1000-a-day visit man" to Dorothy King.

"Staid dowagers wagged their heads and spoke with compressed lips." A descendant of Benjamin Franklin said the Kearsley Mitchells "were ruined socially."

The Case Fizzles

While the public was focused on the Stotesbury family, the district attorney was moving on to other suspects. There were unanswered questions in the case. The elevator operator at Dot King's apartment said he remembered "Mr. Wilson" leaving the building. But he never saw "Mr. Marshall"—a direct contradiction of Mitchell's statement.

Still, District Attorney Pecora became focused on another man. It turned out Mitchell was not Dot King's only boyfriend. Another man was also known to visit Dot in her rooms: Albert E. Guimares. A closer look at Guimares showed that he wasn't the sedate businessman he appeared to be. He was a con man from Boston selling fraudulent stock.

A friend of Dot's reported that Dot had told her Guimares used to beat her up but that she loved him and continued to see him. She even doted on him, spending some of "Mr. Marshall's" $10,000 on an automobile, an $800 raccoon coat, and a $1,500 diamond ring for Guimares.

Pecora developed a new theory of the crime: Someone, he believed, tried to enlist Dot King in a plot to blackmail Mitchell. The night of her murder was supposedly the night the blackmailer would spring the trap. Her maid, Billie Bradford, said Dot King had put letters from Mitchell in a safe deposit box, but one remained in her apartment. That letter was missing. Pecora said he was certain the blackmailer—Dot King's killer— had that letter. Dot had refused to go along with the blackmail plot, and protecting John Kearsley Mitchell had cost her her life.

One of Mitchell's love letters later surfaced. In it, he wrote, "I want to see you, O so much, and to kiss your pretty pink toes."

But if it was Guimares behind the blackmail scheme, he wasn't talking. Guimares had an alibi. Another woman claimed he was with her while Dot King was being murdered.

The woman who gave that alibi would die suspiciously, years later, and on her deathbed she admitted that the alibi she gave was a lie. But no evidence ever materialized that would resolve the Dot King murder case, and it remains unsolved to this day.

The Aftermath

John Kearsley Mitchell disappeared from the headlines as the Dot King murder investigation grew cold. His wife did not leave him. District

Attorney Pecora turned the matter over to the police, saying he didn't have a case to prosecute. Critics charged that Pecora seemed more interested in protecting Mitchell than building a case against him. But the controversy did not hinder Pecora's career. Ten years after the murder, he was appointed chief counsel to the US Senate's Committee on Banking and Currency. He famously uncovered fraud on Wall Street, exposing practices that benefited the rich at the expense of the poor. Ironically, he uncovered the "preferred list" of Stotesbury's partner, J. P. Morgan, which gave steep discounts of stock offerings to influential customers like President Calvin Coolidge. He compelled testimony from wealthy financiers like J. P. Morgan Jr., that they paid no income tax in 1931 and 1932.

The investigation became known as the Pecora Commission after the now-zealous prosecutor. It spurred Congress to enact the Glass-Steagall Act, which restricted banks from speculating in the stock market, and to create the Securities and Exchange Commission. Pecora was appointed an SEC commissioner and later a New York State Supreme Court judge.

As for the Stotesbury clan, their reputation may have been trash in Philadelphia, but they did well enough in Bar Harbor. Much of the older money was already leaving, clearing the way for newcomers. Ned Stotesbury withdrew $55 million from his bank account during the last five years of his life. By the time he died in 1938 his fortune had dwindled to $4 million. But the record shows he and Eva enjoyed their time.

They were active in the Pot and Kettle Club and Bar Harbor Club. And when Meyer Davis, leader of the Meyer Davis society orchestra, played Bar Harbor, he would ask Ned to sit in and take a turn playing drums, supposedly because Ned had been a Civil War-era drummer boy.

Ned Stotesbury died in 1938 at the age of eighty-nine. Lavish spending, the stock market crash of 1929, and the federal income tax had depleted his fortune. Wingwood fell into disrepair after Eva's death in 1946. It survived the fire of 1947 but not the wrecking ball. It was demolished in 1953 to make way for the new Bar Harbor ferry terminal on Eden Street.

Love, Marriage, and Misery

J. P. Morgan Can't Fool Anyone

THERE WERE THREE EASY WAYS TO KNOW IF J. P. MORGAN HAD ARRIVED for his regular summer visit to Mount Desert. You could look for his yacht, moored in one of the harbors. You could wait for his inevitable visit to the Episcopal church in Northeast Harbor. Or you could look for the most powerful financier in the world striding up the Bar Harbor street called Rotten Row.

The original Rotten Row is the coach road in London's Hyde Park reserved for royalty. Bar Harbor locals borrowed the nickname for High Street because Morgan—America's answer to royalty—kept several of his mistresses there over the years.

Bar Harbor and Newport, in their heydays, attracted a similar crowd—wealthy aristocrats from East Coast cities and the South. But they were very different places. In a nutshell, the summer guests at Newport clung more closely to the traditions of society in New York and Philadelphia. In Bar Harbor, many restrictions were relaxed—especially when it came to matters of the heart. As Cleveland Amory put it in his memoir of the two resorts, *The Last Resorts*, "Bar Harbor was where easy-going Philadelphia girls taught slow-going Boston boys how to flirt."

Something about the cool air, hiking, and sports or the distance from the city made mothers and chaperones loosen the grip on their young charges. The result was a constant flirtatious air that invited romance.

Future president Teddy Roosevelt met his first love in Bar Harbor and, legend holds, attempted suicide there in despair at his inability to charm her. The writer Edith Wharton most likely had her first brush with the great love of her life, Walter Van Rensselaer Berry, in one of Bar Harbor's hotels at the tender age of twenty-one.

The flirtatious nature of the place didn't end with the younger guests, either. Mount Desert Island was notorious as a spot for trysts and affairs among rich people of all ages. The island's amorous climate also suited a blackmailer who threatened to expose the secret vices and dalliances of its wealthy visitors.

Few came wealthier and none came more powerful than John Pierpont Morgan.

J. P. Morgan Takes Liberties

Morgan inherited a small banking fortune from his father and turned it into an enormous banking fortune. His wealth placed him notoriously above the rules that governed most people. New Yorkers joked that he underwrote the cost of the hospital for young women there so he would have a place where his girlfriends could get a safe abortion. That probably wasn't the only reason—the doctor who ran the hospital also treated Morgan's depressions and other ailments.

Despite his reputation, Morgan and his money were more than welcome in the parties and dinners of high society, and he was well-placed in the Episcopal Church. He traveled often to religious conferences and enjoyed debating theology.

Each summer at Northeast Harbor he would attend services at the Episcopal Church and make a donation of $100, which Bishop William Doane would announce from the pulpit to appreciative nods. Of course, it took more than $100 to buy the good graces of the church when you were fooling around on Morgan's scale. When Bishop Doane was raising $200,000 for a new cathedral in Albany, he put the arm on Morgan.

Obligingly, Morgan told him to collect what he could elsewhere and he would make up the rest. But he couldn't resist a small jibe: "Father, you are the prince of beggars," Morgan said. Doane had an appropriately sycophantic reply at the ready: "I don't know about that, but I am certainly a beggar of princes."

The flow of cash doubtless eased whatever pangs of conscience Bishop Doane and others in the church might have felt over Morgan's womanizing. He chartered private trains so high church officials could travel with him to West Coast religious conferences—and, of course, he brought along lady friends. When the Archbishop of Canterbury visited Acadia, he dined with Morgan, and one of his mistresses played hostess.

Swapping Mistresses

Morgan's wife, Frances, largely turned a blind eye to his affairs, but in at least one instance she put her foot down. In her diary on April 15, 1894 she noted: "Spoke to P. about Mrs. R." P. of course, was her husband Pierpont. And Mrs. R. was Mrs. Edith Sybil Randolph. Edith, who met Morgan in France, was a young widow, just thirty-six years old, while Morgan was fifty-three.

Morgan was never much to look at. He was afflicted with rosacea, which caused his nose to swell and develop growths, pockmarks, and lesions. It looked like a purple cauliflower. "What would you do if you were me, with all my riches yet having this terrible nose?" he once said to a lady friend. She replied: "I should not mind so much if I were you, as you can never have been very good looking." The tart reply prompted a smile and endeared her to Morgan for life. She and Morgan were merely friends, but in fact Morgan had many girlfriends who were willing to overlook his nose in light of his finer qualities, of which he had roughly $80 million.

Mrs. Edith Randolph was one of his girlfriends. And in 1890, she was Morgan's primary lover, but she was also in need of a husband.

Mrs. Randolph was described in the papers as "popular in society." Lacking money of her own after the death of her first husband, a British military officer, she started a flirtation with William Whitney, former secretary of the Navy. Whitney's wife put a quick end to that. And so, Edith Randolph strayed over to Pierpont Morgan.

Edith insinuated herself into Morgan's circle, even accompanying the family to his father's funeral. Generally, Morgan liked to keep the Atlantic Ocean between Edith and his wife. While his wife was in Europe, he would visit Edith in New York or Bar Harbor and vice versa.

But Morgan had gotten lax, and Edith was hanging around too often while his wife was in town. Hence the wife's admonition: Morgan would have to break things off with Edith. Morgan would not get a divorce, though he had lost interest in his marriage. Edith needed a husband—a wealthy one. Fortune finally smiled on this unhappy threesome. It came in the form of the death of William Whitney's wife.

With no complaining wife to keep Whitney and Edith apart, the two picked up where they left off. The threesome of Morgan and Whitney and Edith Randolph sailed off into the waters around Mount Desert one day, and by the time they returned to shore, Morgan had handed the widow off to William Whitney. The two were married in St. Savior's Church in Bar Harbor in 1896. One gossip columnist reporting on the wedding noted, with some snark, that he was surprised to see Mr. and Mrs. Morgan not on the guest list.

Edith would suffer an unfortunate fate. Just two years after her marriage, she was riding a horse in a fox hunt in South Carolina when she misjudged the height of a bridge. Her horse thundered under the bridge and bounced poor Edith's head off the underside of the structure, costing her both any chance at victory in the hunt and the use of her extremities.

With Edith gone, Morgan faced a new problem: He needed a new girlfriend. Fortunately, one of Edith's good friends, Adelaide Douglas, was ready to grasp the nettle and take over. Adelaide was married, though already heading toward a split. Her husband had injured himself playing polo and had not been right in the head since.

Adelaide soon moved out of her marital home into a New York mansion built for her by Morgan—complete with a private entrance for his use—and the two carried on for many happy years, traveling contentedly on Morgan's yacht.

The Dangers of the Dalliance

Morgan was hardly the only millionaire visiting Acadia under the guise of restoring one's health among the pointed firs—but really for the chance to roll in and out of a variety of beds. In one public instance, a Bar Harbor matron chose an amateur theatrical to reunite her husband with his children. He had been traveling in Europe for three solid years and a backyard pageant seemed the perfect chance to show him how his three children had grown. It was also a perfect opportunity to introduce him to his two new children, both conceived and born while he was away.

All this bed hopping also attracted a different type of opportunist to Mount Desert, the kind who might advance himself by getting in on the secrets of the wealthy. Probably the greatest of these was William d'Alton Mann, who for forty years terrorized Bar Harbor, Newport, Jekyll Island, and other outposts of the wealthy. Mann, a Civil War colonel, used his newspaper, *Town Topics*, to wreak havoc.

The publication focused exclusively on the comings and goings of members of high society. The attacks he launched were designed so cleanly that to today's reader they might not even be understood as attacks.

In one typical example, President Grover Cleveland, a Democrat, won the presidency in the election of 1884. He lost in the election of 1888, but vowed to return in 1892—and he did, winning election again. In early 1893, speculation was rampant about who would win appointments in the second Cleveland administration, and Mann set his sights on his target.

The subject of one story was New York Democratic activist C. C. Baldwin—a strong Cleveland supporter. But the target was G. Creighton Webb, a Bar Harbor regular. Webb would distinguish himself for bravery during the Spanish-American War. But at this point he was merely a society bachelor serving a Republican administration as an aide in Russia and fodder for Mann's newspaper:

I understand that Mr. C. C. Baldwin is likely to be Minister at St. Petersburg. Mr. Baldwin has great wealth, which is a necessity at the Court of the Czar, but just how well fitted he may be for diplomacy remains to be seen. With Mr. Creighton Webb as an able assistant, I shall look for some racy accounts of life in the czar's territory, and even a change of administration need not make a recall necessary . . . I do not see why Mr. Webb may not anticipate a lengthy stay at St. Petersburg. I remember he was always most attentive to Mrs. Cleveland, and ingratiated himself in her good graces in former days at the White House.

In case you missed the knife being inserted, the implication is that Cleveland's wife—who was then just twenty-nine (and twenty-eight years younger than the president)—was infatuated with the flamboyant Webb. Mann also insinuated that the president might be pleased to keep young Webb as far away from Washington as possible even if it meant leaving a Republican in a job that might rightly belong to a Democrat.

The largely Republican crowd at Bar Harbor would have tittered over such gossip. For his part, young Webb said his inability to stop Mann from plaguing him was a terrible embarrassment. On one occasion, he noted, he had to pack his trunks and quietly leave his summer home in Bar Harbor to escape the controversy Mann stirred up.

The Blind Item
For bigger fish like J. P. Morgan, Mann had a more nuanced approach: the blind item. For example, he might report one week that trouble was afoot in a marriage between an American heiress and her Italian prince husband. If properly compensated he would then follow up the next week:

> *I heard, by the way, that the American-Italian trouble to which I alluded last week may possibly be arranged [resolved], the husband promising amendment.*

There was a subtle code to the way Mann constructed his news items. He would place the blind item on one page, suggesting a scandal. Then, several items away in the newspaper he would place an innocuous report, such as a list of dinner attendees, that would include the real names behind the blind item.

To those in the know, the implication was clear. If the subject of the blind item would make a payment to Mann, the blind item need never be connected with the actual name. People being extorted could pay Mann in cash. Or they could buy an expensive subscription to his annual publication highlighting fashions of the rich and famous, *Fads and Fancies of the 400*.

Mann was the 1890s grandfather to today's gossip websites. He gathered his information from all available sources. Many society swells themselves would contribute items, either to smear someone they did not like or to prop up the image of friends. A suspected homosexual could be shown to be straight by having his name appear in Mann's paper, linked to a beautiful young woman.

But much of Mann's information came from the telegraph operators, waiters, maids, and servants at Bar Harbor who augmented their incomes by selling information to him. He paid well, he was always right, and he always got his money. Well, almost always.

In 1905 *Town Topics* sent one of its sales people to call on Edwin Post. Post was a stockbroker, well known on Wall Street. Today we would know him best as the husband of Emily Post, who was America's arbiter of etiquette for forty years. In 1905, however, Emily Post was yet to publish the etiquette book that would make her famous. Back then Edwin was the better-known member of the couple.

When Mann came upon evidence that Edwin Post was having an affair, it only made sense that he would blackmail him. The ask? He wanted $500 for a subscription to Mann's forthcoming annual society guide, and no one would read about Post's Connecticut hideaway where he kept his mistress. Post should be grateful, he was told; others were paying far more.

Unfortunately, Mann's sources had failed him. What he did not know was that, contrary to appearances, Edwin Post was not a wealthy man. He was a lousy investor, and he probably couldn't have raised the $500 if he wanted.

Edwin had no choice but to tell his wife about the jam he was in. Together they decided that Mann would not get away with his blackmail scheme. They contacted the police, and when Mann's agent showed up to collect from Edwin, he was arrested.

Libels and Misdemeanors

After the arrest, the fallout from the *Town Topics* affair began to spin out of control. Mann fired his editor. Shocked, he said, he was shocked to find out anything like this was going on at his newspaper. It didn't wash. A competing magazine blasted Mann and one of his lawyers, who sued for libel, and the whole story came out.

J. P. Morgan, William Vanderbilt, William Whitney, Charles Schwab, and countless others had paid blackmail to keep their dirty laundry hidden. The names of senators and businessmen turned up among Mann's records. Many of the secrets they paid to hide stayed secret, but the taint of paying Mann was damaging anyway. It meant you definitely had something to hide, and people left to their imaginations might dream up stories even more damaging than the real thing.

Mann explained that the payments were loans, or investments—he just never paid them back or they generated no profit for the lenders. The jury laughed off the libel claim, and soon the district attorney was accusing Mann of perjury. Mann beat the case, but it cost him.

In the wake of the trial, it became clear that if you appeared in a favorable light in Mann's publications or advertised in them, you were probably paying him off to hide something. And if you chose not to pay him off, he would set his spies on you looking for any misdeed.

Mann kept up his newspaper until his death in the 1920s, and it wouldn't go out of business until the 1930s. Finally, society at Mount Desert could get some peace.

The Alimony King and
His Alimony Queen

NELLIE KENDALL CLAIMED TO BE SHOCKED WHEN HER MULTIMIL-lionaire husband Lyman gave her a king's ransom in 1919 to end their twenty-five-year marriage.

From her $2 million Bar Harbor mansion, she told a reporter for the *UK Star*, "I'm so surprised that it takes my breath away." *The New York Times* called it "one of the most generous settlements under a divorce decree ever made."

Nellie wasn't even sure she wanted the divorce, she said shortly after news broke of the settlement. "I have a feeling we may patch it up yet."

As usual, she was full of crap.

There were always two versions of the Lyman Kendalls: The public fairy tale of a Wall Street genius and his supportive, doting bride; and the private version that Lyman, and especially Nellie, did their utmost to hide.

But through her lies, one nugget of truth may have tumbled out. Her husband had grown tired of her social pretensions. Still, the question remains whether the marriage would have survived if both Nellie and Lyman hadn't already fallen in love with other people.

Go West, Young Man
Ellen "Nellie" Ballentine was a product of the ambition that drove Americans westward. Her father, James Madison Ballentine, moved from the

Midwest to Idaho, where he succeeded at mining and ranching. Newspapers later described Nellie as the daughter of the governor of Idaho. Failed candidate for governor would have been more accurate. She would claim other imaginary accomplishments. But it wasn't all that unusual for westerners who struck it rich to come East with invented backstories.

Nellie, for example, said she was ten years younger than her husband, but that would make her fifteen when they married in 1895. More likely they were about the same age.

According to Nellie, she met Lyman Kendall in Idaho while her father was running for governor in 1894. She was wearing her first train to a party in Boise, and she got tangled up in it. A handsome stranger came along and helped extricate her. The stranger, of course, was Lyman Kendall, and they were engaged by the end of the evening.

Lyman Kendall was a simple surveyor making only $85 a week, and Nellie wanted more. She said she wouldn't marry him until he had $7,000 in the bank. It was her father, she said, who helped him get government contracts that allowed him to save the $7,000.

But Lyman Kendall was already working for the US government when he came to Idaho.

Lyman Kendall

Idaho may have been a social backwater by Bar Harbor standards, but it was the right place for Lyman Kendall to be at just the right time. When Idaho joined the union in 1890, the US government had only begun to map the state's geography and natural resources. Great fortunes could be made from a knowledge of western geology.

Lyman Kendall was born just south of the Mason-Dixon Line in Hancock, Maryland, on September 16, 1870. He attended Georgetown College in Washington, DC.

He may have still been in college when his big opportunity came along. The US Geologic Survey had been created just eight years earlier to investigate the mineral resources of the West.

In 1888, Congress had ordered the Survey to investigate the possibilities of irrigating nearly half the United States. The Survey badly needed trained field surveyors for the enormous project. It decided to train young men to be temporary field assistants as a way to supplement its workforce.

The USGS selected Lyman Kendall among ten young men of "good education and high general intelligence" for the project. In December 1888 Kendall left Washington, DC, for an instructional camp in Embudo, New Mexico, where he lived in an Army tent and learned his trade.

Kendall would spend the next decade in the West becoming deeply familiar with its natural resources. After five months in New Mexico, he did surveying work in Colorado. By 1891 he was doing topographic work in Idaho—for about $900 a year.

He was surveying the Snake River in Idaho when he became familiar with Nellie Ballentine. Nellie belonged to the social elite of Boise, Idaho. It wasn't a very big elite, as Boise had a population of about twenty-three hundred. But Boise was growing fast, and ambitious people were making money.

It was probably through Nellie Ballentine that Lyman Kendall met the man who would make them rich, Eugene Meyer.

Meyer, who came from a California banking family, became famous much later for buying and resuscitating the *Washington Post*. Meyer was a friend of Nellie's brother. In 1901, he bought a seat on the New York Stock Exchange and offered Lyman Kendall a partnership. It included $20,000 a year and a share in the profit.

Why would Eugene Meyer give Lyman Kendall, a simple surveyor, such a sweet deal, a deal that would make him a multimillionaire? Because Lyman Kendall knew all about the geology and natural resources of the West.

There's Copper in Them Hills
Eugene Meyer was one of the financiers who worked with the Guggenheim family, which was prominent in developing the western mining industry. The patriarch, Meyer Guggenheim, had bought a large piece of the Leadville silver mine in Colorado in 1881. His sons would add to their father's holdings during a time when America had a rapacious appetite for metals.

Ultimately, they would control the largest complex of mines, smelters, and mineral railroads in the country.

Meyer, like the Guggenheims, came from an Alsatian Jewish family. Like many successful Jews of the era, he didn't identify as Jewish. But it's likely the Guggenheims knew of their shared heritage.

On Wall Street, Eugene Meyer was the link between the Guggenheim family interests and J. P. Morgan & Co., their chief financier. Lyman Kendall, meanwhile, was a link between the best mining opportunities in the West and Eugene Meyer.

Within five years of the start of their partnership, the Guggenheims took over American Smelting, a mining and refining company. Kendall and Meyer managed the extraordinary rise in the company's share price, as well as that of the Reading Co., which was also engaged in mining and in railroads.

By 1917, Kendall had made more than $20 million on Wall Street—more than $400 million today. He had an expensive Park Avenue apartment, a Bar Harbor mansion, a yacht, a garage full of luxury cars, and a social-climbing wife.

The key to succeeding on Wall Street in that era was inside information about which stocks would be pumped up and which would be dumped. Kendall and Meyer told the world the secret to their success was a new statistical model for economic forecasting. At least that wasn't as outrageous as Nellie's explanation.

Nellie's Story

When Nellie and Lyman Kendall were newly married, she said, they had been figuring out how they could make a great fortune.

"We watched the newspapers with our whole souls and played the stock market—on paper," she said. "But we succeeded so marvelously we decided to stake our destinies on our good judgment and put our poor $7,000 in Wall Street."

She said Lyman got feverishly involved in stock picking, studying it like a science. Then, according to Nellie, he hit it big. She didn't bother mentioning their connections to the mining and stock market powerhouses of J. P. Morgan and the Guggenheims, nor of her husband's extensive knowledge of western topography and transportation systems. Nope, she and Lyman had just read the newspapers and played the game.

Nellie may have been secretive about how she and Lyman earned the wealth, but she was anything but secretive in how she spent it. The small-town girl from Boise thought she could buy her way into the social elite of Bar Harbor and New York.

She described her own aspirations when she told a reporter how Lyman had encouraged her. "You have wealth, my dear," he told her. "You have all the social graces. You are splendidly equipped to be a great social leader. That is your sphere! There you would shine!"

She poured a fortune into her luxurious Park Avenue apartment, filling it with collectible art and expensive furniture and inviting people to dine with them.

She transformed Sonogee, a forty-room Italian villa on Bar Harbor's Eden Street that they bought in 1911. Built just eight years earlier for hotel heir Henry Lane Eno, the mansion's white stucco and red tile roof supplanted Bar Harbor's shingle style as fashionable architecture.

Nellie converted Sonogee's interior into an Italian Renaissance showplace. In July 1916, she opened the updated mansion to the *Bar Harbor Times*, which cooperated by gushing about the Kendalls' wealth and taste:

> *Internally there are pillared halls, broad marble stairways, with delicate hammered iron balustrade, the ceilings vaulted and tinged with rich dull gold; a noble salon which might be an apartment in an ancient palazzo on the Grand Canal, the ceiling a sixteenth century masterpiece; stone walls hung with medieval tapestries and high windows with brocades; furniture, much of it almost priceless, covered with Venetian damask or tapestried; venerable sanctuary lamps suspended from the ceiling to cast a mysterious glow, with tall renaissance standards to add a stronger light; priceless Chinese and Persian rugs upon the floor, with a vista through a lofty and elegant trumeau of a white marble temple d'amour banked with flowers, and a view through the windows behind of what might be the Bay of Naples or the Adriatic.*

She lived large in Maine, holding glittering entertainments at her remodeled mansion and on the Kendalls' fifty-five-foot yacht, the *Lyel*. But try as she might, Nellie Kendall, parvenu from Boise, didn't shine. Bar Harbor society snubbed Nellie as a social climber.

Lyman, on the other hand, enjoyed a reputation among the elite of Bar Harbor and New York for his investing prowess. He was lauded as a lion of Wall Street.

By the time the United States entered World War I, trouble had started to lurk in the Kendall household.

Lyman Kendall became "fed up with Nellie's social ambitions and with the persons who filled his homes, ate his food and bored him stiff," according to the *American Weekly*. Or perhaps he just got tired of Nellie's failed social ambitions, for he had fallen for someone younger, prettier, and more acceptable to society.

The Divorce

In May 1919, the news of the Kendalls' divorce settlement shattered any hope that they could quietly go their separate ways. Lyman Kendall gave Nellie $100,000 a year, $1 million in cash, their $1.5 million Park Avenue apartment, and their $2 million Bar Harbor estate Sonogee. Bar Harbor society was stunned at the price he paid for his freedom from Nellie.

The astonishing settlement, worth about $70 million in today's dollars, made international news. Lyman Kendall was no longer the Lion of Wall Street. He was the Alimony King. And Nellie was described as the Alimony Queen.

No doubt many surmised that Lyman Kendall gave his ex-wife a fortune because he was so anxious to get rid of her.

Nellie Kendall, ever concerned about her image, went to work. As usual, she told a tale that only the most credulous could believe. She said their friends were astonished by the divorce, because she and Lyman had always gotten along so peacefully.

Surely, Nellie had to admit that he spent more and more time away from home. But she explained that Lyman didn't like the social ramble; he was just a plain fellow who loved solitude and quiet. He liked his corncob pipe, the old fishing hole, and the smell of the stables.

She claimed they wanted to get a divorce because Lyman didn't want to interfere with her social life. Noble Nellie wanted him to be happy in his simple life. She couldn't possibly abandon her social career because such a sacrifice would make Lyman so desperately unhappy.

And so, she said, like two intelligent adults they decided to divorce. But he still cared for her, she insisted. Why, he called her every night. Just last night he had called, concerned that the garage was too far from the house. He wanted to send her a check to move the garage so she could get to the cars with less trouble.

A Chanteuse for Him—a Boy Toy for Her

Over time, the true story of the divorce came out. Though Lyman Kendall denied infidelity, the friends Nellie described as "astonished" had actually noticed him paying assiduous court to the beautiful Betty Lee, seventeen years his junior. Miss Lee, a chanteuse, gave private singing performances in the homes of the wealthy. He "was always in the forefront of those who applauded her crooning melodies," noted his friends.

Two months after the ink on his divorce decree dried, Lyman Kendall married Betty Lee in Atlanta, Georgia. Her real name was Catherine Elizabeth Lee Welch, and she claimed to be a relative of Robert E. Lee. (But so did a lot of people.)

Nellie acknowledged that she knew Lyman was buying expensive gifts for someone, and she suspected another woman. Lyman had actually bought a house near Betty Lee's family in Georgia.

Lyman Kendall also adopted Betty Lee's ten-year-old daughter, Jane, who would grow up to have a much more successful social career than Nellie did. The beautiful young heiress became a fixture of the social pages. She threw lavish parties, married four men, and had a tempestuous romance with Ernest Hemingway.

Contrary to Nellie's assertions, corncob pipes and fishing holes played little role in Lyman Kendall's new life with his second wife. He bought a palatial townhouse in Washington, DC, and enjoyed the high life in Miami and New York. He bought land in Potomac, Maryland, and built a stunning hilltop estate on it.

Kendall also built a small village on his estate for his servants, groundskeepers, and farmhands, along with a two-story garage, a dairy, and a barn for thirty-six cows. The Kendalls moved into the home, christened Kentsdale, in 1926, and filled it with antiques they bought in Italy.

Lyman Kendall's simple plans included subdividing his thirty-one hundred acres into an English village. He never completed those plans because he died suddenly of a heart attack in 1929, just short of sixty. He outlived Nellie by three years.

Nellie's New Beau

Though Lyman's wandering eye may have prompted the divorce, Nellie was not without her own extramarital interests. In January 1920, less than a year after her divorce, Nellie married Eldredge M. Roberts. They were living at her apartment at 520 Park Avenue in New York after they'd gone down to the city clerk's office to tie the knot.

The Kendalls had turned Sonogee into a hospital for recovering soldiers during World War I. It was likely there that Nellie had met Eldredge Matthew Roberts, who served with the British Royal Flying Corps. The newspaper in Bar Harbor noted that the bride was forty and the groom thirty-one. The New York press observed that the couple's romance had begun two years prior, well before Nellie's divorce from Lyman. And newspapers ran wedding photos of the dashing young airman and a rather haggard looking Mrs. Lyman Kendall. The couple planned a honeymoon in Palm Beach and then planned to travel to Europe. Captain Roberts possessed a striking war record; he had shot down several German planes while flying for Canadian forces, had himself been wounded four times, and had won the French Croix de Guerre.

Whatever sniggering the Mount Desert society swells got out of Nellie's second marriage, it was well beyond her hearing. She had already sold Sonogee to the Frederick Vanderbilts. They, in turn, sold it in 1927 to the Atwater Kents, who distinguished themselves by throwing parties at Sonogee on a scale that was lavish even by Bar Harbor standards. The Kents entertained almost daily at the mansion until the eve of World War II. It then changed hands several times and ultimately became a nursing home.

Breaking Up Is Hard to Do— Vanderbilt Style

In 1875, very few Americans had even $1 million. Cornelius Vanderbilt, known as the Commodore, had $100 million. Then in his eighty-first year, he had more money than the US Treasury.

But the Vanderbilt name, a household word today, was nothing special then. It would take the Commodore's grandchildren—and especially his granddaughter-in-law—to put the family name on the front pages.

They did it by spending spectacular amounts of money—in New York City and in New York state, in Vermont, in Newport, in Asheville, North Carolina, and on Jekyll Island in Georgia. And with Mount Desert in the early stages of its resort period, any family intending to dominate high society needed a presence on the island. So that's where the Vanderbilts turned their attention.

Over the next fifty years, the Vanderbilt grandchildren would run through the Commodore's massive fortune. By 1927, no Vanderbilt made the list of the world's wealthiest people. And at the first family reunion in 1973, not a single one of the 120 Vanderbilts gathered could claim to be a millionaire.

But when they had the money, the Vanderbilts spent on a grand scale. Before they were done, they rose to the pinnacle of society and occupied a dozen Bar Harbor mansions—along with mansion-sized yachts. But with that rise in status came a new scrutiny of their behavior.

The press lapped up stories about the romantic misadventures of Mount Desert's social elite, and the Vanderbilt family provided plenty of fodder because their divorce scandals played out on the same scale as their many mansions—enormous.

We'll focus on those who left their greatest impact on Mount Desert among the eight grandchildren who inherited the bulk of the Commodore's fortune: Willie K. and Alva, the social climbers; George, the spendthrift; and Frederick, the unfortunate lothario.

Willie and Alva

In 1875, when Alva Smith married William K. Vanderbilt, known as Willie K., the news barely made the society pages. High society viewed the Vanderbilts as vulgar upstarts, despite their millions.

The Commodore, who founded the family fortune, was an uncouth farmer's son who could barely read. He wore old-fashioned frock coats, chewed tobacco, pinched women's bottoms, and had a collection of cuss words unmatched on the waterfront.

Historian Henry Adams observed that the stingy multimillionaire "lacked social charm." New York's old money set agreed. The Dyckmans, the Stuyvesants, and most of all the Astors kept their distance from the Commodore.

The Commodore was too busy making his fortune to have much truck with high society. Through hard work and sharp business practices, he parlayed a little ferry service into a regional steamship line, then an oceangoing steamship business and finally a railroad empire that included the New York Central.

In 1853, the sixty-year-old multimillionaire decided to finally pamper himself. He built the biggest steam yacht in the world, the *North Star*, and took his family on a grand tour of Europe. He tried to mingle with the English nobility, but for the most part they steered clear of the crass Vanderbilts.

Alva Vanderbilt would change that.

Alva Crashes the Party

Before she became a Vanderbilt, Alva Smith was a pushy Southern belle, born in 1853 to a Tennessee slave owner. The Civil War ruined her father, and Alva needed to marry well. When Alva met Willie K., the Commodore's grandson, she struck gold.

Two years after Alva married Willie K., the Commodore died and left 95 percent of his fortune to his son Billy, Willie K.'s father. The Commodore also gave several million dollars to each of Billy's four sons. Willie K. got $3 million, and Alva went to work spending it.

She built a palatial home called the Petite Chateau on Fifth Avenue in Manhattan and a country manor in Long Island with forty-five bathrooms. And in 1883, the year the mansion was finished, Alva launched her assault on New York society with a fabulous costume ball. She sent twelve hundred invitations to all of New York's elite, with one notable exception: Caroline Astor.

Mrs. Caroline Astor was the queen of New York society, and she had snubbed Alva along with the rest of the Vanderbilt clan. For that, she got no invitation to Alva's stupendous party.

Mrs. Astor held out—for a while. Ultimately, she dropped her hauteur and made a social call on Alva. Mrs. Astor then got her invitation.

Joseph Pulitzer's *World* ridiculed Alva's ball of the century, poking fun at the partygoers' discomfort in their elaborate costumes and mocking its obscene cost—$250,000, about $6 million today. But the newspaper had to admit, Alva had accomplished her mission. The Vanderbilts were now respectable in high society. "Until Mrs. William K's advent, the Vanderbilt family was unheard of in NY society. . . . She took Willie K by the hand and led the way for all the Vanderbilts into the gay world of society, Fifth Avenue, terrapin, Newport, dry champagne, servants in livery, men who don't work, women with no serious thoughts, and all the other charms of fashionable existence."

Shortly after the Vanderbilt fancy-dress ball, a string of exclusive gentlemen's clubs invited Willie K. to join. The following January, Alva and Willie K. marked their ascent into the highest of high society when they attended Mrs. Astor's annual ball.

Bar Harbor

The year after Alva's historic costume ball, Billy took the whole clan to Bar Harbor for the summer. He rented Devilstone, a newly built oceanfront estate on Bar Harbor's Shore Path. In a photograph of the family on Devilstone's front porch, Alva's expression suggests she'd rather be in a less rustic environment.

But some of Billy's eight children took to Mount Desert Island like ducks to water. The fashionable new resort would satisfy their yen to build enormous homes and sail gigantic yachts. George, the youngest, would embark on a mansion-building spree in Bar Harbor even as he started work on his Biltmore Estate in North Carolina. Frederick and Willie K. would ply the waters of Bar Harbor in their luxurious steam yachts.

The year after that first summer at Devilstone, Billy passed away, the world's richest man. He had doubled the Vanderbilt fortune in the eight years since the Commodore died. But unlike the Commodore, Billy didn't give most of the fortune to one son in order to preserve it. Instead, he divided it between his two eldest sons, with Willie K. getting $60 million and Cornelius $65 million.

Cornelius and his wife, Alice, were furious. They expected Billy to give everything to Cornelius. Billy, they believed, gave half his fortune to Willie K. as a reward for Alva elevating the Vanderbilt status. They hated her for stealing half their money. From then on, the Cornelius Vanderbilts were not about to let Alva spend more money than they did.

Mansions, Mansions Everywhere . . .

Refusing to be outdone by Alva and Willie K.'s Petite Chateau, the Cornelius Vanderbilts doubled the size of their Fifth Avenue mansion to make it the largest private home in America. Then Alva built a marble cottage in Newport modeled on the Acropolis at the staggering cost of $11 million. Alice retaliated by rebuilding her Newport home, The Breakers, which had burned down, to be bigger and better than the Marble House.

Billy's other children, still wealthy in their own right, also spent extravagantly on homes and yachts.

George especially liked Bar Harbor, bringing his mother most summers until her death. In 1889, he bought Ogden Point in Bar Harbor, renamed it Point d'Acadie and set to work doubling its size. He added cabins to the property, hired Frederick Law Olmsted to landscape the grounds, and built Bar Harbor's first swimming pool.

George also built another home, Islecote, on the grounds of Point d'Acadie for Margaret Shepard Schieffelin, his niece, and her family. Margaret's sister Edith Shepard Fabbri would build two mansions called Buonriposo on the same site, right next to Uncle Frederick's Sonogee. Their sister Alice would marry the son of the Louisiana Lottery King and inherit the rambling cottage Bogue Chitto. The girls' mother, Margaret Louise Shepard, and her husband would rent the elaborate Mossley Hall.

Willie K. chose to build a palace that floated. The *Alva* was the largest yacht ever built. Once, when Willie K. sailed into the Dardanelles, a Turkish naval vessel shot at the *Alva* thinking it was an enemy warship. It had a thirty-two-foot-wide dining room with white woodwork trimmed in gold, oriental rugs on the teak decks, and bathrooms in every stateroom.

Willie K. and Alva on the Rocks

In July 1892, Willie K. was sailing *Alva* from Bar Harbor to Newport with a fifty-two-man crew. A dense fog rolled in, and the yacht lay anchored off Cape Cod. A freight steamer rammed into the port side of the *Alva*, causing her to sink immediately. "Abandon ship," ordered the captain. Everyone made it to shore safely. But as soon as Willie K. could send a message, he did: to order up an even bigger yacht.

The name of his new yacht spoke volumes about the state of Willie K.'s marriage. He did not name it the *Alva II*, but the *Valiant*. At that point, he and Alva weren't speaking, and they had begun to live apart. Their teenage daughter, Consuelo, had the painful task of carrying messages back and forth between them.

At least one of those messages suggested reconciliation, and in November 1893 the *Valiant* set sail for a ten-month cruise with Alva, Willie K., their children, and an entourage. The voyage to Asia, Africa, and Europe was supposed to bring the family back together. It did just the opposite.

Four months into the trip, Alva stormed off the yacht with Consuelo and went to London, where they stayed until September. Willie K. moved to Paris, where he carried on a flagrant affair with an attractive and notorious American named Nellie Neustretter. He bought her a lavish apartment in Deauville and fitted out her servants in the Vanderbilt's maroon livery. His friends cautioned discretion, but Willie K. ignored them and publicly gave Nellie Neustretter 40,000 francs he won at the Grand Prix de Paris.

At some point, word of Willie K.'s brazen infidelity reached Alva. When she returned to America in September 1894, she made an announcement so staggering it appeared on page one: She wanted a divorce. And in case anyone doubted who was to blame, she specified she wanted the divorce in New York State, where the courts granted divorces for just one reason: adultery.

It was a time when ladies left the room if the word "divorce" was uttered. The Vanderbilts, fearing scandal, hastily left their summer cottages in Bar Harbor and Newport to meet in Boston for a powwow. The clan frantically tried to persuade Willie K. and Alva to merely separate instead of divorce. It didn't work.

The End of Alva

The Vanderbilt clan couldn't keep the divorce out of the newspapers, but they could defend Willie and trash Alva. The Vanderbilts told reporters that Willie K. did nothing wrong, and they predicted he would soon be vindicated (he wasn't). They painted Alva, on the other hand, as a spendthrift virago.

A society matron—prompted by the Vanderbilts if not a Vanderbilt herself—spoke anonymously about Alva to a *Boston Globe* reporter.

"All of Mrs. W.K.'s sisters are divorced from their husbands," she said. "It is said that they all lived too high for their husbands. For example, when Mrs. W.K. went to live at the finest hotel in Paris, the furniture of the apartment given her was not fine enough to suit her, so it was all taken out and the suite refitted."

The *World* had a field day with the story, reporting that any wage reductions for New York Central Railroad employees went to pay for "some trifle for Nellie Neustretter."

Willie K. didn't contest the divorce, and perhaps he wanted it. Rumors spread that he had hired Neustretter to appear daily in public with him so he could force Alva to cut him loose.

Alva vowed she would never speak to Willie K. again, and she didn't. But society didn't speak to her, either. The Vanderbilts cut her dead. She was ostracized from the elite circles she had worked so hard to enter. Society, Alva would later recall, was "stunned, horrified and then savage."

Other Vanderbilt Divorces

Alva's fall from social grace brought into public view some Vanderbilt history that the family wished to keep hidden—a track record of divorce. In 1895, the year of Alva's divorce, a news story appeared about Willie K.'s brother Frederick.

In 1878, the story went, twenty-two-year-old Frederick scandalized his family by secretly marrying Louise Torrance. Louise was not only twelve years Frederick's senior but had only recently—very recently— divorced Frederick's own cousin, Alfred Torrance.

Billy considered disinheriting Frederick, but in the end, he forgave him. "If he had been rich they would have turned him out neck and heels into the cold world—him and his eccentric wife," went one story. "But he was worth only $2,000,000 and they wept when they thought of the dear boy, on the verge of poverty, as it were, wandering about looking for something to do. So they relented, forgave the couple, gave them a few million dollars and set them up in housekeeping."

But Frederick was an unknown young man back then, and his marriage to a divorcee went unnoticed. Alva, on the other hand, was a social lioness. She was criticized for setting a precedent that would encourage other members of the social elite to dissolve their marriages.

Alva's lawyer, Joseph Choate, tried to convince her that divorce would undermine the social authority of the upper class. "No member [of the upper class] must expose another member to criticism lest the whole foundation of wealth be undermined," he told her.

Left unsaid—or perhaps unrealized—was that divorce would dissipate the Vanderbilt fortune. In March 1895, Willie K. was ordered to let Alva keep Marble House in Newport and $250,000 a year in alimony. In the end, his divorce was said to cost him $10 million. He spent the summer of 1895 sailing off Bar Harbor in the *Valiant* and avoiding newspaper reporters.

The Aftermath

Soon afterward, Alva married her newly divorced Newport neighbor, Oliver H. P. Belmont. They held the ceremony at her townhouse in New York because no church would marry them.

But eventually the stigma of divorce would disappear, and divorce would eat away the Vanderbilt fortune, as would bad investments, philanthropy, high living, and conspicuous consumption.

Alva's divorce from Willie K. was followed the next year by one of the most brilliant social events of the season. Edith Vanderbilt Shepard married Ernesto Fabbri in Scarborough, New York. The reception was held at her parents' baronial estate overlooking the Hudson.

Ernesto was half-American and half-Italian. Like his father, he was a partner of J. P. Morgan. The newlyweds moved into a 22,500-square-foot house at 11 E. Sixty-Second St. in Manhattan, a gift from Edith's mother. Ernesto's two bachelor brothers, Egisto and Alessandro, often joined them.

Edith undoubtedly absorbed the lesson of Alva's social ostracism and maintained an outward show of respectability throughout most of her marriage. But not everyone was fooled.

In 1905, Edith and Ernesto built an Italian villa in Bar Harbor and called it Buonriposo. That year, Ernesto was transferred to the Morgan office in Italy. Upon the Fabbris' return from Europe in 1914, they decided to dump the Vanderbilt house on East Sixty-Second St. Instead, they built a new, Italian Renaissance mansion on the Upper East Side. Egisto, an artist with superb taste, helped Edith and an architect design and decorate the house. Egisto's brother Alessandro lived on the fourth floor.

Bar Harbor rumor had it that Edith was having an affair with Egisto, but her cousin-in-law Louis Auchincloss corrected the record. It was brother-in-law Alessandro and Edith who were lovers. The fact that Edith had Alessandro buried next to her in the Vanderbilt mausoleum on Staten Island suggests Auchincloss is correct.

Alessandro Fabbri probably had more of the Commodore's enterprise and inventiveness than any of the Vanderbilt grandsons. He built a radio receiving station at Otter Cliffs in what is now Acadia National Park, and he ran it as an important military installation for the US government in World War I. Today, a plaque commemorating the spot where it stood calls it "the most important and most efficient radio station in the world."

In 1918, the Fabbris' Bar Harbor cottage Buonriposo burned down, and they decided to rebuild it as a more formal Mediterranean villa. Egisto again helped Edith design the mansion. By then Edith and husband Ernesto were largely living apart—and Alessandro was still living with Edith.

At age forty-four, Alessandro caught a cold while duck hunting on Long Island and died of pneumonia shortly thereafter. With Alessandro gone, Edith presumably no longer needed Ernesto as a beard and divorced him a year later.

Though attitudes had changed considerably in the twenty-nine years since Alva stormed off the *Valiant*, Edith did not risk the harsh criticism Alva endured. She stayed away in Europe while news broke about her divorce. There wasn't much.

Three months later, Ernesto married a woman seventeen years younger than he. The *Bar Harbor Times* reported the wedding on the front page, merely stating the friends of the couple would be interested to know of Ernesto's remarriage.

Times Change

Just how much things had changed became evident in the life and loves of the Fabbris' only daughter, Teresa Clark. Said to be the most beautiful woman on Mount Desert Island, she married four different men.

As a child, Auchincloss was friends with Teresa's two children, James and Edith, and joined them at Buonriposo with their grandmother. Auchincloss recollected Teresa's rare visits to her mother when she was between marriages.

> *The telephone at Buonriposo rang constantly for her. There was an extension in my bedroom, and I had the impudence to listen in. Was that really Father's friend Tom Cook, whose amorous tone I heard? It was. Yet he was married to a friend of Mother's and had six children, some of whom were older than I.*

Teresa's last husband, George McMurtry, paid no price for marrying the much-divorced Teresa and succeeded Ned Stotesbury as president of the elite Bar Harbor Club. They lived together in his colonial estate, and she had no need of Buonriposo. In 1963, she had the villa demolished.

Many of the other Bar Harbor houses occupied by the Vanderbilts also fell to the wrecking ball: Islecote, Pointe d'Acadie, Bogue Chitto, and Mossley Hall. Sonogee became a nursing home. Alva's Marble House and Alice's The Breakers became house museums.

Willie K.'s New York houses are gone, and the *Valiant* was bombed during World War II. The Fabbris' mansion is now an Episcopalian retreat. By 1947, just sixty-four years after the first Vanderbilt mansion went up on Fifth Avenue, all ten of them had been demolished.

The Many, Many, *Many* Loves of Cornelia Baxter

IN 1903, NAVY LT. JOHN EDIE CAME ASHORE VISITING BAR HARBOR while his ship, the USS *Indiana*, was in port. He made the mistake of accompanying a friend to the summer cottage of Cornelia Baxter, who would turn his world upside down.

Cornelia, frequently described as the most beautiful woman in America, had a way of making the men who entered her orbit quickly look like idiots. Even a slight brush with the celebrated beauty could feel like being run over by a truck—and it usually guaranteed the poor man would be the subject of gossip for decades to come.

Cornelia started out life in Tennessee, but her family moved west when her wealthy father was appointed governor for the Wyoming territory. She spent her early years on the prairie, but when her dad failed to win election as governor, the family left Cheyenne for Denver.

It was there that she encountered the first of the many men she would leave devastated in her wake. Sixteen-year-old Cornelia became engaged to her childhood sweetheart Gerald Hughes, son of a US senator and a future senator himself. Cornelia was publicly engaged to Gerald, and wedding plans were underway in 1900. The Hughes family had commissioned a silver service for the young couple, and Denver society awaited invitations to the highly anticipated nuptials.

But then Cornelia visited San Francisco with her father. At just seventeen, she met Hugh Tevis, a forty-year-old widower. Tevis's father had led a group that acquired the Wells-Fargo Company, and Hugh was heir to an enormous fortune. Gerald soon learned that his fiancée was no longer his fiancée—through a newspaper announcement of her engagement to Tevis.

From Hughes to Tevis

In 1901, Tevis and Cornelia married. But it wouldn't last long. An eighteen-year-old bride proved too much for Tevis's weak heart. He died during their honeymoon in Japan. When Tevis's daughter from a prior marriage died a short time later, Cornelia found herself in possession of a fortune of some $4 million to $5 million. Needless to say, young men took notice of the rich young widow.

Talk began swirling around Denver that Gerald Hughes and Cornelia might be reuniting. But after a short dalliance, she left Hughes again. This time, Hughes was so furious he hired a straw buyer to purchase Governor Baxter's Denver house at any cost up to $100,000. The jilted lover wanted to be sure the Baxters were gone for good from Denver—or at least from his neighborhood.

Though Governor George W. Baxter probably would not have sold to Hughes, he did sell to the straw buyer for $40,000. The Baxter family then centered its activities in New York, with summers in Bar Harbor and Newport.

It was in Bar Harbor in 1903 that Lt. Edie had his unfortunate run-in with Cornelia. At the Kebo Valley Country Club, Edie was accosted by Ernest Wiltsee. Wiltsee was a friend of Cornelia's from Denver and apparently under the impression that he and Cornelia were engaged. Cornelia had told him that Lt. Edie showed up drunk at her cottage with a mutual friend and engaged in behavior unbecoming of a naval officer. Wiltsee challenged the unruly Edie to a duel. Fortunately, friends stepped in on both sides. Edie returned to his ship, and Wiltsee was persuaded to take a trip to Boston.

Meanwhile, a friend of Cornelia's visited the USS *Indiana* to lodge formal charges against the lieutenant. Edie's commanding officer called a court martial, and Cornelia was brought to the *Indiana* to testify. When she finally told her story, the charge against Edie consisted of this: He sat down on the arm of Cornelia's chair.

The controversy blew over with a reprimand for Edie but not before the Bar Harbor court martial made headlines across the country. Ernest Wiltsee, meanwhile, made his own announcement to set the record straight: He was not engaged to Cornelia Tevis (in case anyone besides himself thought he was).

Cornelia moved on to Knoxville, Tennessee, where she took society by storm. That is, until a dustup with a jeweler about a necklace she hadn't paid for soured the city for her. She then took her act to London and Paris. In London she was courted by the Earl of Rosslyn. But the unfortunate earl didn't know when the party was over. With Cornelia boarding a ferry for France, the earl rushed to the boat to join her and received an eye-roll for a welcome. It would be several months before Cornelia could get shed of him.

Meanwhile, her next target was already in sight. This time she went after a married man.

Hart McKee—Love and Vengeance

Genevieve Phipps and Cornelia Baxter had been best friends growing up in Denver. Genevieve had graciously bowed out of any competition for Gerald Hughes—the boy they both set their sights on—when Cornelia and Gerald were engaged. But when Cornelia jilted Gerald for Hugh Tevis, Genevieve was furious. She worked tirelessly to exile the Baxters from any society events in Denver, thus hastening their departure.

In Paris in 1904, Cornelia saw a chance to even the score. Genevieve, also heir to a family fortune, was involved in a high-profile divorce with her husband. In their divorce he named not one but two correspondents, blackening her name along the way before finally paying $1 million to be rid of her. Meanwhile, Hart McKee was getting a divorce of his own. McKee, the married heir to a Pittsburgh glass-factory fortune, had been named as having an affair with Genevieve in the divorce suit. All that was left was for him to get free of his wife and he could marry Genevieve—or so the world thought.

Cornelia met McKee in Paris and glommed on to him immediately. When he flew to the United States to finalize his divorce, Cornelia surprised him by showing up in Pittsburgh. By the time he finally got his divorce, Genevieve was out, and Cornelia had him firmly snared. They married in a discreet ceremony—but it wasn't discreet enough. Pittsburgh society was so disgusted that the minister who married them had to publicly apologize. He said he was too new to the area to know the history of the parties involved. Had he known, he assured his congregation, he would not have had anything to do with the wedding.

Barons, Counts, and Kings

It was while Cornelia was in Paris that she played a part in one of the odder incidents in her life. As usual, her beauty was at the heart of it. This time it was a straight-up swindle.

Bernie Gruenebaum went by several names. An Austrian huckster of meager means, he introduced himself in the 1890s to New York society as the elegant Baron Gruenebaum. He knew horses, which gained him entrée to New York's horse society, and he was wined and dined by the city's wealthiest families while he scouted for a mark. In 1899 he had been arrested for passing bad checks and spent a year in jail in New York. The experience pointed to only one possible option: He had to take his tattered reputation and go west where he was unknown.

In departing the city, Gruenebaum remembered meeting the wealthy US senator from Colorado, C. H. Hughes. So, he set out for Denver. Hughes welcomed the "baron" and helped introduce him to Denver society, including Cornelia Baxter and her father. Gruenebaum had agreed to procure four carriage horses for Baxter, who had advanced him money for the purchase. Since he never intended to use the money for horses, Gruenebaum chose instead to flee to San Francisco to work on a bigger target—the Wells Fargo millions of the Tevis family.

Imagine his shock when, in San Francisco, he encountered Governor Baxter and his teenage daughter Cornelia. He explained to the governor he was in San Francisco to find the finest horses. A convenient lie. But the next evening he introduced Cornelia to Hugh Tevis, who thanked him profusely for finding him the love of his life.

"When a man has to steal a woman there's a lot more romance in the possession of her," Tevis exclaimed.

Gruenebaum would soon leave San Francisco as the drama between Cornelia and Gerald Hughes played out, but it wasn't the last time he would see Cornelia.

Four years later their paths crossed outside of Paris at the Chantilly Racecourse. The finale of the meet involved a carriage parade of the social elites.

Cornelia, now widowed, remembered Gruenebaum as a horseman, though he was now traveling under the name Count Gregory. Her carriage was to contain King Leopold of Belgium, assorted minor royalty, and her British admirer, the Earl of Rosslyn. Leopold was a noted womanizer well into his sixties who would marry a sixteen-year-old French prostitute shortly before his death. At Chantilly, though, he was swept off his feet by Cornelia, and Gruenebaum saw his chance for a score.

In Cornelia's box at the races, he encouraged the king in his efforts to sleep with Cornelia. He suggested a gift of a jeweled toilet set might be appropriate. Rather than have the king lower himself to shopping, Gruenebaum suggested he procure the gift for him, to which the king assented. Gruenebaum next approached a member of Europe's wealthy Rothschild banking family. He laid out his plans and asked for a letter of credit, which he could leave with the jeweler. Armed with the letter, Gruenebaum visited the jeweler and exchanged the letter for the toilet set. The delighted king paid him 125,000 francs to reimburse the jeweler, and spent the evening trying to charm Cornelia.

Gruenebaum, meanwhile, decamped with the king's money, quite confident that someone would cover the letter of credit to the jeweler—or not.

Gruenebaum's colorful forays through American society led him to the highs of its leading horse shows and banquets and to the lows of jail time for fraud. He died in 1921 in jail in Germany for trying to swindle his landlady. Cornelia Baxter Tevis McKee, however, still had a long career ahead of her.

Break-ups and Younger Men
It probably gave Cornelia great pleasure to have stolen Hart McKee from under the nose of her rival and former best friend. Cornelia and Gene-

vieve met once for a full-out, hair-pulling, eye-gouging brawl in a hotel room, but Cornelia's 1905 marriage to McKee did not last long.

The McKees were spending the winter of 1907 in Paris when Cornelia shocked society by filing for divorce. The proceedings in the French courts made for juicy reading. The couple's explicit love letters were entered into evidence, revealing that when they were apart, they missed making love in the bath most of all. Cornelia painted a picture of a violent home in which Hart fired off pistols, kept pornography, and spent her money lavishly on gifts for women friends while refusing to pay her the $25,000 annual allowance he promised. The household ran through thirty-five maids, all of whom fled to avoid Hart's advances.

Hart countered with charges that Cornelia was unfaithful and brazenly so. She flirted with old flames, prompting him to chase after her and constantly question her whereabouts.

The judge granted the divorce and decried American morality: "These two persons are victims of wealth and idleness," he wrote. "They are spoiled children of the rich and must be treated as unfortunate hothouse plants."

It would be seven years before Cornelia could marry again—this time to English-Argentine cricket player Evelyn Toulmin, who had retired and gone into banking. Their marriage in 1914 was Cornelia's third and longest. Long enough for her son, Hugh Tevis, to accuse the couple of looting his share of the Tevis estate to the tune of $1.8 million.

Her marriage to Toulmin ended in divorce, but Cornelia had one last trip down the aisle in her.

In 1932, at the age of fifty, Cornelia married William Gower. This time it was Cornelia who was the elder statesman. Her new husband was twenty-seven.

Gower already had his own colorful history. In 1928 he married Huguette Clark. Clark was the unusual daughter of William Clark, copper mining mogul and US senator from Minnesota. The couple married when she was twenty-two and he was twenty-three.

Gower was the son of the accountant who helped manage the affairs of Clark's copper empire. The marriage was arranged and doomed from the beginning. Financially, however, it was a success for Gower, who was paid $1 million by her family to marry Huguette.

Apparently, Gower was such a lousy lover that the couple's honeymoon put Huguette off sex and men for the rest of her life, which was long and strange indeed. She made headlines with her passing in 2011 at age 104. She had lived most of her life as a recluse in Manhattan, having spent her final years in New York's Beth Israel Hospital, generally under assumed names.

Huguette left an estate of roughly $300 million, most of it going to charity. William Gower relinquished all his rights to her money at their divorce, which was granted on grounds of desertion. Perhaps Cornelia taught him a few things about the art of love, as her marriage to him was, finally, a success.

The Wealthy Teenage Widow
Who Wanted to Be Alone

IF MADELEINE ASTOR HAD ANY HOPE THAT THE PAPARAZZI WOULD leave her alone during her engagement, it left her when she survived the sinking of the *Titanic* on her honeymoon.

Eighteen-year-old Madeleine hoped to settle down quietly with the forty-seven-year-old man she met and married in Mount Desert's exclusive summer colony. But he was one of the richest men in the world—and then he went down with the *Titanic*.

She was a socialite at a time when socialites were celebrities, and her marriage at the age of eighteen to a wealthy—very wealthy—divorced man caused a sensation. The celebrity press of its day loved the story of the beautiful teenager, the rich scion of a storied family, and the April-November marriage with a whiff of impropriety to it.

Madeleine was born Madeleine Talmage Force in 1893 in Brooklyn, New York. Her father, William, was the wealthy owner of a shipping company; her mother, Katherine Talmage, was the granddaughter of a Brooklyn mayor.

Still, the Forces were considered nouveau riche by New York's old money set. Katherine's social ambitions earned her the nickname "La Force Majeure."

Madeleine was sent to elite private schools: Miss Ely's in Greenwich, Connecticut, and Miss Spence's School for Girls in Manhattan. Her mother took her and her sister to Europe several times. She learned to dance, to ride horses, to play tennis, and to sail her father's yacht. She appeared in several society plays and made her debut in New York at the age of sixteen—attracting little attention.

Husband Hunting on Mount Desert

Madeleine's anonymity disappeared when the press pounced on her romance with Colonel John Jacob Astor IV. The couple met in Bar Harbor, though exactly when is unclear. They were seen together in Bar Harbor in September 1910 after his divorce in March by his first wife, Ava Willing, a domineering Philadelphia socialite.

Madeleine and her mother joined Astor on his yacht, in his opera box, and at his homes in Newport, Manhattan, and the Hudson Valley. The gossipy newspaper *Town Topics* in 1911 noted, "Mother Force has let no grass grow in getting her hook on the Colonel."

Astor was one of the richest men in America, the son of William Backhouse Astor and Caroline Schermerhorn Astor, the grande dame of New York's old-money elite. Caroline Astor was the queen of the so-called "Fashionable 400," believed to be the number of people who could fit into her ballroom.

Her son earned the title "Colonel" for his involvement in the Spanish-American War. Though he was considered a dilettante he managed to expand the family's considerable real estate holdings in Manhattan. He invested in a hotel that would become the Waldorf-Astoria, wrote a science fiction novel, and patented several inventions, including a bicycle brake and a device to produce gas from peat moss.

The news of his engagement on August 2, 1911, sent the media into a frenzy.

The *Washington Times* editors observed that Madeleine was admitted to the best of Brooklyn society but "never stepped through the sacred portals of wealth and culture until her meeting with Colonel Astor."

So, when her engagement to Colonel Astor was announced, this eighteen-year-old girl was lifted from the comparative seclusion of the "younger set" in New York society to the eminence of a girl whose future as a social leader is secured. In the full glare of publicity the

*women who now are the arbiters or New York society since the death
of Colonel Astor's mother have scrutinized her.*

Madeleine Makes a Splash

The press breathlessly covered her arrival at the Astor family cottage,
Beechwood, in Newport. "Mrs. Ogden Mills was the first to call at
Beechwood to present the official welcome to Miss Force and her family," reported the *Boston Globe*. "That means there is no social power in
America which can oppose the Astors' social standing." Madeleine and
the colonel would learn, to their chagrin, that the *Globe* was premature in
its conjecture. Madeleine's position in society was anything but secured.

The paparazzi caused Madeleine to collapse due to "nervous and
physical strain." When she secluded herself in her parent's home in
Brooklyn, reporters turned their attention to her family. They staked out
her house, once eavesdropping on an argument between Madeleine's
mother and Colonel Astor through an open window. Her father was said
to have used his cane to chase away a photographer who tried to take his
picture outside of a jewelry store.

William Force, however, was willing to speak to the press about the
ministers who wouldn't marry his daughter. A Newport minister, the
Reverend George Chalmers Richmond, had refused to perform the ceremony. Madeleine's father was quoted saying he was lacking in Christian
spirit. Richmond retaliated by denouncing the wedding in a sermon,
"Sins of Society." Its subhead: "The Astor-Force Alliance—a Threat at
the Foundations of Our American Morality."

Richmond accused Madeleine of selling herself to the highest bidder
in a sermon shocking to today's ears. "Let me tell you who are responsible
for the scandals, divorces and demoralization of American society, the
women of this country," he preached. "They are money-mad, clothes-
mad. They hunger and thirst for the limelight. The home is just a place
in which to eat and sleep. They scheme for automobiles, for notoriety.
They dress with such immodesty that their limbs and bodies are exposed
to the gaze of all who wish to look. They lust for wealth and for the evil
leadership in fashionable society."

The engagement was even considered fair game for the opinion pages. The *Evening Post* editorialized about the pending nuptials, referring to them as the "selling of daughters to worthless inheritors of wealth or rank." Madeleine's former school principal, Miss Clara B. Spence, agreed with the *Evening Post*. She wrote a letter to the editor shortly after the engagement was announced on August 7, 1911. Miss Spence blamed Madeleine's mother and the "leaders of society" who encouraged her.

"Not only should we be indignant with the arranged marriage of a young girl with a "notorious roué," but the so-called leaders of society, who, perfectly understanding the terms of the marriage, continue to send flowers and congratulations, must share with parents the responsibility of encouraging a marriage which can lead only to unhappiness and scandal," wrote Miss Spence in righteous indignation.

Miss Spence was, at the time, living with her longtime companion and assistant principal, Miss Charlotte Baker, in a cottage on the grounds of Kenarden. Baker was the niece of Emma Kennedy, the widow of John Stewart Kennedy.

The Wedding Wreck

Madeleine and Colonel Astor were married in the Astor mansion's ballroom in Newport on September 9, 1911. To throw off the press, they leaked the news that they'd be married in a country inn. *The New York Times* fell for the ruse. On the front page, the *Times* reported a clergyman had been found who was willing perform the ceremony, "probably in Connecticut."

Colonel Astor's son by his previous wife, twenty-year-old Vincent, was his best man, though he would later make no secret of his hatred for his stepmother. The Congregationalist minister who married the couple was criticized so severely he resigned from his pulpit.

Perhaps to avoid the press, the new Mr. and Mrs. Astor took an extended honeymoon, first to Paris, then to Egypt. Madeleine became pregnant on the journey, and they decided to return to America. They booked passage on the *Titanic*, bringing with them a maid, a nurse, a valet, and their Airedale dog.

John Jacob Astor IV was easily the richest man on the ship, worth more than $2 billion in today's money. When he learned the ship struck an iceberg, he went to tell Madeleine in her stateroom. He said he didn't think it was serious. They went to the gymnasium to sit on the mechanical horses and chat. They wore their lifebelts, but he found an extra one and cut it open with a knife to show her what it was made of.

When it became apparent the ship was sinking, he helped her through a porthole on A deck into Lifeboat 4. He asked if he could join his wife in the boat to protect her, as she was in a "delicate condition." He was refused. A survivor standing nearby later recalled, "Mr. Astor then said, 'Well, tell me what is the number of this boat so I may find her afterwards,' or words to that effect. The answer came back, 'No. 4.'"

Madeleine Astor was rescued by the *Carpathia*. John Jacob Astor IV and his valet died in the disaster. Astor was either crushed by a falling smokestack as the ship sank or drowned in the icy water.

His body was recovered a week later. He was identified by the initials J.J.A. on the back of his flannel shirt collar. On his body were found a gold watch, gold and diamond cufflinks, a diamond ring, $2,240 and 225 pounds sterling, and gold coins.

Madeleine gave birth to their son, John Jacob Astor VI, on August 14, 1912, at the Astor mansion in New York City. He inherited from his father a trust fund worth $3 million.

An Inheritance of Trouble

Madeleine's son was immediately under attack; his legitimacy was questioned by his half-brother, Vincent Astor, who had inherited $75 million, the bulk of his father's estate. Vincent was by all accounts a difficult and irascible person. He blamed Madeleine for his father's death and refused to have anything to do with his half-brother.

John Jacob Astor IV bequeathed to Madeleine $100,000, income from a $5 million trust, and use of the Astor's Fifth Avenue home and Beechwood in Newport. She would forfeit it all if she remarried.

For several years she ventured out rarely, described as the "girl widow" by the press.

Her situation was summed up by a headline that appeared in newspapers across the United States: "Social Ostracism in a Lonely Fifth Avenue Palace, Harassed by Fears for the Safety of Her Tragic Babe."

In 1913, Madeleine Astor returned to Bar Harbor, where she rented a waterfront cottage built for a Pennsylvania coal baron. La Selva was an 8,600-square-foot chateau overlooking Frenchman Bay. There she tried to resume a normal life, doting on her young son. By the time he was three years old, she had spent $6,000 on toys and clothing for him, including a mink coverlet and an ermine robe.

There was widespread interest in the "Titanic Baby," and speculation about whether his health had suffered because of his mother's grief and terror. "Newspaper photographers were assigned the task of getting his picture; but it proved to be a hard one, lasting more than a year and extending from New York to Newport and Bar Harbor," wrote photographer Edwin N. Jackson for the *American Magazine*. Few photographers ever got a glimpse of the child. One photographer hid himself before sunrise in the bushes near La Selva. He waited until 10 a.m. and finally snapped the baby sitting on a bench nearby, but he had turned his head just as the shutter opened.

Jackson, the photographer, then had more luck. He stood in front of the Astor residence on Fifth Avenue every day from 8 a.m. to 5 p.m. without seeing the child. Finally, he saw the nurse with a baby carriage leave from the servants' entrance, and he stalked them. Eventually she took the child out of the carriage and let him play on the sidewalk with a toy horse. Hiding his camera, Jackson sneaked up to the child and called his name softly. John turned around, he snapped the picture and the nurse rushed up and cried, "How dare you!" Jackson snapped another shot of the baby, which appeared in every major newspaper in the country.

The Burdens of Wealth
John Jacob Astor IV's other son, Vincent, was hounded by crowds of people asking for money and then threatening him when he didn't give them any. On the day he turned twenty-one and inherited his father's money, crowds gathered outside his offices just to catch a glimpse of the

richest young man in America. He was forced to hire a bodyguard and carry a revolver to protect himself.

The press was again stirred to frenzy when Madeleine announced in 1916 she would marry a childhood sweetheart, William Karl Dick, a banker who had inherited $3 million from his grandfather. They were married in a simple ceremony at the St. Saviour's Episcopal Church in Bar Harbor while a crowd of reporters and photographers waited outside. They managed to fool the press by sneaking out the back door of the church and driving to Ellsworth, Maine. There they boarded a train for New York, where they started their honeymoon.

After they returned from their honeymoon, they lived in the rented Islecote Cottage on the George Vanderbilt estate in Bar Harbor. Madeleine had two sons with Dick: John and William. The marriage lasted until July 1933, when Madeleine filed for divorce in Reno.

Four months later she married an Italian prizefighter, Enzio Fiermonte, who taught her sons boxing. She was forty, he was twenty-five, only four years older than his stepson, John Jacob Astor VI. Fiermonte had left an ex-wife in Italy, who in February 1935 left her job in a shirt factory to demand money from Madeleine. When Madeleine hired an Italian lawyer to protect herself, it made international news—as did the story that Enzio Fiermonte had stormed out of their hotel room after a fight.

Madeleine divorced him in 1938, citing extreme cruelty. She charged that he beat her and demanded money.

Two years later, Madeleine Force Astor Dick Fiermonte died of heart failure at the age of forty-six in her Palm Beach, Florida, mansion.

Political Bad Boys

Daddies Dearest

THE PRESIDENTIAL ELECTION OF 1884 WAS ONE OF THE DIRTIEST, AND closest, in history. And smack in the middle of the mud was James G. Blaine, influential Maine politician and regular summer swell in Bar Harbor.

The 1884 race was Blaine's third try for the presidency. His first two efforts were stopped short by his record of corruption. But in 1884 he finally secured the Republican nomination for president against Democrat Grover Cleveland.

The result was a mud-flinging contest like few had ever seen. Allegations of bribery, religious slurs, and sex scandals all received a full airing.

The revelation that Grover Cleveland had an illegitimate child has long been remembered as the most salacious issue in the campaign. But Blaine had his own sex scandal that also kept people gossiping at the time. What people have forgotten was James Blaine's love child.

Bar Harbor and the Blaines

The Blaines were fixtures in Bar Harbor, especially during the last summers of James Blaine's life. He joked that as a young man serving in the Maine Legislature in 1856, he had visited Mount Desert Island for the first time. He then had the chance to buy it for $500—the entire island. Over the years he and his family became more attached to the island, and in 1885 they built a palatial cottage of their own called Stanwood.

But in 1884, Blaine was still renting in Bar Harbor while looking for land to build on. More importantly, he was in the midst of a presidential election. Blaine had lived in the public eye most of his adult life and his fortunes—both political and financial—had risen steadily.

By then, Blaine was a household name and one of the most influential politicians of the post–Civil War era.

He was born January 31, 1830, in West Brownsville, Pennsylvania, to a family of some wealth and status. His great-grandfather, one of the wealthiest men in Pennsylvania on the eve of the American Revolution, had served as George Washington's commissary general.

Blaine graduated from his father's alma mater, Washington College (now Washington & Jefferson College).

According to a biographical sketch written in 1884 by George Alfred Townsend, "Jim Blaine" was noted in college for two things: He was a skilled debater and a great player at shinny, an informal form of hockey. "He has a long, Irish-boned spine, legs and arms, and you can fancy him jumping into the middle of a crowd even on the floor of congress, and get in his crooked stick and yank out the ball and give it a lick that sends it whirling away, and then see him laugh, opening his mouth wide, and enjoy the game," wrote Townsend. His classmates said his style of speaking hadn't changed since his college days. He would cross over to his opponents' side and get very close to their faces.

Blaine began his career as a schoolteacher at the Western Military Academy in Blue Lick Springs, Kentucky. After three years he became part owner and editor of the *Kennebec Journal* in Maine. Under Blaine's leadership, the newspaper became a house organ of the Republican Party and helped launch his career in politics.

Running for President

Blaine won a seat in the Maine Legislature, then Congress. He rose quickly in the Republican Party and became Speaker of the House at just thirty-nine in 1869, serving until 1874. He won a US Senate seat from Maine in 1876. He also sought his party's nomination for president that year, but he was tripped up by a scandal known as the Mulligan Letters.

Blaine had a history of accepting bribes, especially from railroad executives who needed Congress to give them the land to build railroad lines across the country. In one deal alone Blaine made more than $110,000 for securing a land grant for a railroad company.

A railroad company bookkeeper named James Mulligan revealed the details of how Blaine had been bribed in a series of letters that outlined the operation. The clincher seemed to come in a letter from Blaine that carried the instructions: "Burn this letter." Blaine stonewalled, though the evidence against him was convincing.

Blaine again ran for the Republican nomination for president in 1880 but lost out to James A. Garfield, who won the general election and named Blaine US secretary of state. Blaine, secure in his new status, commissioned an architect to build a palatial mansion in Washington's ultra-fashionable DuPont Circle. "Here the rich parvenu, anxious to enter the swell society of Washington, builds his house," reported the *Boston Globe*, no fan of James G. Blaine. Blaine's ostentatious house was the biggest in Washington, next to the British ambassador's residence. It cost an exorbitant $85,000 and was nicknamed "Blaine's Folly."

Blaine moved out of the showy mansion after Garfield was assassinated. He had literally been standing next to Garfield when the killer shot him. Blaine then took up residence on Lafayette Square in a home once owned by William Seward, secretary of state to Abraham Lincoln. Blaine already owned a stately home in Augusta that had belonged to his wife's parents. Eventually it became the Executive Mansion for Maine's governor.

Controversial and Congenial

Blaine cut a fine figure in public. He was tall, handsome, charismatic, and well dressed. In 1888, a newspaper article devoted a paragraph to his appearance: He was dressed in a "black cutaway coat, with a pair of light striped trousers and gaiters of the same material, buttoned over a pair of fine French calf shoes. He wore a standing collar of ecclesiastic height and whiteness, and the regulation four-in-hand scarf."

One of his many nicknames was "the Magnetic Man." Another was "the Plumed Knight." But he was reviled as well as revered. To his detractors, he was the "Continental Liar from the State of Maine."

The *Boston Globe* opined there were two James G. Blaines. "One is a know-nothing, a stock jobber and a monopolist; the other a philanthropist." He was both the soul of chivalry and the abettor of scandals, the *Globe* editors wrote. They mocked him for his pious claim to be a friend to labor. "One Mr. Blaine has always been poor but honest, having steadfastly refused even to have anything to do with coal and iron lands in Ohio, lest he should seem even remotely to be opposed to the dearly beloved miners, whose good will and friendship were more to him than any amount of gold or other goods of this transitory world. The other Mr. Blaine bought liberally of the stock of one of the most grinding monopolies in Ohio."

Mrs. Harriet Blaine also had her admirers and detractors. In Augusta, she was known as an avid reader, generous to a fault, and a friend to the poor. In Washington, she was viewed as stiff and distant. Newspapers reported that in the nation's capital she was considered exacting and imperious, indifferent to the feelings of others, a woman who thought she was better than anyone else. And as her husband rose in stature, she only got worse. By the time James G. Blaine was elected to the Senate she, "shut herself behind such a barrier of exclusiveness that there were few people brave enough to try to penetrate it." When Garfield named Blaine secretary of state, no woman in Washington was more disliked, the *Globe* reported. Her autocratic nature was alluded to even in her obituary, where the flaws of the deceased are rarely mentioned. The *Boston Globe* obituary read:

> During her husband's long political career, from which he derived a very large fortune, Mrs. Blaine is said to have cared nothing for the social opportunities that came to her, and she was generally regarded in Washington as exceedingly cold and reserved. She always remained thoroughly domestic in her tastes and preferred to be queen in her home circle rather than shine in more public surroundings.

Third Time Lucky

In 1884, Republicans made James G. Blaine their candidate to run against Democrat Grover Cleveland for the presidency of the United

States. The race shaped up as a contest between the corrupt Blaine and the squeaky clean reformer, Cleveland.

Blaine's opponents taunted him with allusions to the Mulligan Letters with shouts of "Burn, Burn, Burn this letter." Blaine's blustery stonewalling against the charges of corruption were seen as signs of strength by his supporters.

In a convention speech nominating him for the presidency, his fiercely argumentative style was lauded: "Like an armed warrior, like a plumed knight, James G. Blaine marched down the halls of the American Congress and threw his shining lance full and fair against the brazen foreheads of the defamers of his country and the maligners of his honor."

"The Plumed Knight" was adopted as a term of mockery by his enemies. Blaine's Republican supporters, meanwhile, unearthed an interesting item about Cleveland. He had an illegitimate child. When confronted, Cleveland admitted the fact. Now the Republicans had their own charge to make. They disrupted speeches by Cleveland surrogates chanting, "Ma, Ma, Where's My Pa?"

In late August of that year, the Democrats decided to bring out an old story that had first appeared years earlier in the *New York Times*. Using a newspaper in Indianapolis as the vehicle, the story of James Blaine's love child came out.

The Love Child

At the heart of the scandal is one simple date. James Blaine married Harriet Stanwood of Augusta, Maine, on June 30, 1850, in Millersburg, Kentucky—or so his official biographers would tell you. His marriage certificate, however, is dated March 29, 1851 and was issued in Pittsburgh, Pennsylvania. A minor discrepancy in the scheme of the world, but for the people of Maine—and much of the rest of the country—it was all they were talking about in August of 1884.

The story was crafted to show Blaine in the absolute worst light. It told of Blaine's days as a young schoolteacher in Kentucky. His future wife, Harriet, was also a teacher in the neighboring town of Millersburg. Blaine was quite the partier in 1849 and made the rounds of the girls in town, including Harriet. It soon became clear that Harriet was pregnant.

But Blaine refused to marry her and continued his dating, leaving Harriet to live on her own. The town was scandalized to have a pregnant, unmarried woman teaching at the girls' school, and she was told she would have to resign. Still Blaine refused to take responsibility for the baby.

Finally, Harriet's uncle or brother came to town, the newspaper reported, and confronted Blaine and threatened him. The exact nature of the threats was not known, but Blaine admitted he had impregnated Harriet and agreed to marry her.

The couple traveled to Pittsburgh and were married. Harriet continued on to her family home in Maine while he detoured to New York. In Maine, Harriet gave birth to a son—Stanwood—in June of 1851, just three months after the shotgun wedding had taken place.

The baby died after only three years and was buried in Augusta. And the shameful secret that Blaine had impregnated and at first refused to marry Harriet Stanwood seemed to die with him. One of the most appalling charges that the newspaper leveled was that Blaine had chipped the baby's birth date off his gravestone with a chisel, defacing his son's grave to keep his secret.

Blaine Speaks

Reaction to the story was predictable. Blaine's enemies relished the way he was smeared, just as his supporters had smeared Cleveland. The leading libertine, he was dubbed by some. The seducer of the Republican Party.

The pressure grew on Blaine to vindicate himself or be dropped from the ticket. He had no choice but to respond. From Bar Harbor he telegraphed a terse denial of the story, and then he sued the newspaper that started it for libel. The suit was filed, he said, to defend the honor of his wife. Then Blaine took to his bed. His doctor insisted he had a cold and sore throat and required at least a week of total rest.

The lawsuit was welcome news to the Indiana newspaper, which repeated its story and now would have a chance to question Blaine. In the discovery stages of the trial, Blaine tried to clear his name as best he could.

Yes, he acknowledged, his son's gravestone had been defaced, but he did not know who did it. Yes, the boy had been born in June of 1851. And yes, he had married Harriet in March of 1851 in Pittsburgh.

But, he said, he and Harriet had been married secretly in a small ceremony with only two witnesses, both of whom were now dead. The second wedding was conducted because, he said, he realized he had not obtained a marriage license for the first, and its validity might be challenged. It was not a shotgun wedding, he said, forced by Harriet's family.

Blaine's story of the secret wedding drew howls of laughter, and the press took great pleasure in pointing out the ludicrous nature of the denial. Marriage licenses were required by law, they noted. No one would perform a wedding without one. What possible reason would Blaine have for letting the town think Harriet was an unwed mother? They brought forward more witnesses who said Blaine introduced himself as a single man in 1851 and even dated other women.

One writer cheerfully pondered: "Is Blaine insane?" Blaine's response, he noted, was "striking evidence that he has become mentally addled."

The newspaper crowed that he should have come forward and admitted the truth—as Cleveland had done with respect to his child—rather than fabricate a story.

The Final Slur

Though the love child damaged his campaign, it was an anti-Catholic slur that probably tipped the scales against Blaine. A speaker at a Blaine campaign stop rallied his supporters with the warning that a vote for Cleveland would put the country under the sway of the Catholic Church. He called Blaine's opponents advocates of "Rum, Romanism, and Rebellion."

Cleveland operatives spread news of the slur widely in Catholic communities and produced a strong turnout against Blaine. In the tight election, nearly ten million votes would be cast, and Cleveland would win by fewer than sixty thousand. His supporters chanted gleefully, "Ma, Ma, where's my Pa? Gone to the White House, Ha, Ha, Ha!"

Two days before Christmas, Blaine dropped his libel suit. He didn't believe he could get a fair trial, he said, and his critics laughed again, noting that the honor of his wife must have seemed somehow less important after the election.

Blaine briefly retired from public life. He decided to build a villa in Bar Harbor befitting a man of his stature. Stanwood, named for his wife's family, took two years to build from 1885 to 1886. He hired a famous architect, Frank Furness, to build the huge Queen Anne style house with oversized turrets and enormous stone veranda.

Blaine filled the house with the mementos and souvenirs he acquired during his career. Among them was a valuable punch bowl that had belonged to George Washington. When the Blaines moved into Stanwood, Harriet Blaine hired a carpenter to unpack their furnishings and told him if he found anything broken, he shouldn't tell Mr. Blaine. The carpenter found the punch bowl broken in two pieces. She gave it to him. The carpenter repaired the bowl and showed it off to his visitors.

Stanwood, meanwhile, became a regular stop for Republican politicians. In March of 1889, President Benjamin Harrison named James G. Blaine his secretary of state. That summer Blaine entertained Harrison for six days at Stanwood. The visit was reported in minute detail by the press: How Harrison and Blaine arrived on the brightly decorated steamer *Sappho*, wearing overcoats on the deck. How the revenue cutter *Woodbury* fired a national salute, while nearby yachts joined in. How they were cheered by crowds of people on the wharf and in the streets, which had been decorated for the presidential visit. How they proceeded in a stylish landau to Stanwood. How they were received by Mrs. Blaine on the doorstep while Mr. Blaine's big mastiff looked calmly on.

Harrison was treated to a flurry of receptions by Bar Harbor society, including US senators Henry Cabot Lodge and Eugene Hale; author Mrs. Burton Harrison; the Potter Palmers of Chicago; George Vanderbilt; John Stewart Kennedy's partner, Morris K. Jesup; and foreign ministers of France, Turkey, and Italy.

Blaine served as secretary of state for three years, resigning in June 1892. He died on January 27, 1893, leaving nearly all of his considerable wealth to his widow. The Atlantic Eyrie Lodge now sits on the former Stanwood Estate.

No Dynasty for Jimmie

AFTER HAVING EIGHT CHILDREN, JAMES AND HARRIET BLAINE MIGHT reasonably have expected to build a family dynasty. One of their four sons, presumably, could have stepped into Blaine's shoes and built upon his legacy. Perhaps one of the boys could even win the tantalizing prize that had eluded their father: the presidency of the United States.

But the Blaines' oldest son, Stanwood, passed away as a young child. Of the remaining sons, Walker Blaine was the one most likely to have a future in politics. Walker was an accomplished attorney who at thirty-four served as solicitor to the State Department when his father served as secretary of state.

In 1890, however, the Blaines' second and most successful son died of pneumonia. With Walker's passing, two sons remained—Emmons and James Jr., the youngest, aka Jimmie or Jamie.

Emmons was a moderately successful businessman, jumping into the railroad business, where his father had substantial holdings. But he was not groomed for politics. And his only appearance on the national political stage probably hastened his death.

Emmons attended the 1892 Republican National Convention in Minnesota, where he worked tirelessly as his father's representative. Too tirelessly, it turned out. Two weeks later he died, probably from an infection aided by exhaustion. Like his brother, he was thirty-four when he passed away.

That placed the burden on Jimmie, if there was any hope for a Blaine political dynasty. And a slim hope it was.

Jimmie the Wild Child

Jimmie established his credentials as a wild child early on. He had been thrown out of two exclusive private schools and a prep school. In 1886, at age seventeen, he was being tutored privately at home and, his father hoped, preparing for college.

James Blaine would later describe his son as: "The most helpless, least responsible member of my family; erratic but controllable through his strong affections; an object of constant watchfulness to his parents, his brothers and his sisters, a source of constant anxiety, but not despair, because he is of good abilities, as readily influenced to the right as the wrong, and because the patience of love can never know weariness."

Perhaps. But in the summer of his seventeenth year, Jimmie's constantly watchful family had decamped to Bar Harbor for vacation and left him in Augusta with a tutor. Enter Marie Nevins, a minor actress one year older than Jimmie.

Nevins's family was also visiting Bar Harbor from New York. They were reasonably well off—after all, they were summering in Bar Harbor. But they hadn't spent a lifetime in politics seeing their opportunities and taking them. In other words, the Blaines were far richer.

Marie and her sister spent a few days in Augusta, and that's where Marie met Jimmie. The two fell in love. When Marie rejoined her parents in Bar Harbor, she spilled the news about her new romance. Her parents were appalled. Young Jimmie was wild, had no prospect of a career that would support a wife, and, on top of all that, they doubted his sincerity.

Lacking a blessing from either set of parents, Jimmie and Marie eloped and married in New York. A Catholic priest, friend to the Nevins family, performed the ceremony in his rectory. His two servants acted as witnesses. A rectory wedding of two young people with no family or friends in attendance, he assumed, suggested a child was on the way. With a promise that the couple would raise their children in the Catholic Church, he agreed to conduct the wedding.

To choose just one word to describe the marriage: Short. Ugly would be another apt choice. The couple separated soon after having a child, and the marriage ended in 1892, but not without acrimony. In fairness to both sides, following are Jimmie's and Marie's versions of the relationship.

The Divorce—He Said, She Said

Marie Said	Jimmie Said
After she met Jimmie in Maine, Marie's parents abruptly hustled her back to New York. However, Jimmie pursued her there and persuaded her to marry him against her parents' wishes.	Marie began scheming to marry the wealthy Jimmie Blaine within a week of meeting him, arranging the priest and the ring and encouraging him to research the laws about marriage.
The marriage was a happy one until the couple had a baby. At that point, Jimmie relapsed into his old ways, drinking, fighting, and chasing women.	The couple first moved to Pittsburgh and then New York, where Jimmie worked as a reporter. The marriage was a dismal failure, with the young couple hopelessly in debt and living beyond their means. They were offered the use of the Blaine home in Augusta and a substantial stipend while Jimmie found work that could support his family.
The couple went to Augusta in the summer of 1888 with their new baby to spend some time with Jimmie's family. Here, Jimmie abandoned the family to travel to Bar Harbor and carouse with the rich summer girls, though he told her it was to help his father in his campaigning. Trapped in Augusta with Jimmie's mother, Marie was barraged with the older woman's hostility as she repeatedly claimed Marie had "stolen my baby."	The couple went to Augusta, penniless, to discuss their future. This was when the Blaines offered the house and a stipend. Jimmie wanted to accept it, but Marie declined. Jimmie had left Augusta to help his father, and was in Bar Harbor alone, but only because his business had been delayed by rough weather.

Marie Said	Jimmie Said
Marie returned to New York, and wrote to Jimmie seeking support and asking him to join her. He ignored her letters. She returned once more to Augusta to try to see him, but he refused. Jimmie's mother, meanwhile, furious that her grandson was being raised as a Catholic, tried to persuade Marie to give up the child.	Jimmie refused to go to New York and had told Marie that she needed to settle in Augusta with him. He agreed that he did not provide any support for her, but says his mother's offer to take their child was merely a kind gesture and that, had the couple surrendered the child, it would have been with the understanding that they could reclaim the boy any time they liked.
With no money from Jimmie or his father, Marie turned her hand to acting and announced she planned to take to the stage using the name "Mrs. James G. Blaine." This produced the desired result of shocking the Blaines into action.	James G. Blaine, Jimmie's father, visited New York. However, the visit was far from an attempt to bring about reconciliation. He told his daughter-in-law in a letter that there would be no support, nor would there be a reconciliation with his son.
Marie sued. She would not seek a divorce, for her Catholic faith forbade it. Instead, she sued Mr. and Mrs. Blaine for alienation of affection. They had turned their son against her, she said, and tried to steal their child so he wouldn't be raised Catholic. She wanted $100,000.	Jimmie's specific response to this is unrecorded, though he denied the allegations. But apparently the lawsuit opened the Blaine checkbook and negotiations began in earnest.

Marie Said	Jimmie Said
Terms were not disclosed, but Marie cast aside her religious objection to divorce and moved to South Dakota (where divorce laws were liberal).	James G. Blaine announced he was never pleased with his son's marriage, but was satisfied that the divorce was the best outcome. His son, he concluded, was "more sinned against than sinner."
Jimmie was concerned that Marie intended to charge him with infidelity and cruelty. He hired detectives to follow her. In the end, Marie simply charged him with abandonment and failure to support his child. Jimmie did not contest the divorce, his lawyer sitting silent during the proceedings. Marie won $100 per month alimony in perpetuity. The case was final in 1892.	

The divorce might well have ended as a he said/she said affair, except with the benefit of hindsight that makes it pretty clear who was the sinner and who was the sinned against.

Marie's health suffered during the divorce. She was nursed back to health by a physician who had been a friend of the Nevins family. She married that doctor in 1893, and the couple lived happily until his death sixteen years later.

Blaine Back on the Loose

With a wife no longer holding him back, Jimmie Blaine began splashing in again among eligible young society women.

For a time, Jimmie Blaine held a clerkship in Washington, DC, thanks to his father's influence. He eloped with a congressman's daughter, however, bringing shame upon the family when he abandoned her after three weeks in New York.

For a time, he dabbled in journalism, reporting for the *New York Tribune*. Jimmie Blaine was well known in Manhattan as a charming, if somewhat wild, man about town. It wasn't uncommon for Jimmie Blaine to stir up nightclubs by clattering his hansom carriage right up to the front door, and even inside the building if he could manage it. The show delighted his friends. The club owners, not so much.

Stories circulated of wild times with actresses and models, night-long revelries and orgies, and all-out brawls, all with Blaine's name attached.

He got engaged to the exotic sculptor Kuhne Beveridge of Chicago. She, too, had been married as a teenager, and her marriage also ended badly. Beveridge had married actor Charles Coghlan. Unfortunately, she discovered Coghlan already had a wife—and a daughter. Coghlan argued over whether he had actually married the wife in question, or whether they were simply married under common law. The distinction seemed lost on Beveridge. She divorced him. On the rebound, she was squired about by Jimmie Blaine.

The relationship did not last, however, and Blaine set about looking for a new love. Meanwhile, Blaine also took "the gold cure" at least once. It was a method of treating alcoholism by eating gold. It didn't take. He told the world that his heartbreak at the loss of Miss Beveridge was so great that he wanted to join the US Army and serve in the Spanish-American War. That way he could drown his sorrows with the thunder of guns. Commissioned as a captain by the War Department (most likely on the strength of his father's connections), Jimmie Blaine was sent to the Philippines to become assistant adjutant general to General Wesley Merritt, who would become the first American military governor of the island country.

But this was Jimmie Blaine. Was it possible for him to get from Washington to the Philippines to assume his duties without causing scandal? Of course not.

Go West, Young Man

Jimmie's first prolonged stop on his way to the Philippines was in San Francisco. There he got into a very public argument in a restaurant over money. The argument ended with an agreement that the combatants would meet for a duel at dawn. (Knowing Blaine, noon would have been more likely.) In the morning, dried out and in the stark light of day, cooler heads prevailed. The duel never materialized, but not before the newspapers reported the whole affair.

A stop in Hawaii proved an even bigger disaster. There, Blaine was invited to a luau. He brought the wine and presumably drank plenty of it. When he groped another man's wife, Blaine was beaten to a pulp and had to be hauled back to his ship.

With Jimmie Blaine already wounded before battle, the War Department called him home. But not before he apparently managed one more romantic entanglement. He announced he intended to marry Hawaiian Princess Victoria Kaiulani. At one time she was in line to be queen of Hawaiian Islands, before the monarchy fell and the country joined the United States. The marriage never happened.

Jimmie Rings the Belle

Returning to the East Coast, Blaine set his sights on one of Washington's most sought-after, and beautiful, young women: Martha Hichborn.

Martha, the daughter of Rear Admiral Philip Hichborn, was nicknamed "The Heliotrope Belle" because she loved to wear gowns the color of heliotrope, a pinkish-purple flower.

Chauncey Depew, a wealthy senator from New York, was so smitten by the much younger Martha that he declared her the most beautiful woman he ever saw. Depew was the leading suitor for her affections, but he had a lot of competitors, including Jimmie Blaine.

Martha was wary of Jimmie. When he got involved in another street brawl in New York City, she gave him an ultimatum. He must give up his vices if he wanted to marry her. He agreed, of course, but Martha was still cautious. If he could prove that he could behave himself for one year, she would accept him.

"Could Love for an Admiral's Daughter Reform Young Jimmie Blaine?" blared one headline. The world was skeptical.

But Jimmie proved everyone wrong. In June of 1901, Jimmie Blaine and Martha Hichborn married. It looked as if Jimmie Blaine had finally reformed. Perhaps the Blaine dynasty was merely delayed. Or not. Their marriage progressed in tumultuous fits and starts for five years.

In 1906, Martha Hichborn Blaine was having lunch with a friend in a New York City restaurant. Jimmie Blaine barged in and attacked her friend and set about tearing up the restaurant. Martha hopped a train to South Dakota without delay. After a short stay and with a return train to catch for Washington, she made it in and out of a courthouse in under an hour. She revealed that Jimmie Blaine had deserted her, failed to support her, and treated her cruelly. She cut the story short and dashed down the courthouse steps in time to catch the train back east, divorce in hand.

The Final Years

By all accounts, Jimmie Blaine possessed the psychotic charm necessary for success in politics, but none of the discipline to conquer his demons. He apparently made a mediocre journalist, clerk, and stockbroker—but he never rose to the pinnacles of power that his father and mother might have hoped for. Still, he did make one final trip down the matrimonial aisle.

In 1920, he proposed to Mrs. Beryl Whitney Graydon Wheeler. As her name suggests, Beryl was not a newcomer to the marriage game either.

"Will Peace Come at Last to These Matrimonial Careers?" a newspaper headline asked, complete with a flow chart diagramming the prior marriages and divorces of the happy couple.

Beryl Whitney was a wild child from a wealthy family herself. As a young woman at Ely's Boarding School in New York, she frustrated her minders by running away from school to have fun down on Broadway. As punishment, the school banished her to a cottage in the Connecticut woods where incorrigible girls could be corralled with a chaperone.

But Beryl, who was heir to a sizable fortune, proved too sharp for her guards. She telephoned her boyfriend, Harvard College football quarterback Tom Graydon, and he showed up to keep her company, pretending to be her brother. A sharp-eyed chaperone caught on that the couple was a little too cozy for brother and sister and sent Tom packing.

The pair's second attempt at running away was foiled when a school chaperone spotted a ladder at Beryl's window. But, third time lucky, the future Mr. and Mrs. Graydon eloped. Tom, though, had chosen a career as a Cincinnati cobbler. He couldn't support her in the style she desired, so she divorced him.

A second trip down the aisle with J. C. Wheeler proved no more successful for Beryl, and it, too, ended in divorce.

To say the public was skeptical of the third union for Jimmie Blaine and Beryl Wheeler was an understatement, but this one took. The couple moved to California in 1923 because of Jimmie's declining health, and he died in 1926, still married.

Lacking the senior Blaine's ambition and intelligence, one newspaper noted, "The father was destroyed by Rum, Romanism, and Rebellion. It only took rum to bring down the son."

The Duchess of Dix Island

JANE BEALS WAS AN ACTUAL DUCHESS. AND SHE OWNED A TINY MAINE island that had produced a very large fortune. But by the time she gave it to her gigolo husband in Bar Harbor, the island had become a national symbol of scandal.

The story of the Duchess of Dix Island begins with a bad investment. In 1839 Horace Beals became a partner in the Franklin Granite Company. After just eighteen months, the firm—with quarries in Quincy, Massachusetts, and New York—foundered, leaving Beals with nothing.

It wasn't the only time Beals would fail, but he was determined to succeed. Beals would later accept a piece of land in Maine—the fifty-five-acre Dix Island and some smaller neighboring islands—as payment for a debt. That decision would make him a millionaire many times over.

At first glance, Beals wasn't in love with Dix Island. If someone were looking for a good place to commit suicide, he concluded, Dix with its high granite peaks would be a fine choice. Over the next fifty years, tiny Dix Island's population would explode and contract, topple a political dynasty, and give rise to a Spanish duchess before finally slipping into the hands of her flamboyant Bar Harbor gigolo and once again returning to obscurity.

Dix Island is about three miles off the coast of Rockland, Maine. Today it's home to a handful of summer houses. While private, its owners welcome polite visits from day-tripping boaters. When Beals acquired it, along with several neighboring islands, Dix was just a potential granite quarry. But it also put Beals at the nexus of an unusually ambitious and corrupt group of politicians and businessmen.

Beals was the operations man at Dix Island. Others provided political and financial clout. Courtland P. Dixon was essential to Dix's first big job—providing granite for the Charleston Customs House in far-off South Carolina.

Dixon was son of a US senator from Rhode Island and brother to a New York congressman. He lived in the South and had a strong network among the politicians there. So, it was no surprise the final design of the Custom House in South Carolina included Maine granite in its specifications. In those times, senators got to sign off on the details of federal construction jobs in their states.

The work at the quarry slowed during the Civil War, but Beals and Dixon were perfecting their operation. They would join together with three others and form the Granite Ring—a scandalous business association that rigged public construction contracts for decades.

How the Ring Worked

The ring was made up of General Davis Tilson's Hurricane Island Granite Company, Mark St. John of Clark Island Company, J. R. Bodwell of the Bodwell Granite Company of Vinalhaven, and Dixon's Dix Island Granite Company. Bodwell would go on to become a governor of Maine, but for the most part these men relied on (that is, bribed) two of Maine's notoriously corrupt Republican leaders, Rep. James G. Blaine and Sen. Eugene Hale, to handle the politics. Beals's ties to a Massachusetts congressman, Benjamin Butler, also helped them rig the deal.

The team worked a multipronged approach. Buying off US senators, they would get the federal architects to specify Maine granite for major new buildings. By working together, they could rig the bids and direct the work where they wanted, setting prices as they pleased.

In the earliest days, corrupt government architects would simply contract with a specified quarry to provide granite. Congress began protesting this outright mishandling of money, so the operations got more sophisticated. Government architects would solicit bids. The quarry owners would get together and decide who would get the work and submit bids that generated a predetermined winner.

If some outsider were nosing around and possibly bidding, one quarry would submit a lowball bid that would guarantee it would win. Then, when all the finalists were revealed, it would be clear who the second lowest bidder was. If it was a member of the Granite Ring, the winning bidder could step aside leaving the job to a friendly quarry at a higher price.

And that was just one of the ways the members of the Granite Ring lined their pockets. To make the deal even more lucrative, the quarry contracts were known as "15 percent contracts." The quarry owners would supply finished granite and charge the entire cost of mining and finishing it plus 15 percent. This provided every incentive to produce the granite as expensively as possible. And to make sure the operation was under friendly control, Blaine had the government architect in charge of all buildings appoint one of Blaine's friends to keep track of expenses at Dix Island.

Investigations Begin

By 1871, Alfred B. Mullett, the government's chief architect, was under constant investigation by Congress for the money he wasted. He would resign, but the Granite Ring would proceed without a hitch.

Over time, other states demanded to get in on the action enriching the Maine Granite Ring. With federal construction projects exploding following the Civil War, there was plenty of money to spread around.

Congress decided that town after town, no matter how small, needed a post office, customs house, or other federal building. Looking back on the Granite Ring scandal, Alfred Mullett was rueful in an interview with the *Cincinnati Inquirer*.

"This new contracting for the public buildings is a steal clean through. The quarry men put it up and paid Ben Butler fifty thousand dollars to get it done."

"Tell me, Mr. Mullet," I said, "all about that quarry job, and who were in it?"

"It was a Maine job," said Mullett, "engineered by that little villain Eugene Hale. Originally they designed to let in only Maine

quarries, but Condit Smith, General Sherman's old quartermaster you know, Big Smith, he found they were going to count out his quarry, the Westham (Richmond, Virginia) quarry, and he burst it open. They had to let him in and Jonas French, Ben Butler's quarryman of Cape Ann. The Bodwell granite company is in it on behalf of the Cincinnati post office. They own the Fox Island quarries. Then the Hurricane Island and the Dix Island quarries join in, too.

"That granite ring is an offshoot to the lime kiln ring that governs Maine politics. These fellows sold me out," he said.

Blaine and his cohorts made Mullett the fall guy when the Granite Ring was exposed in 1874. They then turned to his assistant, William Hill, to keep the Granite Ring running for another ten years. Hill, Mullett said, was a "pusillanimous, illiterate cuss."

Labor Shortage

With the politics in place, the only problem the quarries had was finding enough labor to deliver the enormous edifices on time. Workers flocked to Dix Island from Mount Desert and all over Maine. Wages on the island were roughly twice what a man could make elsewhere. Still there weren't enough men.

Dix Island and the other Maine quarries advertised internationally and soon attracted interest from Scotland and Ireland. The first men to arrive were well paid and well treated. The word spread rapidly, and soon stonecutters from Europe were flooding into Maine by the hundreds.

At its peak, more than fourteen hundred men were living and working on tiny Dix Island, mining and finishing the huge blocks of granite for federal projects. Some estimates put the island population as high as two thousand. The US Treasury building in Washington, the New York City Post Office, and the Philadelphia Post Office were built largely of Dix Island granite. Countless smaller projects were made of the stone, as well.

The more skilled workers were put to work carving eagles and other decorative architectural elements. The unskilled workers polished and finished stones or pulled the blocks from the quarry with fifty-two oxen that called the island home.

More than a thousand workers lived in island boardinghouses and hotels. The Dix Island Hotel had 250 rooms, The Aberdeen, 200, and largest of all, The Shamrock, had 350 rooms. In addition to the workers, the hotels played host to congressmen and businessmen when they came to visit.

Boats made their way daily from the coast carrying even more workers—ferries and small rowboats alike leaving in the dark morning hours and returning home in the afternoon. On one side of the island, a steady stream of schooners arrived to carry the granite south to the cities. The island was outfitted with a school for the children of the workers and a church. Forges produced tools, and stores supplied necessities.

There was a seemingly limitless demand for labor. More workers meant more money for the Granite Ring. The monthly payroll at Dix Island alone topped $100,000. A lot of that money found its way back to Ireland and Scotland, but plenty stayed local. In addition to driving prices up for land and goods, it fueled illegal liquor sales and gambling houses.

For the Granite Ring, the quarry was a thing of beauty. For every dollar they paid out, the government paid them $1.15.

The good times couldn't last forever, however, and they didn't. In the early 1870s, reformers in Congress were pushing for a cleanup. But they were bungling it badly.

For example, in one contract with Dix Island, the government made an agreement: If the work on the island required more than a hundred men, it would pay for buildings to handle the excess workforce. By 1874 the government had paid roughly $150,000 (plus 15 percent) to have housing and other buildings erected on the island as the workforce ballooned. Under pressure from Congress, the architect's office renegotiated its contracts. To untangle itself from Dix Island, it put the buildings it had paid for up for auction. The Dix Isle Granite Co. bought them for $1,400. Roughly six months later, Dix Island had won more government business and the government bought those same buildings back for $150,000.

Congress also mandated an end to the 15 percent contracts, instead demanding fixed prices. Now the quarry owners had every incentive to cut wages, and quarrymen found their $4.50-per-day wages cut to $2. Profits were soaring as the quarries squeezed their workers. Before the "reforms," the quarry owners might make $180 on a ton of granite. Now they cleared $600 to $800 a ton.

Though outright strikes were rare, the workers were angry about the company stores they were forced to buy from. In addition, the health effects of inhaling granite dust year in and year out were becoming apparent.

The election of 1878 focused everyone's attention on Maine when the unthinkable happened. A stonecutter who worked on Dix, Thompson Murch, ran against and defeated Congressman Eugene Hale. Both Republican and Democratic newspapers were shocked that a labor rabble-rouser could win in Maine. And even though the Legislature responded by later installing Hale in the Senate, the election marked a turning point as the Granite Ring began to crumble.

The Duchess Departs

Horace Beals didn't live to see his Dix Island quarry reach its greatest heights, nor did he see its decline. He died in 1864 when the quarry was profitable but not yet enormous. His wife would be the beneficiary of his good fortune, hard work, and hustle.

Jane Cornwall married Horace Beals in New York. He was fourteen years older than she, and together they had four children. While Horace and his family lived on Dix Island, he hired architects and gardeners and gave them carte blanche to build a mansion and estate. He hired plenty of servants to try to make island life more appealing for Jane.

But Jane Beals never developed the affection for Dix Island that Horace hoped, and when he died, she couldn't leave the island fast enough. She turned her back on the mansion and all its ornate fixtures, leaving them to spoil. It would serve as a barn for sheep before finally yielding to time.

Free of the island, Jane Beals remarried, and remarried, and remarried. She first married a doctor. Then she married the Spanish Duke della Castellucia, which made her Jane Tamajo, Duchess of Castellucia.

There was one last gasp of adventure ahead for Jane. In 1893 the duke died. Splitting her time between Florida and New York, she would encounter her final husband: Edward Leonard Dwyer. Jane was seventy and by all accounts a shrewd woman. Dwyer was forty-three, an unapologetic adventurer well known to Mount Desert society.

In the six months of their marriage in 1895, Edward would manage to extract $350,000 from Jane. The duchess shocked Bar Harbor when she gave her new boy-toy the small group of islands off the coast of Maine. Unbeknownst to many, the once-valuable islands were now largely uninhabited and stripped of much of their granite.

In her last years before her death in 1895, Jane made five wills, each revision adding in children and grandchildren or disinheriting them as her moods swung. In the end, her family divided up more than $7 million and generated more than 1,200 pages of legal filings as they feuded among themselves.

For husband number four, his final inheritance was just $10. He sold Dix Island, and the other islands, for $135,000. He used the proceeds for his final adventures, and the quarries slowly wound up business.

The Louisiana Lottery King
Builds a Seaside Mansion

NEAR THE HULLS COVE ENTRANCE TO ACADIA NATIONAL PARK YOU'LL find an unassuming building, now owned by the National Park Service and used as a park ranger's residence. It was built as the caretaker's house for an enormous mansion across the street called Bogue Chitto, an unusual name for a Maine mansion. Bogue Chitto means "big creek" in the Choctaw Indian language. It's the name of a river that flows through Louisiana, and that's where the mansion came from, or at least the money to build it.

Bogue Chitto was an oceanfront palace built by the proceeds of one of the great scams of the post–Civil War era, paid for by suckers from around the world. It was built by John Morris, better known as the Louisiana Lottery King.

The South was full of scam artists after the Civil War, but John Morris, who lived from 1836 to 1895, was incredibly corrupt even by the loose standards of Louisiana after the war.

How corrupt? He routinely maintained a slush fund (estimated at $500,000) for buying political favors whenever he needed. And he needed a lot of them. At the height of his influence, he shelled out enough cash to bribe virtually the entire Louisiana Legislature in just one night.

King of the Carpetbaggers
The Louisiana Lottery King was a carpetbagger, one of the northerners who poured into the South after the Civil War. Some were appointed

to political office to oversee Reconstruction. Others were businessmen who saw opportunity in legitimate business as the South reestablished its economy. Others were flimflammers who saw the chance to make a fortune in the politically destabilized region. That was Morris.

Morris was originally from New Jersey, but he found himself a local partner, Charles Howard, who had the right pedigree to be his point man in Louisiana. Howard was another ambitious northerner, originally from Baltimore. He had moved south before the Civil War and established some bona fides fighting for the Confederate army.

Howard had established the Louisiana State Lottery Company before Morris got involved. Howard didn't have any money, but his partners did. By spreading it around in the right places, Howard won a charter from the Legislature in 1867 to operate a lottery in the state. When the governor refused to sign off, Howard's friends in the Legislature had the governor arrested.

The new governor they installed approved the creation of the Louisiana Lottery in exchange for an annual payment of $40,000 to the state. Then Howard and Morris double-crossed the first financial backers of the lottery. Howard refused to turn over the charter to his investors and brought in his friend, John Morris. Together they elbowed out the smaller investors.

The "Octopus" Is Born

At the start, the lottery struggled. But Howard and Morris quickly hired a lottery manager who knew what he was doing. He used newspaper advertisements and posters to promote the lottery, and partnered with street-corner betting shops to handle sales. Over time, the lottery ballooned into the largest lottery in America and quite possibly the world.

How was it possible for a small state like Louisiana to have the largest lottery in the world? For starters, most states wouldn't run lotteries, viewing them as blatant rip-offs. And the shadowy, illegal lotteries were notorious for being rigged.

Morris and Howard knew that making the lottery appear honest was essential. The state charter helped. They then hired two former Civil War generals to serve as lottery commissioners. They oversaw the very public drawings of numbers at the company's downtown New Orleans head-quarters. Morris and Howard even hired children from a nearby school for the blind to draw the lottery numbers as another stunt. How could a blind child cheat when he couldn't see?

The two then spread word of the fabulous lottery in newspaper ads and stories that ran throughout the country. The Louisiana Lottery sold tickets across America through a network of newsstands and betting shops. Before long, in-state sales from Louisiana accounted for only a tiny portion of the lottery's revenue.

Lottery Finances

The modest monthly prize that the lottery started with soon multiplied into a wide array of betting options that included weekly, daily, and twice-daily prize drawings as well as loads of special lotteries. Prizes ranged from small $10 and $50 jackpots up to $300,000 and $600,000 prizes. Ticket prices started at less than a dollar and went as high as $50.

Roughly half the money collected was included in jackpots, and the house kept the other half. A cut that big would make any modern casino operator faint. In Las Vegas, slot machines can keep no more than 25 percent of the money wagered. In Mississippi, it's 20 percent. In New Jersey, 17 percent. In today's state-run lotteries the state keeps on average one-third of the money for itself and returns two-thirds to the bettors.

Even while keeping half the money themselves, Morris and How-ard still employed some other sleight of hand to increase their take. For starters, the lottery kept any unsold tickets for itself. Instead of rollover jackpots that kept growing when nobody won, the Louisiana Lottery simply cashed in leftover tickets for itself. If nobody's ticket number was drawn, the lottery itself pocketed the jackpot.

Sharing the Wealth

The Louisiana Lottery hit on another scheme to soften the blow of paying out winnings. It began selling shares of a ticket, especially for its larger drawings. A $50 ticket might be divided into fifty $1 shares, and a customer could buy just a part of the ticket. The idea appealed to gamblers. For example, a gambler might spread a $50 bet over ten tickets, giving him ten chances to win a portion of the jackpot.

The concept appealed to the lottery even more because it could retain a share of the large tickets. So, while it might have to pay out $300,000 on a $50 ticket, it could recoup $30,000 for itself if it held onto 10 percent of that ticket.

Some historians who have studied the lottery say there was never an instance where it paid an entire large jackpot without keeping at least a small share of the money. There are no records of how much money Morris and his backers made from the lottery, but in its peak years the prize money awarded was between $20 million and $28 million. That means the lottery kept at least $20 million to $28 million, not counting the prizes it actually paid to itself.

And what did the state get out of this? A paltry $40,000 per year. No income tax and no sales tax. But the outcry against lotteries began growing louder as the lottery became more successful. People who had never even heard of a lottery would find out fast what it was when the family breadwinner gambled away the rent.

That public pressure generated one of the lottery's biggest expenses: a slush fund for bribes. Morris and Howard always had several hundred thousand dollars on hand for payoffs, and they were quick to provide a job to anyone connected to the state legislature.

Politics, Louisiana Style

The controversial presidential election of 1876 inspired the Louisiana State Lottery Company to make its most blatant show of force ever. Rutherford B. Hayes lost the popular vote to Samuel J. Tilden, but twenty electoral votes in four states were disputed. One of those states was Louisiana. It wasn't until 1877 that a deal was brokered to give Hayes, a Republican, the presidency. In exchange, the Republicans agreed to withdraw federal troops from the South, ending Reconstruction.

But even before Hayes took office, President Ulysses S. Grant had gotten fed up with Louisiana. For years he had tried to impose order on the state, where elections were dominated by fraud, intimidation, violence, and corruption. In frustration, Grant gave the order to withdraw federal troops, leaving the state to sink deeper into chaos.

The election of 1876 also brought a contested election to Louisiana. Two men were claiming to have won the 1876 election for governor. One was from the Democratic Party and the other, a lottery opponent, was a Republican. As part of the deal brokered by Hayes and Tilden, Louisiana was to turn Democratic. The problem, though, was that the Republican-controlled Legislature had to be paid off to go along with the plan and switch parties. The Democrats had no cash to make the payoffs.

It looked as if there would be a new Republican governor, and he would revoke the charter held by Morris and Howard to run the Louisiana Lottery unless something was done.

The Big Bribe

In 1877, the Louisiana Lottery Company bought the entire Legislature. Morris and Howard bundled up $65,000 and sent it to the opening session. The sergeant-at-arms handed out stacks of cash to each legislator—as soon as he registered as a Democrat.

The large-scale bribery wasn't well reported and didn't inspire much indignation. But the churches were pushing to outlaw the lottery, and the outcry against it grew.

In 1879, the Legislature proposed eliminating the lottery. Morris played his trump card. He revealed the receipt for the $65,000 he had paid out to the state lawmakers. And one of his best friends in the Legislature stepped to the podium in the House of Representatives. He asked his colleagues if they were really prepared to put out of business the man who had saved Louisiana from political chaos. Morris carried the day. He had the lottery added to the state's constitution, though he did have to up the annual payments to the state from $40,000 to $1.2 million.

Over the next six years, Morris and Howard fended off their Louisiana opposition relatively easily, but the lotteries were now under fire on the federal level. Armed with new federal laws, the Post Office declared that using the mail to distribute lottery winnings, or aid the lottery in any way, was illegal. The decision jolted the Louisiana Lottery.

Postal Fraud

Each day an enormous volume of mail arrived in New Orleans full of lottery entries. It made up a huge portion of the mail at the New Orleans post office.

Morris was indicted in South Dakota, West Virginia, and Texas for using the mail to illegally run his lottery. The lottery had to begin using private individuals traveling by train to deliver their money and lottery entries to New Orleans. By 1894, the Louisiana State Lottery Company finally was snuffed out of business when its charter expired.

But the "Octopus," as the press called it, was hardly dead. Morris relocated the business to Honduras. He set up a US office in Tampa to take advantage of a Florida law that outlawed Florida-based lotteries but not foreign ones.

Still, a number of forces were working against the lottery. Other states had begun chartering their own lotteries. Though Morris was able to bribe the Florida Legislature into letting him operate in the state, the Honduran government was tougher to buy off. The leaders of the banana republic, not as easy to manipulate as US politicians, demanded steep payments.

The lottery would go underground and by the time both its principals died—Howard in 1885 and Morris in 1895—it was much smaller than it was at its height. But the lottery had made Morris and Howard kings.

Living High in New Orleans

Howard preferred living the good life in New Orleans. He especially enjoyed lording his money over the local society doyennes, many of whom had snubbed him in prior years. Howard had been rejected from a veteran's group when he exaggerated his Civil War military service. Other clubs snubbed him for his lack of Louisiana roots. Howard, though, gave as good as he got. When he was denied entry to the Metairie Jockey Club—the most prominent in the South—he bided his time. Eventually he bought the celebrated Metairie Race Course and converted it into a cemetery. The cemetery today is a favorite of tourists for its ornate, gothic mausoleums—including the graves of Charles Howard and John Morris.

Howard was generous to institutions that served commoners, and his philanthropy extended to building a public library. In addition, he was an early member of Krewe Rex. New Orleans's Krewes are the organizations that run the city's famous Mardi Gras celebration, and Rex is the most prestigious of them all. Each year, even today, it chooses the king of Mardi Gras, who serves as a master of ceremonies. Howard, naturally, was one of its early kings.

Membership in the Krewe was closely restricted, allowing Howard and others to pay back those who kept them out of New Orleans social clubs.

Howard died in 1885 at only fifty-seven years old following a carriage accident near a home he maintained in Dobbs Ferry, New York.

Morris's Nine Mansions

Morris, meanwhile, chose to spread his fortune in Texas, Massachusetts, New York, and Maine. He had been born into a wealthy family. His father was a horse-racing enthusiast who bred horses. Morris kept the tradition alive by owning thousands of acres in Texas for his thoroughbreds. In New York, he rose to the very pinnacle of horse-racing royalty. He built Morris Park Racecourse in the Bronx, which at its peak hosted both the Preakness and Belmont Stakes. He poured record amounts into acquiring thoroughbred bloodstock and won the major races of his day.

Morris was a short, avuncular, heavyset man who drew a wide circle of friends with his charm. Fifteen years before he died, he suffered a stroke and gave up drinking and smoking at his doctor's suggestion.

By the time he died of a second stroke at age fifty-nine, Morris owned nine lavish mansions. In Mount Desert, Morris was mostly known for his arrivals on his grand yacht *Cora*. The vessel weighed eighty-eight tons and was one of the first to be electrified. A massive battery array lit the yacht from every window. It made a marvelous show sparkling on the harbor as guests partied late into the night. Morris brought his party boat into the very backyard of one of his greatest political enemies, James Blaine. As Speaker of the US House of Representatives, Blaine had pushed through laws that outlawed the use of the mails for lotteries.

Morris's money also built Bogue Chitto, the opulent mansion at Hulls Cove that would later belong to his son David and his Vanderbilt wife. It took nearly two years to build and was finished by 1887.

The Last Lottery

When Morris died, his money-making machine lived on. Though his sons David and Alfred were largely known as legitimate businessmen and politicians, they were both indicted in 1907 with a large group of investors in the Honduras national lottery. The company, successor to the old Louisiana State Lottery Company, had continued operating illegal lotteries, generating sales as high as $500,000 a month.

David and Alfred denied having an ownership stake in the lottery. But the case ended with David and Alfred and roughly thirty other men pleading guilty to conspiring to distribute lottery advertisements in the United States. The men paid fines of $284,000 and agreed to hand over all records of the company for destruction, as well as the printing plates that had turned out lottery tickets for decades.

The *New York Journal* newspaper was puzzled by the apparent inconsistency in the Morris brothers' statement. They said they did not own the lottery but still agreed to plead guilty and pay fines of $10,000 apiece. When the newspaper sent out reporters to find an explanation, a caretaker at David's New York house explained that he was in Bar Harbor. Alfred was traveling in the South.

The Morris family attorney, who had recently married David and Alfred's sister, explained the matter the next day. David and Alfred inherited their shares of the lottery from their father. The sons had given up any ownership stake in the lottery in 1906, before the indictments. But they pleaded guilty because the indictments included crimes that occurred while they were still affiliated with the lottery.

With that, the Louisiana Lottery died. By 1910 all lotteries were outlawed in America. It wouldn't be until 1964 when a state-chartered lottery would finally begin again, this time in New Hampshire. All that's left to remind us of John Morris's time in Maine is the caretaker's cottage and the odd name—Bogue Chitto Lane—on a street off Eden Street at Hulls Cove.

Mount Desert Welcomes the KKK

CROSSES BURNING? WHITE ROBES AND HOODS? RACIST RALLIES? Northeast Harbor? Yes, yes, yes, and yes. It was 1926, and Fulton J. Redman ran for the US Senate from Bar Harbor with the promise to support the principles of the Ku Klux Klan.

Heading into the Roaring Twenties, the KKK was largely moribund in Maine, as elsewhere. But a dramatic image makeover brought the organization to life, and its growth was eye-popping. Maine, it turned out, was fertile soil for its message.

Redman, a summer resident of Bar Harbor since childhood, thought he could take the KKK's message of hate all the way to Washington. F. Eugene Farnsworth, a charlatan with a gift for public speaking, would show him the way.

In 1923, Farnsworth had moved to Portland to run a local chapter of the Ku Klux Klan and serve as the state's King Kleagle. Farnsworth gave his first speech in Portland in January of that year, and in twelve months he built the Hooded Order's membership to twenty-three thousand. The Klan reached its peak in 1925 with more than a hundred thousand members in Maine.

In fact, during the 1920s, Maine had the biggest Klan chapter in the country outside of the South. Nearly one in five Mainers was a dues-paying member. Its popularity didn't last long, just long enough to stain the reputation of the state—and of Mount Desert.

That Old-Time Religion

Unlike the South, where African Americans bore the brunt of the KKK's bigotry, their primary target in Maine was Catholics.

Decades before the KKK experienced its resurgence, another politician who summered in Bar Harbor was perfecting the fine art of religion baiting. As Speaker of the US House of Representatives, James G. Blaine introduced an amendment to the US Constitution that banned the use of tax dollars to fund parochial schools.

The Blaine Amendment passed the House in 1875 but failed in the US Senate. The proposal caught on in the states, however, and passed as a law or constitutional amendment in all but eleven states. (Ironically, Maine was one of the eleven that didn't adopt the policy.) Blaine's exploitation of anti-Catholicism came back to haunt him when he ran for president of the United States in 1884. He aligned himself with anti-Catholic voters, and his attacks on "Rum, Romanism and Rebellion" cost him the Irish vote and the election. Ironically, Blaine's mother was Catholic, and his sister was a nun.

Maine's history of anti-Catholicism goes all the way back to the arrival of the English Puritans, no fans of the French nor the Pope. Hostility toward Catholics blossomed again with the influx of Irish immigrants beginning in 1830, and it continued with the wave of French Canadians from Quebec starting around 1840. By the 1850s, the anti-immigrant Know Nothing Party was flourishing in the state.

For decades in the nineteenth century, spasms of violence erupted sporadically against Catholics in Maine. For example,

- In 1834, an anti-Catholic riot broke out in Bangor.
- In 1854 in Bath an anti-Catholic mob set the Old South Catholic Church on fire. When the Catholic bishop tried to lay the cornerstone for a new church on the site a year later, violent anti-Catholics chased away the congregation.
- Protestant temperance advocates fueled tension as Irish immigrants viewed prohibition laws as attacks on them. A rum riot

broke out in 1855 when Portland's working-class Irishmen learned their saloon-raiding mayor had stashed booze in City Hall.

- In 1854, a Swiss-born Jesuit named John Bapst was tarred and feathered in Ellsworth. He survived his ordeal and went on to become the first president of Boston College.

A Movement Builds

On May 30, 1919, the notoriously racist film *Birth of a Nation* was screened at the Star Theater in Bar Harbor. The film presented the hooded Knights of the Ku Klux Klan as heroes and demeaned African American characters. The movie was held over by popular demand, according to the theater advertisement in the *Bar Harbor Times*. It was a harbinger of the Ku Klux Klan's resurgence in Maine and helped pave the way for the arrival three years later of Eugene Farnsworth, Maine's new King Kleagle.

Farnsworth claimed he'd been born in 1868 in Columbia Falls, a small town in Downeast Maine. He began his checkered career in Fitchburg, Massachusetts, as a Salvation Army recruiter, a barber, and a stage magician traveling under the name Frank Farnsworth. Then a large rock he used in his act slipped and killed his assistant, so Farnsworth had to find a new career and a new name. He went to South America for a while, then returned to the United States as F. Eugene Farnsworth. He tried giving magic lantern shows and failed as a film producer before he finally found his true calling as Maine's King Kleagle.

Farnsworth gave his first Klan speech on "Americanism" in January 1923. That same month, Boston's Irish-Catholic mayor James J. Curley called the Klansmen "morons," "public enemies," and "cowards hiding under their hoods." What Curley didn't know was that the rabidly pro-American Farnsworth was probably Canadian.

Farnsworth took his show on the road all across Maine. He claimed the Catholic Church held political prisoners and railed against Catholics getting jobs as teachers and policemen. He called the pope "that Guinea in Rome." In Farnsworth's cockeyed view, Portland Bishop Louis Walsh was "the political dictator of the state."

And when Farnsworth said "the scum of Europe had been dumped on the United States," his audience understood him to mean immigrants from Ireland and Quebec.

The Klan held its first daytime parade in Milo during the summer of 1923. Farnsworth claimed, "Everybody belongs to the Klan, including 600 citizens, town officials, and the sheriff." Later that year, the Klan's state convention in Waterville drew fifteen thousand people.

The KKK Arrives on the Island

In the fall of 1923, the KKK began recruiting in private homes on Mount Desert Island. Farnsworth spoke at a Klan meeting at Neighborhood House, Northeast Harbor's community center, in October. The Klan featured a Protestant minister on the program, its usual practice, with regional Klan leaders introduced by Alvah L. Reed, a prominent local citizen. Reed was a justice of the peace, a trial judge, a civil engineer, and charter member of the Northeast Harbor fire company.

"The Catholics, Jews and Negroes are clannish and stick together, while the native born Americans are constantly rowing with one another," Farnsworth told the Northeast Harbor crowd.

By April 1924, Farnsworth was drawing large crowds on Mount Desert Island. He lectured that month to six hundred gathered at the Casino in Bar Harbor, but he showed some restraint. Farnsworth probably knew Bar Harbor had popular Catholic and Jewish merchants, office holders, and summer visitors. Most of his audience came from other towns, and the *Bar Harbor Times* reported that people from Bar Harbor were there out of curiosity.

"If we had to make a list of all the things that Bar Harbor could do without, we would head the list with the K.K.K.," the editors wrote in an editorial denouncing the Invisible Empire.

Yet they mocked the Klan as unlikely to have much of an impact.

"If a few of our neighbors want to pay $10 for the privilege of parading in a white nightie and really think it worth the price, then perhaps they are entitled to this form of diversion."

The *Bar Harbor Times* editors were wrong, however, about the Klan's influence. The KKK's candidate for governor that year was Owen Brewster, a Mayflower descendant from Dexter who opposed taxpayer funding for parochial schools. He was running against another Mayflower descendant, William Robinson Pattangall. Brewster never openly acknowledged the Klan's support, but he was unquestionably their candidate.

Pattangall attacked Brewster for the Klan's endorsement, making it the centerpiece of his campaign. Brewster was also denounced by members of his own party. Despite splitting the Maine Republican Party, Brewster won the election. Later, Maine voters elected him to the US Senate, where he became a close friend and ally of Senator Joseph McCarthy, the demagogue who led the witch hunts against alleged Communists in the 1950s.

To celebrate the election of Owen Brewster, the Klan sponsored a free Klam bake on the Graves Farm in Trenton. Turnout was huge, with as many as eight thousand in attendance, and fifty bushels of steamed clams were given away.

"Fiery crosses were kept burning from nightfall until late in the evening," reported the *Bar Harbor Times*, citing one of the Klan's favorite intimidation tactics. The Maine Kluxers, though, lacked the penchant for secrecy embraced by their southern brethren. Only a small portion of the Klansmen and women at the Trenton gathering wore the robes of the Invisible Empire, and they wore their hoods thrown back.

In the South, the Klan infiltrated the Democratic Party, just as it had the Republicans in Maine. And in the South, as in Maine, the KKK was splitting its chosen political party in two. At the 1924 Democratic National Convention in Madison Square Garden, a motion to condemn the Klan was defeated. Tens of thousands of hooded Klansmen celebrated in a field nearby. Klan convention delegates urged violence, burned crosses, and attacked effigies of the party nominee, Al Smith, a Roman Catholic.

But worse than the Klan's political antics was the growing awareness of its connection to murder, lynching, torture, and mob violence. As far back as 1906, Northeast Harbor's Henry Hoyt had won a US Supreme Court case against a Tennessee sheriff for letting a mob lynch a black man accused of rape. And in 1922, KKK Imperial Kleagle Edward Young Clarke put paid to the Klan's pledge to support law and order and protect the purity of womanhood. Joseph Pulitzer's *World* reported the Kleagle was arrested in his pajamas in a notorious underworld resort with a woman not his wife. Clarke quickly resigned.

In November 1924, newspapers reported a Klansman had committed a crime against a woman on Mount Desert. A Bar Harbor dress shop owner named Lottie Hamilton was bound and gagged in her apartment. Her assailant was a white man in a hood and a white robe.

Nevertheless, Maine's Klan membership continued to grow, reaching its peak at 150,141 by the end of 1925. Mount Desert Island had about a thousand members.

On Christmas Eve that year, the Knights of the Ku Klux Klan burned a cross near the Union Church in Bar Harbor. Their white robes gleamed in the firelight as they held a short service. They prayed and sang hymns.

They did it again on Christmas night under a moonlit sky in Northeast Harbor. A large crowd of hooded Klansmen burned a cross on the lawn of the Neighborhood House as they sang hymns and prayed.

No one disturbed the Kluxers in their bedclothes, but the burning crosses undoubtedly terrified the town's French-Canadian and Irish residents.

Redman Joins the Movement

The Klan's surge in membership did not go unnoticed by Fulton J. Redman. Redman did, however, fail to grasp that the Klan had reached its zenith in 1925.

Redman's big opportunity came on August 23, 1926, when Republican US senator Bert M. Fernald suddenly died at his home in West Poland. Fernald's death left the US Senate deadlocked, with forty-seven members from each party. The seat could not remain unfilled, and a Democratic victory would weaken the power of Republican President Calvin Coolidge.

Fulton J. Redman, a Democrat, decided to run for Fernald's seat on the wave of Ku Klux Klan activism.

But that activism was waning. The charismatic Farnsworth had been removed as King Kleagle in 1924 over a dispute about spending money. The Klan, it turned out, suspected him of pocketing $4 of every $10 he collected. The KKK's large auditorium in Portland also burned down that year. Other Portland properties were expensive to keep up, and the Klan was struggling with finances.

The forty-one-year-old Redman was the son of an Ellsworth lumber dealer and grandson of the county sheriff. Since his youth, he had spent summers in Bar Harbor. He graduated from Bowdoin College and Harvard Law School, and practiced law in New York and Portland.

He had dabbled in Democratic Party politics, serving a term in the Maine House of Representatives and as a delegate to the Democratic National Convention. But locally he was mostly known as a genial summer resident at Salisbury Cove who actively supported a national park on Mount Desert.

Redman quietly sought the support of the Klan. He made it clear that his wife, Florence Murphy, belonged to the Episcopal Church, the *Lewiston Daily Sun* reported.

He should have heeded the *Bar Harbor Times*, which reported on one of the last KKK meetings at the Casino. A speaker from Portland had come on behalf of a Klan candidate for the empty Senate seat. But local voters were tired of the hate mongering.

Only about two hundred people came to the meeting. Afterward, the *Bar Harbor Times* concluded, "In the future no candidate for public office in this State will dare to enter a campaign beneath the banners of the Ku Klux Klan."

Redman won the Democratic nomination for the Senate seat, while the Republicans rejected the Klan candidate and chose Arthur Gould, whose wife was Catholic. Gould ran a campaign against the KKK.

Race to the Wire
The special election was to be held on September 13, 1926. It was a red-hot campaign, generating national money and attention because its outcome would tip the balance in the US Senate.

Just three weeks before the election, a Methodist minister who worked for the Klan accused Arthur Gould of spending more than the $1,500 allowed on his campaign. Owen Brewster, the Klan's man in the governor's office, repeated the charge.

Gould fired back at Brewster with both barrels. "No other explanation can be made than that he has lost his sense of proportion by his
connections with and subjection by Imperial Wizard [Hiram] Evans and
others of his lesser satellites in that hooded organization known as the
Ku Klux Klan," said Gould.

He further slammed Redman for pledging to support the principles
of the Ku Klux Klan if elected.

In its election coverage, the *Lewiston Evening Journal* quoted a voter
in that heavily Catholic city. He said he planned to work for Gould. "I
want to see Mr. Gould elected by a majority so sweeping that the Klan
will fade entirely from the political picture in Maine," he said.

He got his wish. Maine Democrats voted in droves for the Republican Arthur Gould to break the power of the Klan. Gould carried every
city and county in the state. The Republican state committee chairman
said his victory showed "the sinister influence of an oath-bound organization no longer threatens the welfare of Maine."

By year end, Klan membership had fallen by more than half to
61,136. By 1927 it was at 3,168, with only 226 members in 1930.

Fulton Redman ran for governor of Maine in 1940 and lost. Two
years later he ran for US Senate and lost. For a time, he published the
Portland Evening News, then became the newspaper's columnist. He died
in Bar Harbor in 1969.

An Epitaph for the Klan

A local resident named Ray Foster in 1974 described the Klan's activities
on Mount Desert Island in 1928.

> *The Ku Klux Klan was active then [1928] and a lot of us joined it
> thinking it was kind of like a cross between the Masons and the Boy
> Scouts. We liked the encampments [at Barcadia near the Trenton
> Bridge]. . . . It wasn't long before we were told we had to hate the
> black people. We weren't excited by that, but there weren't many blacks
> around MDI then, so it didn't make much of a practical difference.
> Besides, society was different then. Next, we were told we had to hate
> Jews. Guys started to get uncomfortable, then. There weren't many*

Jews around, but there were people like Dan Rosenthal, a peddler who came in summer. Everybody liked Dan. He was a good man.

Then we were told we had to hate Catholics. Well, that did it. There were a lot of Catholics around. We knew damned well they were good people. A Catholic priest in Northeast—Father Kinney—was active in the fire company, for example. There was a Catholic church on Lookout Way in Northeast Harbor. The Catholic church had just bought one of the old local houses on Summit Road and was renovating it for a rectory. The Catholic church was enlarging that story-and-a-half little house into a larger three-story rectory.

Well, just about all the workmen in Northeast Harbor donated at least a day's work on that rectory job and we all signed our work. That was our message to the Ku Klux Klan, from every damn one of us. You'll find our signatures all over that house. That was the end of the KKK for Northeast Harbor.

Nelson Rockefeller Lands on the Rocks

On Mount Desert Island, being a Rockefeller meant you were royalty. An open affair with a married woman could be chalked up by island society as just some friskiness brought on by too much fresh air. But when the rest of the world learned of it, the reaction was quite different.

Nelson Rockefeller was born on Mount Desert in 1908, and it's fitting that he died there in 1959—died politically, that is. His actual death was a full twenty years down the line.

Rockefeller ran for president three times—in 1960, 1964, and 1968. Of all of the races, however, 1964 held his only realistic hope for securing the job he believed he was perfect for. He had been elected governor of New York in 1958. In the 1960 presidential primary campaign, which no one expected him to win, he had shown deft political skills, charisma, and grace in a bid against Richard Nixon.

With Nixon's loss to John F. Kennedy, Rockefeller was poised in 1964 to step in as the fresh face of the Republican Party. Positive, progressive, a problem-solver. As the public saw it, the prize was virtually his for the taking.

But in addition to politics, Rockefeller had another great appetite that got in the way: women.

Making the Man
Nelson Rockefeller was successful at almost everything he put his mind to. He was a persuasive and gifted businessman. Though he inherited a

fortune, that didn't deter him from expanding it. In the 1930s, with the nation mired in the Great Depression, he spearheaded his family's efforts to get its latest investment—Rockefeller Center—filled with tenants and generating income.

As a young man he overcame dyslexia. In an era when little was known about the disorder, Nelson persevered and overcame it using all sorts of methods to memorize what he could not read. He had letters typed by secretaries and forced himself to plod through written speeches no matter the difficulty.

Nelson stunned his father by winning election to the governor's office in New York. The Rockefeller name was synonymous with obscene wealth, and John Rockefeller did not believe people would ever vote for a Rockefeller. But he didn't count on Nelson's charm, which carried him to four victories in a row.

It can be confusing to think of Nelson Rockefeller at the end of his life—heavy-set, gray haired, with giant Harry Caray glasses—as being a magnet for women, until you recall that in his youth he was movie-star handsome.

As a boy in high school, Nelson reported that he had nine girls all asking him to visit them over holiday break. His popularity continued as he grew older. In college at Dartmouth, he declared that he intended to marry early and get on with life.

Marriage and Happiness

His choice of a mate was an odd one. He met Mary Todhunter Clark in the summer of 1925 while he and his family visited Mount Desert. She went by Tod and was a year older than Nelson. But she had the outgoing personality of his mother and a try-anything-once zest for life he found compelling.

Their romance slowly blossomed as she accompanied the Rockefeller family on a trip to Egypt. Even in the early days of their romance she showed the good sense to doubt his sincerity.

"For heaven's sake," she wrote him in 1929, "get all that flirtatious-ness out of your system before you and I get married if we ever do. If we should be married about a year and you came to me with a love confession about falling in love with some charming woman—well—it would break my heart that's all."

For his part, Nelson assessed Tod's weaknesses: She was taller than he, a year older and he found her not terribly attractive. Still, he concluded, she was a worthy match.

After a ten-month, round-the-world honeymoon, the couple settled into married life. He went to Cleveland for a short time to get started in the real estate business and then quickly returned to New York. There, he and Tod had four children and soon settled into a rhythm: They spent winters in New York's Pantico Hills and summers at their twenty-one-room Seal Harbor estate.

Rockefeller had constructed The Anchorage in 1939 at Crownin-shield Point, Seal Harbor. Standing right at the mouth of the harbor, the mansion matched the man—bold and prominent.

By all accounts, Rockefeller was incredibly generous, quick to help out when friends found themselves facing medical bills or other expenses. Generous on the Rockefeller scale meant handing out thousands or even tens of thousands of dollars as loans, which he routinely forgave. But it was never quite clear if these "loans" were simply generosity or if he gave them out knowing they would generate silence and loyalty.

The Rift

To all outward appearances, the marriage was a success. By 1939, however, an important change crept into the family routine. Nelson would dine with the family, but he began sleeping in the guest house.

He undertook a series of jobs in Washington in the departments of Defense and Health, Education, and Welfare. These gave Rockefeller even greater freedom. While he worked in the city on the issues of the government, he found himself with a staff of pretty young women assistants.

During this period, Rockefeller had a parade of young women to choose from. Gifts of cars and cash made it all the easier to accept that their duties included visiting his home, where he liked to work in bed.

Whether it's a testament to Rockefeller's checkbook or the genuine affection his mistresses felt for him, very few details of these relationships ever crept out—maybe a love letter here or a sly reference there.

Washington socialite Joan Ridley—whose family would inspire the hit sitcom *Eight Is Enough*—would write that Nelson once followed her playfully into the shower. Ridley was one of a string of aides who would take over as Rockefeller's favorite for a while. But she had no illusions, because he told her exactly where things stood with Tod: "We will never get divorced, but we will live our separate lives."

Nancy Hanks, who would later head the National Endowment for the Arts, was another woman romantically linked to Rockefeller. She worked on his Albany staff until political advisors exiled her for fear of damaging Rockefeller's reputation.

To the public, Rockefeller's reputation remained above reproach. But among those who knew him, his weakness for philandering was an open secret. "He can't keep his pecker in his pants," observed journalist Arthur Massolo of the *New York Post*.

By the mid-1950s, Rockefeller had grown tired of Washington. His forceful style had him butting heads with bureaucrats, and he moved much faster than Washington's painfully slow processes allowed. He wanted to run his own show, but not just in business. Rockefeller was a progressive Republican who had ideas on a grand scale about how the United States should conduct both its foreign and domestic affairs. He wanted to rule.

The Love Governor

Rockefeller set his sights on the 1958 New York gubernatorial race. Incumbent Averill Harriman seemed well entrenched, but Rockefeller jumped into the race. The public was fascinated by this multimillionaire who retained the common touch. "Hi ya," he'd shout in greeting, happy to listen and exchange ideas with anyone and everyone. He was dubbed Rocky—a name the headline writers who were pressed for space loved, but one that he detested (though he embraced it in public).

His close aides called him Nelson. To the staff at home he was Mr. Nelson. And to everyone else he would soon become Governor.

During the 1958 race, a new lady entered Rockefeller's orbit: Margaretta Murphy, known to most by the nickname "Happy." But this girl was different. Though she was young (eighteen years younger than Nelson), she wasn't a secretary who could be easily sent away with a check and a kiss. She was on his staff, but she was also a social acquaintance.

The Rockefellers had sold land to Happy and her husband on their Pocantico Hills estate so the couple could build a home. Dr. James Murphy worked for the Rockefeller Institute researching cancer. He was a friend of Nelson's, and the governor appointed him to his New York council on mental hygiene. And in Seal Harbor, the Murphys' estate was near the Rockefellers'.

Exactly when Happy's affair started with Rockefeller isn't clear, though 1958 or 1959 seem like good guesses. Happy volunteered on his gubernatorial campaign and followed him to Albany as his confidential secretary—a well-worn path into his bed. Neither chose to advertise the affair, and it was kept tightly under wraps in New York. But in Seal Harbor it was not a secret. The two were frequently seen cavorting about. And even before he met Happy, Nelson had spoken about a potential divorce to close friends.

Tod was, for public consumption at least, still in the dark. She would tell the wife of columnist Drew Pearson she had no worries about Nelson's faithfulness to her: "I don't have to worry about Nelson. Whenever he gets those urges, he just goes outside and moves some great tree around."

Meanwhile, Tod would reluctantly play her part at campaign events, though she wasn't a natural extrovert. Occasionally, however, she would resist. The reason, according to aide Kershaw Burban: "She was terribly embittered by his philandering."

By 1961, the Rockefeller marriage was all but over, though none of his staff knew it at the time. Happy was negotiating with her husband over visitation rights to their four children if or when they divorced.

Dr. Murphy himself may well have been ready for the marriage to end, but he was not inclined to give up his children, and there matters stalled.

A Political Suicide

In November of 1961 Tod and Nelson were prepared to break the news to the world: They planned to split. Nelson wanted his freedom. The first outsiders to learn the news would be Rockefeller's lieutenant governor,

Maxwell Wilson, and his wife. In Albany, Nelson sat down to dinner with Max while Tod dined with Wilson's wife in Pocantico Hills.

Wilson, a staunch Catholic, pleaded with Rockefeller to reconsider. He was throwing away his career, destroying any chance he had to run for president in 1964. Rockefeller would not be swayed. In March 1962, Tod got the divorce in Reno, Nevada. Nelson, meanwhile, coasted to reelection as governor in the fall.

Rockefeller's backers, especially in the conservative South, were gobsmacked by the news. The only silver lining, his people said, was that there were no scandals involved. This was simply a case of a couple growing apart after thirty years, especially because Tod disliked the political life. There would be no bimbos coming out of the closet. Many of Rockefeller's supporters believed that line right up until it became clear it was a lie.

Happy was kept out of the limelight on the national stage. In Seal Harbor, however, it was a different story. In the small town, Happy and Nelson were conducting their affair very much in the open, driving around town in a gold Studebaker and openly making a show of their affection.

The developments shocked even President Kennedy. Not that Rockefeller was cheating. He was shocked that it was Nelson who pushed for the divorce, refusing to believe it until Tod's brother told him personally.

"I don't believe it. No man would ever love love more than he loves politics," he said. For Kennedy, it was great news. A young, vigorous, and charismatic potential opponent for 1964 had just imploded.

In 1963, the last stage of the drama played out. Happy Murphy divorced her husband. Her husband demanded, and she agreed, to give up claim to her own children as the price of divorce. Rockefeller's plans to marry her then surfaced.

The criticism was instantaneous. Former Connecticut senator Prescott Bush—father and grandfather to two presidents—said: "Have we come to the point where a governor can desert his wife and children, and persuade a young woman to abandon her four children and husband? Have we come to the point where one of the two great parties will confer its greatest honor on such a one? I venture to hope not."

Business Week was blunter: "If he marries Mrs. Murphy, he might as well take the gas pipe."

But the marriage proceeded and Rockefeller was now not just divorced, he was a philandering home-wrecker.

The Slow-Motion Wreck

Nelson Rockefeller went into the Republican presidential convention of 1964 a dead man walking. He lacked the delegates; it was clear Barry Goldwater would be the nominee. But Rockefeller took to the floor of the convention anyway, excoriating the party for falling into the hands of such radical groups as the John Birch Society.

He was roundly booed, but he refused to give ground. No one pushed Nelson Rockefeller off the stage. He was immune from the rules of marriage, divorce, and politics (or at least he behaved as if he thought that was the case).

Rockefeller refused to end his speech and shouted down his critics, while Goldwater fumed. The longer the show at the convention went on, the worse the party looked. It set Goldwater up for a landslide loss in 1964.

Back in New York, Rockefeller cruised to victory in 1966. If Happy—or anyone else—thought that changing wives would change Nelson's ways, they were wrong. He quickly took up with a new string of mistresses.

He would win election again in 1970. Four-time governors aren't just unusual, they're practically unheard of. But New York loved Nelson.

With Richard Nixon on the ropes in the Watergate scandal, Rockefeller handed over the reins of government to his lieutenant governor, the long-suffering Max Wilson. His goal, he said, was to give Wilson a chance to establish a record for himself and, hopefully, win the job on his own despite the damage Nixon was doing to the Republican brand.

Rockefeller didn't stay retired long, though. When Nixon resigned, the new president needed a vice president. Gerald Ford called Rockefeller at Seal Harbor. Rockefeller had experience, and he had access to Republican talent that hadn't been tainted by the Nixon scandals.

Nelson agreed. Though he always said he did not want the job, perhaps now he realized it was his last shot at the presidency. His philandering now was, if anything, more brazen.

Vice Presidency

Ken Riland, Rockefeller's longtime aide, cautioned that he needed to be ready for questions about his affairs if he became vice president.

"The rumors I've been asked about and haven't been able to honestly deny—would fill a book," he said. Nelson's press secretary and speech writer, Hugh Morrow, was most familiar with cleaning up after Rockefeller. But through Rockefeller's checkbook and Hugh's guile, Rockefeller avoided most of the scandals.

In 1959, Nelson's son Steven had married the family's maid. After the marriage soured and dissolved in divorce, Nelson's former daughter-in-law mailed him the manuscript of a memoir she planned to publish about what she'd seen during her life with the Rockefellers.

Without bothering to read it, Rockefeller tossed the manuscript to his long-suffering public relations man: "Here Hughie, tell me how much this is going to cost us."

But the Senate overlooked any rumors about Rockefeller's sex life in confirming him. After a quick confirmation process, he was settled in as vice president. Even the intense scrutiny of high office didn't slow him down.

His aide James Cannon would recall a young blond woman being smuggled in and out of Rockefeller's Washington home under the watchful eyes of the Secret Service. "I thought, you're really taking a gamble there, Governor," he said.

There were hints of problems. Happy had dodged a dinner with the president, fleeing to Seal Harbor instead to watch her son play in a tennis tournament.

Joan Ridley, who would later tell of Nelson pursuing her into the shower, rode to the rescue in an article designed to buff up Happy's image: "It's important for her to keep the family together," she said, apparently with no irony intended, "and she works hard at it. During all this excitement, she wants to provide security for the kids, letting them know this won't change their whole life."

As 1976 approached, Ford began contemplating reelection. He had needed Rockefeller for his connections and image two years earlier, but now he needed conservative bona fides more. He turned to Senator Robert Dole of Kansas to be his running mate, sending Rockefeller back head home to New York. Ford would later say it was one of the most cowardly and shameful things he had ever done.

Fang at Home

With his political prospects behind him, aides said Rockefeller grew slightly more caustic in his final years. His staff created a new nickname for him that reflected his crotchety temperament: Fang. His trysts, meanwhile, became more open.

The boasting about his sexual conquests, which were always part of his personality, became more embarrassing. He would abruptly leave a meeting and return after only an hour saying, "I guess I'm not as young as I used to be."

Rockefeller also put two of his properties up for sale—his Washington home, which he would no longer need, and his Seal Harbor summer estate. Though he remained wealthy, the 1970s recession took its toll and Rockefeller needed money. To get it, he launched a line of reproductions of some of the many famous artworks he had acquired.

To make matters worse, his doctor began treating him for a weak heart.

The stage was set for his final scandal. On the night of January 26, 1979, almost exactly two years after he left the vice presidency, Rockefeller died of a heart attack.

To this day it's still not exactly clear what happened when Nelson died. The heart attack was suffered at 10:15 p.m. Police and an ambulance were called at 11:15 p.m. He was pronounced dead shortly afterward at Lenox Hill Hospital.

Long-suffering Hugh Morrow had one more mess to clean up for the boss—and he mishandled it quite badly.

Meeting with reporters outside the hospital, and with scant information to go on, Morrow told the press that Rockefeller died alone working at his office at Rockefeller Center—editing a book about his art collection that he was writing.

That was three mistakes (or lies, depending upon who you believe) in one sentence. *The New York Times* printed the story, only to be embarrassed to find out it was not correct. Furious, the *Times* put a team of reporters on the story, which was fueled by New York's tabloid newspapers. Journalists with wilder imaginations speculated that Rockefeller might have been murdered.

Morrow tried to explain his mistakes in an effort to extinguish the fire, but he couldn't tamp it down. It turned into a serial story, running for days as dribs and drabs of information slowly came out. Finally, a narrative emerged that serves as all anyone will probably ever know about Rockefeller's final hours. His body was found in his apartment on West Fifty-Fourth Street. He had not been alone.

As the news spread that Nelson Rockefeller had died, Senator Howard Baker put feelers out to the family about whether they wanted the former vice president to lie in state at the US Capitol. Then he quickly retracted the suggestion. He learned that, contrary to the first reports, Rockefeller had not died at work in his office, but rather he had "died in the saddle," as his aide James Cannon put it.

The speculation ran rampant and a slew of lurid questions came out. Was he naked when he died? Had the body been moved? Had his security team been involved before police were called? Mayor Ed Koch would soon fire a doctor in the medical examiner's office, accusing him of claiming that Rockefeller had died having sex. The firing would later be overturned.

Then there were the jokes: "Nelson thought he was coming, but he was really going." "How did Nelson Rockefeller die? Low blood pressure: 70 over 25." And a favorite among his staff: "What were Nelson Rockefeller's last words: 'Good luck, Hughie.'"

Crimes and Misdemeanors

A Royal Mess: The Harry Oakes Murder

On July 16, 1943, two Miami police officers cruised into Bar Harbor and down the long, tree-lined drive to The Willows, a Regency-style mansion on a bluff overlooking the ocean. Captain Edward Melchen and Detective James Barker had traveled from Nassau in the Bahamas to visit Lady Eunice Oakes.

Police surrounded the house to keep away gawkers and the press, and the front gate was locked. The sensational story of Sir Harry Oakes's murder eight days before had made world headlines. Even a glimpse of a family member merited a mention in the press.

That morning Lady Oakes had buried her husband of twenty years in a simple ceremony near his birthplace in rural Maine. He had been killed at his home in the Bahamas, she wasn't sure how, and the plane carrying his body home had turned around mid-flight. By the time Sir Harry Oakes's remains finally arrived in Maine, his widow was in a state of profound shock.

As soon as she buried her husband, Lady Oakes returned to Bar Harbor and took to her bed. She had asked the detectives to call on her that afternoon. They had, after all, been asked to investigate her husband's death by his friend, the Duke of Windsor.

The police officers were admitted to the bedroom. They found Lady Oakes surrounded by several of her children, including her eldest daughter, nineteen-year-old Nancy de Marigny.

Nancy had learned of her father's death when she was on her way from Miami to Martha Graham's dance studio in Bennington, Vermont.

Her friend Merce Cunningham gave her the news. Nancy changed her plans and flew to Bar Harbor to be with her mother at the funeral.

Nancy and her mother listened with rising hysteria to Melchen and Barker as they told their tale. The killer, they said, took a stick from the garage, climbed the outside stairs to Sir Harry's bedroom and bashed his head in. Then the killer sprayed the unconscious baronet with insecticide and set the bed on fire. Sir Harry revived and tried to fight off his killer. He lost the struggle and died, probably in terrible agony.

And then the two police officers described how they intended to frame Nancy's husband, Count Alfred de Marigny, for the murder of Sir Harry Oakes.

Mining for Millions

No one knows exactly how much money Harry Oakes had, but in 1943 he was one of the richest men in the world and easily at the top of the Bar Harbor summer colony. He owned the second-largest gold mine on the planet. Some put his value at more than $200 million.

Quiet, stubborn, driven, generous, proud, short-tempered—all these could describe Sir Harry Oakes. At the time of his death, at age sixty-eight, some saw a mellowing multimillionaire finally relaxing into his wealth and status. Others saw a tyrannical drunk tilting at decades-old slights and insults and bent on self-destruction.

Before he was Sir Harry Oakes, Baronet of the British Order, he was just plain old Harry Oakes, son of a successful country lawyer from Sangerville, a small mill town in rural Maine. Born in 1874, Oakes had left the state in 1896, shortly after his graduation from Bowdoin College. Though he had no gold as yet, there was no shortage of brass in young Harry.

As a student, when asked what he planned to do after college, Harry was direct: "I plan to make a million dollars."

Perhaps the glittering wealth on display in Bar Harbor and environs had fueled young Harry's ambition. Newspapers of the day avidly reported the comings and goings of European nobility, Gilded Age millionaires, Boston Brahmins, and Main Line Philadelphians in the fabulous summer resort. Readers found no detail too small about the fashionable season just two hours from Harry's home town.

Harry was awkward and pugnacious as a college student. Not hated, but not well liked either. Harry's friends and relatives didn't know what to make of his boastful plans. His future brother-in-law bluntly said: "Harry Oakes is not going to make a fortune."

After Bowdoin, Harry attended Syracuse University for two years, studying at its medical school. But the lure of gold caught up with him there, and he left the school to begin prospecting for gold in Canada in 1899.

What followed was a fourteen-year odyssey that carried Harry from Canada to Alaska to New Zealand to Africa to the Philippines and back to Canada. Along the way, he worked as a miner in other peoples' mines, as a medical technician in hospitals, and for over a year as a flax farmer in New Zealand—his most profitable occupation up to that point.

But he continually returned to prospecting, making a study of what types of soil and rock indicated the presence of gold and the ways in which gold mines fanned out in veins. With each passing year, Oakes grew more determined to find his millions and angrier at any perceived slight.

He dodged all the typical barriers to success that tended to slow other businessmen. He didn't drink excessively. He had little to do with women, guiltily paying for prostitutes when he needed affection, and abandoning a pregnant woman in Australia. All in pursuit of gold.

Why gold? He wanted to be rich without exploiting the work of weaker men—part of a personal code of honor. The year 1918 found Harry back in Canada in Ontario's Lake Shore District.

Harry begged and borrowed money to operate. His brother and sister sent money religiously. He sold shares of the mine he knew he would one day own to pay for his tools. And along the way he built his enemies list of anyone who slighted him.

In 1912, Harry struck a rich vein of what would be the second-largest gold mine in the Americas—the Lake Shore. It would be years before he could fully commercialize it, though. He sunk shafts, invested in equipment, and pleaded with bankers and backers to fund him.

When success finally arrived, Harry was fond of pointing out that other prospectors might be smart enough to find gold, but they almost always had to sell out because they couldn't navigate the complicated process of getting a mine actually up and running. With the Lake Shore Mine on the way to producing what would become 266 tons of high-grade gold, Harry made millionaires of his backers—his family and merchants who had accepted his mine shares as payment for services.

Some shares that had been given out at forty cents would one day be worth $64 each. Meanwhile, it didn't pay to be an enemy of Harry Oakes. Harry issued an edict that no one connected with his mine should do business with one particular shop. Its owner had denied Harry credit and embarrassed him in the process. When the shopkeeper went bankrupt, Harry laughed.

When he needed the road improved to the mine—and local suppliers balked—Harry ordered that the road be paved by his own men with ore from the mine. He later gleefully scoffed that he could get a million dollars' worth of gold out of that road if he wanted to.

In the mining business, he was a tyrant. A meddlesome and micromanaging boss, his top managers routinely quit within months of being hired. Those who managed to stay with him he eventually fired.

In 1923, Harry met Eunice McIntyre, a bank clerk from Sidney, Australia, on a cruise to South Africa. Harry's contemporaries joked that the only way he could get a girl would be to corner her on a deserted island. Eunice, though, looked past his rough exterior and manners. Just twenty-eight, she married Harry, who was now fifty, and moved to Ontario. There the richest man in Canada and his wife began raising children.

Harry angled for a seat in Canada's upper house of Parliament. He went so far as to renounce his US citizenship, but he was denied by the prime minister. He became increasingly furious at Canada's tax system and at the failure of the government to appreciate the wealth he generated.

In 1935, he announced he was leaving Canada to become a citizen of the Bahamas, which was still part of the UK, but with no income tax. The uproar in Canada was instantaneous as its richest citizen decamped. Had he known his fate in the Caribbean, he might have stayed in Canada.

Who Murdered Harry Oakes?

Harry's arrival in Nassau was no less cacophonous than you'd expect, as he continued to make enemies in the Bahamas. One would eventually kill him.

He bought huge swaths of the remote island at depressed prices and set to building houses, a golf course, a country club, and an airport. He reshaped the place without restraint.

In the poor island nation, Harry was not only friends with the former King Edward VIII, he could be king himself. One day he stopped at the British Colonial Hotel for lunch. The maître d' decided to seat Harry at the back of the restaurant because of his shabby clothes. Harry got up and left, bought the hotel, and fired the maître d'.

He decreed that only black employees could work in the hotel, infuriating many of the white employees. When he found out there weren't enough black workers who knew how to run hotels in Nassau, he set up a training center to teach them to run his new business.

Determined to spite the Canadian politicians who had passed him over for friendship, Harry began a campaign to win a knighthood. A steady flow of charitable gifts to British institutions made the king take notice. Harry donated more than $1 million to charities in the Bahamas, and in 1939 he won a knighthood, 1st Baronet of Nassau.

Harry and Eunice now had houses in London, Florida, and Ontario in addition to their main homes in the Bahamas. But Eunice was not a fan of the sweltering Nassau summers. She wanted a cooler summer location for the family.

The Baronet of Bar Harbor

You can travel from Sir Harry's birth place in Sangerville, Maine, to Bar Harbor in two hours. But Harry Oakes definitely took the long way. There were sixty years between Harry's birth in 1874 in rural Maine and his arrival to buy a summer cottage in Bar Harbor. Sir Harry bought the gracious twenty-seven-room cottage called The Willows in 1938. The purchase of The Willows set the pattern for Harry's life until his murder in 1943. The family would spend the cold months in Nassau, and Eunice and the children would return to Bar Harbor in the spring, followed by Harry later in the summer.

In Bar Harbor, Harry continued to spread his money—and to show stuffed-shirted summer swells how his money insulated him from the customary requirements of polite society.

By this time, Bar Harbor was past its heyday as a summer resort for the wealthy families of Philadelphia, New York, and Boston. Letters to the local newspaper complained of the number of empty cottages. Storefronts were vacant. A public solicitation was created to shame the Congregational Church on Mount Desert Street into cleaning up trash and debris that accumulated in the churchyard.

But vestiges of the robust summer colony remained. Two of the Oakes's neighbors—the Atwater Kents and the Ned Stotesburys—happily squandered their millions on furnishing their mansions and throwing lavish parties during the Great Depression.

Harry and family attended the birthday parties, talent shows and dinners. He occasionally let his rough side show. He often ate using only a knife and spat pits and seeds across the banquet table.

Some said he simply spent too many years in rugged mining camps to knock off the rough edges he picked up. Others said he just didn't care to.

Nevertheless, the Oakeses fit in at Bar Harbor. As America went to war in World War II, there was an intense interest in foreign affairs. And along with the usual fashion shows, charity soirees and concerts, the Malvern Hotel, where the Oakeses occasionally stayed, played host to a summer series of public affairs lectures supported by Harry Oakes.

He often gave generously to charities, demanding only anonymity in return. And he pursued his passion for golf when he visited Maine. A hole at the venerable Kebo Valley Golf Club is named in his honor.

As the war started, discussions of charity drives like Bundles for Britain gave way to investigations into who was abusing fuel coupons and the dangers of black markets forming. And the downtown Criterion Theater began featuring somber fair such as *Guadalcanal Diary*, *Somewhere in France*, and *Hitler's Hangmen*.

But Sir Harry Oakes's murder on July 8, 1943, literally knocked World War II out of the headlines.

When Harry Met Freddy and Eddy—It Was Murder

It was in the Bahamas that Harry Oakes met the two European aristocrats who would play central roles in the scandal surrounding his murder and the aftermath: Count Alfred de Marigny and the Duke of Windsor.

When he arrived in 1935, the Bahamas were little more than a colonial backwater. But as World War II ravaged the cities of Europe, the Bahamas suddenly became very desirable. Wealthy Europeans looking for refuge from the war funneled into the islands. British wives, looking to escape the dangers of the cities, moved to the Bahamas where they could relax and play safely out of the range of German bombs—and their husbands.

Further adding to the intrigue, the Duke of Windsor arrived in 1940 to take on the role of colonial governor. The Duke had previously been Edward VIII, the king of England. He created a sensation when he abdicated the throne to marry Wallis Simpson, a twice-divorced American. The Duke had embarrassed the British government by showing sympathy for the Nazis and favoring appeasement before the war. He was stationed in the Bahamas—an unusual post for a royal—where he could be kept out of sight of the British people.

Though the Duke and Duchess of Windsor were admired as icons of style, the Duke would be found wanting on matters of law enforcement.

Upon arriving in the Bahamas, the Duke and Duchess immediately declared the governor's residence to be uninhabitable. It needed a complete overhaul. Sir Harry Oakes rode to the rescue. He had several homes on the island, and he offered the Duke the use of his best house while the governor's mansion was renovated. Sir Harry had bought island property for a pittance before the war and soon found himself sitting on a gold mine of a different kind.

By then, another aristocratic European had already entered Harry's orbit when Alfred de Marigny—or Freddy—landed in the Bahamas. He, too, left war-torn Europe for the peace and sunshine of the Caribbean.

Freddy had a title of his own and a reputation as a playboy. He was a count from his mother's family. He had amassed some savings working in finance, divorced his first wife, and slept with, then married, his banker's wife.

When Freddy and his new wife moved to Nassau, Freddy was in love—with the Bahamas, not with her. A brief and stormy marriage gave way to a quick divorce. In the fall of 1940, Sir Harry's wife, Eunice, extended a dinner invitation to Freddy, then well known around Nassau as an eccentric, as well as an accomplished sailor.

Freddy dined with the Oakeses, including daughter Nancy. He was thirty; she was fifteen. Later he said he noticed her beauty but didn't give her much more thought. She, however, had a serious crush. Later in the year, she visited him at the hospital in New York where he was being treated for stomach pains. And a year later she would again flirt with him at her coming-out party.

Nancy flattered Freddy by revealing she knew all about his sailboat racing, and he was smitten. A long-distance courtship ensued, with Freddy traveling again to New York in 1942. There, Nancy proposed. Freddy accepted.

There would be no Bar Harbor society wedding for Nancy Oakes. The day after she turned eighteen, they eloped in New York City. Lady Eunice Oakes collapsed at her summer home at The Willows when she learned of the wedding.

It's easy enough to imagine how Count de Marigny, with his French accent and cultured manners, would appeal to Nancy, who was horrified by her own parents' manners. And it's easy enough to imagine how a lithe and beautiful seventeen-year-old would appeal to the thirty-two-year-old Freddy.

It's much harder to imagine what happened next.

By most accounts, Freddy and Harry's relationship was neither especially friendly nor unfriendly. After announcing their elopement, Freddy and Nancy were invited to Bar Harbor for their honeymoon. There, the Oakes family welcomed them politely, if not warmly. Freddy got along well with Nancy's four siblings, taking them sailing off the Maine coast.

A trip to Mexico ended badly, with Nancy contracting both typhoid fever and trench mouth. The marriage was then stressed by a pregnancy, which Nancy, at the urging of her parents, terminated.

Further trouble soon arrived in the form of a letter from Freddy's second wife, Ruth. It accused him of being unscrupulous and immoral. The letter turned Lady Oakes against her son-in-law, and a feud ensued between mother and daughter. Nancy demanded that the family welcome Freddy.

On July 8, 1943, the final crisis was to occur in Sir Harry's life. He was ticketed to fly from the Bahamas to Bar Harbor the next day to join Eunice and the children at The Willows. He never got the chance. That night during a torrential tropical storm, someone killed him, bashing him on the head and then setting him on fire.

The murder made international headlines—that is, after the Duke finally let the news out. Faced with the sensational crime on his turf, Edward, Duke of Windsor, proved to be at the least incompetent and perhaps unscrupulous. Rather than rely on the local police or Scotland Yard, the Duke invited a Miami detective he knew to come to the island and handle the investigation.

The Duke's first thought was that Harry had killed himself. Sir Harry had been riding around his golf course recently on a bulldozer, toppling trees. He seemed more than usually unhinged. The Duke pondered: Eunice wanted to leave the Bahamas, so perhaps Harry had gone insane.

Disabused of this notion by the gruesome facts surrounding the death, the Duke then came to suspect Freddy, whom he loathed.

Alfred de Marigny had, in fact, had several arguments with Sir Harry. But so had almost everyone who knew Sir Harry. Freddy didn't have an airtight alibi for the murder, but no one had seen him around Sir Harry's house the night of the murder. The question arose: didn't he and Nancy stand to inherit millions if Sir Harry died? Police pounced on Freddy and charged him with murder.

The case against Freddy went to trial. It was a gift to the tabloid press, with the elements of private investigators, crafty lawyers, and beautiful young Nancy against a backdrop of an island paradise where the wealthy fled to avoid the war.

The case unraveled fast. Freddy testified that he had renounced any claim to Nancy's future fortune. Further, under the terms of her father's will she would only receive $1,000 a month until she was thirty-seven, when the residue of his estate would finally be distributed among his children.

Then under questioning, the validity of the single piece of physical evidence the police had against Freddy—a fingerprint from a screen next to Sir Harry's body—was crushed.

The two police officers had blundered. When they made that unforgettable visit on July 16 to Lady Oakes in her Bar Harbor bedroom, they told her about the fingerprint. But they testified in court that they didn't identify the print until July 19.

Unable to present a clear picture of how and where the fingerprint was found, the defense created the impression that the police lifted the print from a drinking glass and fabricated the evidence. The detectives, Freddy's lawyers suggested, pretended they had found the print on a shade in Sir Harry's room to frame him.

In truth, it appears the detectives believed Freddy was guilty and would confess if confronted with enough "evidence." But Freddy, in his memoirs, said he simply knew the lie would have to surface because he had not been anywhere near the bedroom on the night of the murder.

The aftermath of the case was probably inevitable. The jury found Freddy not guilty, but he was thrown out of the Bahamas as an undesirable. He fled to Cuba and spent a few months palling around with his old chum Ernest Hemingway. Nancy, meanwhile, was more interested in Ernest's young son Jack, and the two began a brief, torrid affair.

While able to match Nancy's appetite for sex, Jack said he was unable to match her funds, and so the two parted. He headed off to Montana and college.

Nancy traveled to Montreal, and Freddy pursued her there. He wound up sleeping with a journalist who splashed his name across the newspapers. She reported his pillow talk that the Canadian government soon planned to deport him.

Nancy announced she planned to have their marriage annulled. He announced he would fight. He lost and spent the next twenty years trying to find a country that would take him in, finally securing US citizenship in 1975.

For Sir Harry Oakes, there was no tidy ending. His body was flown back to Maine and buried. His death remains unsolved to this day. He had many enemies, but none seemed likely—or able—to kill him. Freddy speculated that it was Harry's real estate partner who killed him upon learning that Sir Harry planned to leave the Bahamas. He also alleged the Duke of Windsor deliberately muddled the investigation for fear that if Freddy were cleared, investigators would begin looking elsewhere. The Duke, Freddy found, had been illegally squirreling money away in Mexico in violation of currency control laws. The Duke planned to use the money after the war—assuming the Germans would win.

With numerous theories floating around, there is to this day no definite answer to the question: Who killed Harry Oakes?

He did leave a legacy of sorts in Bar Harbor. Eunice—Lady Oakes— donated The Willows to Bowdoin College as a conference center. The college sold the Oakes Center to a developer, who turned it into a hotel now known as Atlantic Oceanside Hotel & Event Center.

The story of Harry Oakes has been told in film and books, and he finally came full circle, buried in a cemetery near the place of his birth in Sangerville. Lady Eunice Oakes died in Nassau in 1981.

A Serial Killer Is Born

MASS MURDERER WILLIAM THORESEN SHOCKED THE WORLD WITH HIS bloodthirsty madness during a criminal career that started, rather mildly it turned out, in Bar Harbor. His childish prank at the Bar Harbor Ferry Terminal in 1959 was just the starting point for a decade-long spree of gun-running, drug-dealing, and murder.

In September 1959, twenty-one-year-old William Thoresen III and his girlfriend, Louise Banich, stole six posters from the Bar Harbor terminal for the Canadian National Railroad ferry to Nova Scotia. They were thrown into jail and charged with larceny of goods more than $150. With no money for bail, they stayed behind bars for ten days.

Thoresen was a spoiled rich kid, the son of William E. Thoresen II, founder and president of Great Western Steel Company of Chicago. The younger Thoresen was charming and handsome with a volcanic temper and a severe stutter. Louise was a teacher and speech therapist from a working-class family.

Later she would describe herself as "naive, impoverished, willful, and ambitious."

William and Louise made an impression on the Hancock County sheriff. Fifteen years later he remembered they had a cat named Wee. Louise wore hot pants and strolled around the jail in a leotard. She also kept a diary that revealed they had stolen two canoes from the Old Town Shoe Factory and a trailer from Blotner Trailer Sales in Veazie.

Dad to the Rescue

Young Thoresen hired a lawyer, who called William's father. The father came to Bar Harbor with bail money, fired the lawyer, and talked to the district attorney. He told the DA he was worried about his son and thought he should be locked up in a mental institution. He suggested a suspended sentence and probation so the young man could return to his home in Illinois and seek treatment. William Thoresen III agreed to plead guilty and was released.

But he didn't go to a mental institution. And he would pay a steep price for his guilty plea for the theft of six travel posters in Bar Harbor.

William Thoresen III had been troubled from an early age. He saw his first psychiatrist at age three. He developed an early fascination with guns and claimed to be a crack shot by the age of nine. As a teenager he had been stabbed by a service station attendant during an argument. In 1958 in his hometown, the wealthy Chicago suburb of Kenilworth, Illinois, he was fined $50 for shoving a man.

William Thoresen married Louise Banich on New Year's Day, 1960, in Indiana. Two years later they had a son, Michael. They moved to Tucson in a series of nomadic stops around California and the Southwest. In 1964, William was accused of setting off dynamite explosions near a radio station with a University of Arizona student. Louise, who helped him, said it seemed like fun. William was arrested, but the charges were dropped when witnesses refused to testify.

In 1965, William's father swore out an arrest warrant for his twenty-five-year-old son Richard, whom he accused of burglarizing his Kenilworth home. The day before Richard was to stand trial, he was shot to death. He was found in a rented car in the posh Chicago suburb of Lake Forest with a bullet hole behind his right ear. He was left handed. The coroner didn't rule it a suicide.

The weapon, a .357 magnum pistol with one cartridge missing, was found next to his body in the car. Louise Thoresen had purchased it two days earlier. She explained she did it because she had a "thing about guns." So did her husband.

Airport Arrest

By the time of his brother's death, William and Louise were gallivanting around the country on a wild weapons-buying spree. Then in January 1967, they were arrested at John F. Kennedy International Airport after airport authorities confiscated their luggage. Inside, they found papers describing an enormous cache of weapons at their home in the tony Pacific Heights section of San Francisco.

San Francisco police and federal authorities raided their mansion and found a cache of firearms including bazookas, hand grenades, machine guns, and rifles. They learned of warehouses where William had stashed more weaponry and a garage where he kept a cannon. They found anti-aircraft guns, cannons, parachute flares, and more than a half-million rounds of ammunition. In the end, the federal agents uncovered seventy-seven tons of guns and ammunition.

Under the law, convicted felons can't traffic in interstate shipment of firearms. William and Louise had been convicted of a felony—the theft of six travel posters in Bar Harbor. They were indicted in federal court on multiple counts of federal firearms violations. William, dubbed the "gun-happy millionaire" by the press, said he collected the guns because he liked them. He also said he collected rocks and stamps. Both he and Louise claimed they collected the guns for a gun shop and museum they were planning to open.

There were no restrictions on the Thoresens while they awaited trial, and they moved to Phoenix.

All along, William Thoresen's violent temper had continued to get him into trouble. He fought with a bartender over the check. He broke a woman's nose in Las Vegas, then tried to bribe two police officers with $5,000. He led police on a high-speed chase in his Ferrari.

Louise wasn't exempt from his temper. She took to wearing large sunglasses, she said, to hide the black eyes he'd given her. She filed for divorce in Phoenix but didn't go through with it.

The Trial

Their trial was moved to Fresno because of all the publicity surrounding their enormous weapons cache in San Francisco. It began in April 1969, and the Thoresens lost their case: William was convicted on multiple gun counts, fined, and sentenced to six months in jail and nine and a half years' probation. Louise was convicted of aiding and abetting him, fined, and put on probation for three years. They appealed.

As part of their appeal, Thoresen tried to get their conviction for stealing posters overturned. His lawyers argued the posters cost only $26.25—well under the $150 threshold for larceny.

That fall, the Thoresens bought a white stucco mansion in Fresno and filled it with a little bit of furniture and a lot of large, unopened crates.

On June 9, 1970, the Thoresens' attorney called to tell them they'd scored a legal victory: A federal appeals court ruled they were entitled to a new hearing because of questions about the legality of the search and seizure of their weapons.

At 8:30 the next morning, Louise Thoresen shot her husband five times as he lay naked in bed. She ran out of their home to a neighbor's house, crying, "I shot Bill."

He was pronounced dead on arrival at St. Agnes Hospital twenty minutes later. Louise was taken to another hospital for treatment. An orthopedic surgeon found recent injuries: two broken ribs, bruises, and a half-inch puncture wound caused by a needle or knife. William had tried to kill her the night before. He beat her and tried to force her to swallow a bottle of sleeping pills.

Louise was charged with murder.

Madness Explained
The sordid details about her husband—and about his increasingly violent, bizarre behavior—soon emerged in the press.

On the day he was killed he had purchased a plane ticket with an unidentified woman for a trip to Spain, Lisbon, London, Paris, Gibraltar, Fez, and Tangiers. Police found a brand-new weapons cache in his home, including mortars, machine guns, rifles, shotguns, land mines, hand grenades, five thousand rounds of ammunition, dynamite, and a collection of knives.

Police also found fifty pounds of marijuana in the house, needle marks on his arm, and traces of LSD in his system.

Louise pleaded self-defense. She took the witness stand and described his increasingly bizarre and violent behavior. He beat her with his fists, with a cattle prod, with a boxing glove. But he did it all quietly and made sure their son's bedroom door was closed while he beat her.

Her last year with him had been a living hell, she said. She knew by then he was mentally unstable and pleaded with him to seek psychiatric help. He refused, fearful that his guilty secret would come out under the influence of truth drugs.

One Last Bombshell

And then Louise let drop a bombshell: William Thoresen was tormented by guilt because he'd hired a hit man to kill his brother.

Then, she said, he killed the hit man a year after his brother's murder. William said he hired Lewis Dale Stoddard to kill Richard. When Stoddard came to the Thoresen home demanding more money, William told her, he hit him on the head with a hammer. "There was blood all over the kitchen," he had said. "I finally got a gun to put him out of his misery." He then put Stoddard's body in a weighted sleeping bag and dumped him in the ocean.

There was still more: He had tried to hire a hit man to kill his parents. He had offered three hit men money to kill Louise. He plotted to bomb Caesar's Palace and to kidnap the child of a man who owed him money.

Well after his death, the FBI revealed William Thoresen III had been a prime suspect in the 1966 murder of US senator Charles Percy's twenty-one-year-old daughter, Valerie. She was asleep in her bed shortly before her father's election to the Senate when an intruder stabbed her to death. The Percys lived a block-and-a-half away from William Thoresen's boyhood home. The murder remains unsolved, and police never cleared Thoresen from involvement in the crime.

More details about Louise's life with the gun-happy millionaire came out in a book she later cowrote. The book described her gradual deterioration at the mercy of a man who wanted to destroy her. "He used to tell me a man was more important than a woman and he certainly convinced me he was more important than I was," she told the *New York Times*. "He used to say, 'Be quiet, I created you.' And I said to him, 'Look what you created. I'm not very proud of it. Why should you be?'"

By the time Louise gunned down her husband, she said she was "destroyed and hollow," her husband's "personal robot." He taught her to steal—glasses, canoes, guns, dynamite. He forced her to take sleeping pills with him.

At her trial, she pleaded not guilty on the grounds of self-defense. A jury agreed with her and she went free. She titled her book, *It Gave Everyone Something to Do*. She had wanted to call it "William, Sweet William."

The Flatiron Murder

Visitors to Mount Desert undoubtedly know of Flatiron Road in Tremont. Connecting with routes 102 and 102A, it forms a triangle—the shape of a flatiron that you would use to iron clothes. But there's another Flatiron on the island as well—Flatiron curve on Route 3, just after you pass the village of Otter Creek on the way to Seal Harbor. It looks nothing like a flatiron, and to figure out how it got its name you have to dig back to 1916.

Late on the night of August 4, 1916, Guy Small stood by that corner on the road in Otter Creek and waited for a doctor to arrive. Earlier in the night he had been recruited with the other men of the area to search for a missing woman. Just a few feet into the woods from where he stood, the body of Emma Turnbull lay dead. Emma was Guy's aunt, and he stayed behind while the others went to get the doctor and more police. What no one knew at that time—except Guy himself—was the man left to guard the body was the same man who had put it there earlier in the day. That fact would take another month to emerge.

All police knew when they first got the call to Otter Creek was that Emma Turnbull was missing. Her eight-year-old son, Howard, came home in the afternoon to find the house empty and blood and broken glass on the kitchen floor. At first, neighbors surmised Emma had cut herself and gone to Seal Harbor to the nearest doctor for help.

As the hours passed, they called police, who organized a search party. It wasn't long before the searchers found Emma in the grass behind her house. Posting Guy to stand guard, the police went to get the doctor who served as medical examiner. Once the body was removed, the police went home to wait for daylight.

Murder Theories Multiply

The following day the physical evidence surrounding the murder began emerging. Emma was partially clothed, but not assaulted. A bloody flatiron was found in the grass. Guy was brought to formally identify his aunt, and he broke down, nearly hysterical. Had the police interrogated him at that moment, they might have gotten a confession. Instead, he said nothing.

Word spread that a group of black men had been seen walking in Otter Creek, and they came under suspicion. Others put forward the idea that a woman was involved, since a flatiron was a woman's tool. Weeks would pass and the townspeople grew anxious. They had one strong suspicion: Guy knew more than he was telling.

Guy Small wasn't particularly successful, working at odd jobs and farming a little. He was a well-known drunk and unhappy with his life. He had a wife and four children—Stewart, six; Lawrence, five; Eleanor, three; and two-year-old Katherine. To help make ends meet, he brought a boarder into the house. Guy told the boarder he hoped to soon join his brother living in the West Indies. "And what of his wife and children?" the boarder asked. "To hell with her and the brats," he replied. His only problem was that he needed money.

Emma Turnbull had very little money. She had been widowed four years earlier and left to raise eight children. Her eight-year-old son, Howard, worked as a gardener to help support her. Just days before the murder, Howard had come home with his monthly pay—$50.

As they learned of Guy's desperation to leave, the police developed a theory of the case: Guy, thinking the money was in the house, had decided to rob his aunt and use the money to run away. When Emma surprised him, he panicked and killed her. Police correctly surmised that was just about what happened. But how to get the story out of him? How to get the evidence needed? There was precious little cooperation coming from Guy Small and his family.

The police, though, were under pressure to make an arrest. And so, without a lot to go on, Guy Small was charged with murder.

Guy Small in Jail

At Guy Small's first hearing, the prosecutors managed to hold him in jail on $10,000 bail, but his defense attorney scoffed at the paltry evidence. Guy had been seen walking to his aunt's house that day in plain sight, the defense attorney said. Was that the behavior of someone planning a murder? Guy's lawyer planned to paint the picture that robbery was not the motive. Rather, he would suggest, someone had plotted to assault Emma, which led to her murder. Her clothes were disturbed and partially missing when the body was found, Guy's lawyer pointed out, suggesting the attacker had planned to rape her but got frightened away.

About then, police had a stroke of luck. In nearby Ellsworth, the C. L. Morang dry goods store was robbed. Someone had broken into the safe and taken a considerable amount of money. Bad news for the shop owners, but a golden opportunity for the Hancock County sheriff.

In early September, a young private detective from Boston stepped off the train at Bangor. The sheriff took him into his car. When the two law enforcement officers reached Ellsworth, the sheriff didn't introduce the man as a detective from Boston working for the police. Instead, the sheriff had him arrested for the robbery of C. L. Morang. The detective was hauled before the municipal court and sentenced to jail to await a hearing on the charges. Once inside the jail, the detective gradually got close to Small. It took more than a month, but the detective managed to pry information out of him.

A Visitor in Otter Creek

Back in Otter Creek, Miss Ellen Gardner arrived in town. She was looking for work and told the sad story of having been recently widowed. She found a room with another of Small's aunts.

Without raising suspicions, Ellen managed to slowly gain the confidence of the Small family and learn details of the murder. Finally, she learned from six-year-old Stewart that he had seen his father come home the day of the murder wearing blood-stained clothes. The boy had watched as his father went inside to change his clothes and burn the bloody outfit.

Ellen Gardner was no random visitor to Otter Creek. She was working for the sheriff, as well. Small was presented with growing evidence of his guilt in the murder. Finally, he cracked and wrote out a confession.

Small revealed that on the day of the murder he had stopped at the Russian Tea House, then located on Ocean Drive. The Tea House was a restaurant that primarily served the rusticators and cottagers on the island. And even though Maine was dry, it was a place where liquor could be purchased.

Small said that on the morning of the murder he had bought a quart and a pint of whiskey and had drunk most of it by the time he entered Emma Turnbull's kitchen. He did not admit why he was there, but he said Emma had raised a knife at him. Panicked, he said, because he had been cut with a knife in the past, Small lost his head. He reached out and grabbed the flatiron and threw it, striking his aunt in the head.

With his aunt bleeding on the floor, Small said, he was in shock. He didn't remember carrying her body outside, but did remember being outside and seeing her on the ground. It was then that he regained his senses. He slunk home, burning his clothes to hide the evidence of his crime.

The confession obtained, a judge ordered the Boston detective officially released so he could return home.

Small pleaded guilty to first-degree murder on October 14, 1916. His attorney asked the judge to consider the extenuating circumstances—that Small had lost his head while under the influence of cheap liquor.

It took but a few minutes for the judge to sentence Small to life in prison. He appealed for clemency from the governor for many years. As late as 1947, he was arguing that jail had reformed him.

Guy Small's 1947 appeal for clemency was the last known record of him. He presumably died in prison. Meanwhile, a stretch of road on Route 3 in Otter Creek has been called Flatiron Corner for more than a hundred years because of the gruesome murder that took place there one August day.

Prohibition Follies: Three for the Road

Mount Desert Island has always had a messy relationship with alcohol. Right from the get-go, the first European settlers on the island aggravated the leaders of the resident Indians by selling alcohol to their young men. That set the tone for the next four hundred years.

In its heyday as a resort, the easy flow of alcohol was looked upon mostly as an idiosyncrasy of the island. In 1888, Congress agreed to spend more than $800,000 building the breakwater from Bald Porcupine Island. Whether it was to stop J. P. Morgan's yacht from rocking in the harbor and spilling his drink (as legend has it) is open to question. But the island definitely had a reputation for liking its liquor. As the price tag on the breakwater rose, a joke passed around Washington, DC, about a visitor to Bar Harbor who was impressed by the growing breakwater. "That's not a jetty," he was told. "That's our bottle dump."

You could write an entire book about the dustups and scandals of Mount Desert in which alcohol played the central role. We'll look at just three:

- **H. N. Pringle and the Mob**: The story of a teetotaler minister who came to town looking for trouble and found it;
- **The Real Liquor Wars of Bar Harbor**: These had nothing to do with outlawing liquor. They were all about who would profit from it; and

- **The Unlikely Threesome:** The rumrunning kingpin of Bar Harbor, the sheriff who looked the other way, and the zealot who ultimately tamed the island's thirst, at least for a time.

H. N. Pringle and the Mob

Let's begin with the story of the Rev. H. N. Pringle's visit to Mount Desert in the spring of 1907. Pringle was a do-gooder from Waterville, Maine. He rose to be secretary of the Christian Civic League of Maine, which operated as a watch society. The members flushed out lawbreakers whenever they could, and for decades Pringle actively tried to root out sin in the state: gambling; working on Sundays; and, of course, alcohol.

Pringle was visiting Bar Harbor to collect dues from local members. He stayed at the Florence Hotel on Main Street—not the town's grandest hotel, but a nice enough place. Orrin Haynes, nineteen, approached Pringle with a proposition. Haynes had a bottle of champagne (most likely stolen) and offered to sell it to the minister. The offer stirred a budding Elliot Ness within Pringle, and he offered to buy some of the champagne, one dollar's worth. The minister stashed the champagne inside a valise in his room, called Deputy Sheriff Bloomfield Higgins and went to eat dinner in the hotel dining room while waiting for the lawman.

When Deputy Higgins arrived at the Florence Hotel, Pringle accused Orrin Haynes of peddling illegal alcohol. The young man denied everything. In a bit of showmanship, Pringle led the sheriff to his room and popped open his suitcase, planning to reveal the evidence in a grand "gotcha" moment. But it was empty. It later turned out that another hotel guest persuaded a chambermaid to open the door to Pringle's room and swipe the champagne. With no evidence and conflicting statements, Deputy Higgins dropped the matter. But that was not the end of the story.

When you came to a Maine island in those days and decided to make trouble for a local boy, you were treading on thin ice. And there's one more thing to know about the young man in this story, Orrin Haynes. He was what they called in 1907 mentally deficient. The people of Bar Harbor were protective of Orrin Haynes, as they would be of one of their own, and didn't appreciate the attempt to entangle him with the law. As word of the confrontation over alcohol spread, some of the men in town took offense.

The Rev. Warren Hanscom of the Methodist Episcopal Church had dined with Pringle on the day of the confrontation with Orrin Haynes. Walking along School Street he first got wind that some townspeople planned retribution against the out-of-town minister. He heard Otho Jellison shout to another man, "Hurry up and get the gang together." At first the minister thought Jellison might be getting a group together to play a ball game. But he soon concluded the men had more sinister plans.

Eggs at Ten Paces

H. Russell Emery, a high school sophomore, figured out what was up when a man gave him money and told him to go find some eggs. At about eight o'clock, Hanscom found Pringle at the corner of Mount Desert and School streets. He warned Pringle to be careful. By now the gang of men was growing. Later estimates placed the size of the mob at between forty and seventy-five men.

Walter Roddick, Jr., a young school boy, was playing at the Village Green. He began heading toward the Florence Hotel, following the mob. He would later admit he did it out of curiosity, "to see them egg this feller."

Pringle was scurrying along Main Street, attempting to reach the safety of his room, when the first eggs began to fly. Several missed the target before the crowd improved its aim. As he approached the hotel, Pringle was confronted by a man who began grappling with him.

Fred Chandler at the drugstore up the street heard the fracas and remarked, "He's hollering like a loon!"

After one or two attempts to fend off the attacking mob with his umbrella, Pringle was pushed to the ground and knocked unconscious. When he regained consciousness, he lay in a pool of egg and blood. His coat was ruined; a three-inch gash in his head gushed blood. The mob had disappeared. Wesley Paine found Reverend Pringle and helped him to his hotel. "Now," Paine said, "I guess you won't get any more foolish boys to sell you champagne."

In the aftermath, Dr. George Phillips was summoned, and he stitched up Pringle's head. Undeterred, the minister went searching the town until he spotted the man who attacked him: Otho Jellison. Otho Jellison was a local legend in Bar Harbor, a larger-than-life figure who would go on to become police chief as well as postmaster. But Pringle charged he was just a vigilante and had him hauled to court.

In a five-hour trial, the Rev. H. N. Pringle accused Jellison of attacking him, and the county attorney pleaded with the judge not to turn a blind eye to mob rule. But even though some forty to seventy-five men witnessed the fight, no one could quite recall who had attacked Pringle. Witnesses were sure of one thing, though. They swore Otho Jellison was well up the street talking with Fred Chandler at the drug store while the fight took place.

In a scene foreshadowing the O. J. Simpson trial, the county attorney made an attempt to link Otho Jellison to a hat found at the scene of the attack, but when Jellison placed the hat on his head it was far too small. The judge decided that since the hat didn't fit, he must acquit. And with that bit of island justice, the teetotaler minister was sent packing.

The Liquor Wars

As the summer trade blossoms on Mount Desert each year, there is a healthy competition for the tourist dollar in all things: transportation, lodging, and of course food and drink. In 1851, the sale and manufacturing of alcohol was outlawed in the state. That was one of the many gyrations in the liquor laws that would continue for another eighty years. In some periods, alcohol could be brought in from out of state; in other years wine and cider were illegal, but not beer or spirits. Finally, in 1881, a constitutional amendment was passed that outlawed all alcohol except cider. But thirsty customers usually found a way to wet their whistles. For instance, while an individual could not buy or sell liquor in the state of Maine, one could purchase liquor from a warehouse distributor out of state and have it delivered, unopened, and not be in violation of the law.

Thus, regardless of the laws, alcohol was generally available for most of the period before the start of nationwide Prohibition in 1920. The sheriff and police had a general understanding with the island businesses.

Drunkenness and alcohol-related crimes were punished, but the sheriff rarely went out of his way to look for alcohol. Some towns even adopted a system named for the City of Bangor, where it started. Under the "Bangor system," bar owners would come to court once a year, admit they sold liquor, and pay a fine. Then they could go back to business for another twelve months, unmolested.

But 1895 and 1896 represented a notable break from the usual detente. Maine's temperance advocates were growing tired of the nonenforcement of the liquor laws and began pushing for arrests.

In May of 1895, the newspapers reported that in Bar Harbor, "The gutters ran with beer last week near the vicinity of Aaron Bunker's carpenter shop on Main Street when the contents of sixteen barrels of beer, recently seized, were emptied onto the ground." Still there was a Keystone Cops element to the raid. When news spread that beer was being dumped, neighbors came running to fill buckets with the excess before it could disappear into the ground.

In most years the rules for running a saloon had been fairly simple. Close up shop by 10 p.m. Stay closed on Sundays. Don't sell to children. Don't sell to drunks. Saloons that stayed on the right side of those rules had little to fear. But in 1895 the rules went out the window. The local judge began issuing search warrants for the saloons and coffee houses along West Street that discreetly sold liquor.

The business owners were furious. Why were their shops being raided and fined (as much as $500 and $1,000) when the summer visitors were still free to swill booze at the luxurious hotels and finer restaurants?

The saloon owners banded together and went to court to swear out complaints against the hotels. But they didn't count on opposition from the local judge, who refused to issue warrants. It seemed it was OK to harass the businesses selling to locals, but the hotels and restaurants that served the tourists were something of a golden goose for the island. The judge was reluctant to kill it off by enforcing the liquor law too scrupulously.

The saloon owners would not drop the matter, and they found allies in an unlikely place—among the summer visitors. Many had joined the politically fashionable temperance movement. The saloon owners reached out to them for help. Together, these strange bedfellows went to Ellsworth to hire a lawyer. There they found an off-island judge willing to issue search warrants for the grand hotels. That forced the sheriff into action.

One by one, Bar Harbor's hotels for the summer swells fell to the sheriff. He raided the marvelous Malvern Hotel and the luxurious Louisburg Hotel, leaving them high and dry. He carted their wine and liquor off to the lockup. The sheriff also raided Sproul's Cafe, world-renowned for its fine dining. He emptied its famous wine cellars, forcing Sproul's patrons to do without the grape.

Local business owners grew increasingly alarmed by this scorched-earth approach to drying out Mount Desert. Threats were made to poison the water supply at Eagle Lake to get back at cottagers on the temperance side who were interfering with the hotels and restaurants. Even the president of the Maine Central Railroad reached out to political friends. Worried that a dry Mount Desert would mean empty trains, he urged that local judges be left to set local enforcement policies.

In 1896, the liquor wars subsided somewhat, but they continued to rankle. They surfaced again in 1900. This time Dan Herlihy, was behind the backbiting. Herlihy and his Woodbine Club had been cited for staying open too late and creating a public nuisance. The bootlegger returned fire, lodging complaints against the large hotels. Dan Herlihy knew better than anyone that the liquor business on Mount Desert was a gold mine.

The Unlikely Threesome: Dan Herlihy, Howe Higgins, and Ward Wescott
To say Howe Higgins had his hands full is an understatement. Appointed to the Customs Service in 1919, he was assigned to Southwest Harbor. His mission was to enforce Prohibition starting January 1, 1920. He had no car and a sheriff with limited concern about the booze flowing through Mount Desert.

Picture this scene: A fishing boat late on a cloudy night steams along the ocean toward the coast of Mount Desert. It has just traveled three miles out to sea into international waters, where it rendezvoused with a Canadian supply ship, and it's now returning. The fishing boat runs fast, weighed slightly down by a full load of liquor cases brought on board from the Canadian vessel.

With the Coast Guard bearing down, our little fishing boat captain confidently urges his boat toward a shoreline he knows better than anyone else alive. The tide is going out fast. The boat barely grazes the top of a rocky ledge that the tide is about to expose. Our captain knows that any boat pursuing him will have two choices: risk running on the rocks or turn back. The fishing boat will be emptied and the cargo of liquor well-hidden ashore before any pursuer can even reach land.

That scenario played out time and again up and down the coast of Maine during the state's prohibition years when alcohol was illegal. Mount Desert was a favorite place for the rumrunners to put in. For the most part everyone was OK with that.

The sheriff talked about going after rumrunners, but that was about all he did. As the *Bar Harbor Times* opined in 1915, "Two deputies could entirely stop the sale of liquor in Bar Harbor if they tried. . . . Any ordinary man can get enough evidence in one summer to put every dealer in the ardent [spirits] out of business if he wanted to, and the county attorney was willing to have that evidence used before the Grand Jury. The present plan seems to be to do just enough to fool the temperance element and not enough to seriously interfere with the liquor business."

By 1915, everyone on the island seemed to know there was mainly one man to see if you needed liquor: Dan Herlihy. Herlihy had come to the island from Bangor with his family decades before. His father had sold liquor. And Herlihy had taken to the business. He had gradually gobbled up the lion's share of the liquor trade on the island.

The implementation of nationwide Prohibition was a huge boon for Herlihy. He had decades of experience bootlegging liquor from Canada under Maine's prohibition laws, and his market suddenly expanded exponentially. There was now an entire country looking for illegal booze. Herlihy would put together a network of local contacts to land his liquor, store it in businesses around the island and distribute it locally. He would also ship it to points around New England and beyond.

Herlihy's main opposition was Hancock County Sheriff Ward Wescott. Wescott was an old political war horse. After serving in the Legislature he first won election as sheriff in 1916. Sheriff Wescott, like his predecessors, did not view rumrunning as a top priority. There seemed no reason why the liquor business couldn't proceed as it always had.

The Feds Arrive

When customs officer Howe Higgins came on the job, for the first time a serious prohibitionist was enforcing the laws. Wescott and his Bar Harbor deputy, George Clark, pledged to help. But Higgins had serious doubts about where their loyalties lay. So, Higgins worked on his own. For nearly three years, Herlihy booze flowed through the island and to points around New England without a hitch. Higgins was outmanned and without resources.

In the fall of 1922, Governor Percival Baxter summoned Sheriff Wescott to a meeting and berated him for his performance. There was no end to the complaints coming from Hancock County about illegal liquor. Wescott promised he would do the best he could and headed home. But did he do the best he could? Deputy Clark would later say that as soon as Sheriff Wescott returned from the meeting with the governor, the sheriff called Dan Herlihy to warn him trouble was brewing.

No figures exist that show exactly how much Dan Herlihy made, but his haul was in the hundreds of thousands of dollars. And his associates also profited handsomely by investing in liquor and driving it off the island. A driver could get $35 for carrying a passenger to Augusta from the island. For that same trip in a car loaded with booze he could get $125 and more. Could there be a sweeter deal?

But one of Herlihy's drivers, Willie Cunningham, had a falling out with the boss. Cunningham hadn't been paid for a trip he had taken— or at least he hadn't been paid what he thought was fair. Cunningham and Herlihy argued. Suddenly things started to change around Mount Desert. Now Howe Higgins apparently had a new contact with useful information. Instead of always showing up looking for liquor at the wrong place or just after it had been moved, Higgins and federal law enforcement officials suddenly started finding liquor on the island.

In the fall of 1922, the US Coast Guard accosted the ship *Kanduskeag* making its way to Mount Desert with more than one thousand cases of whiskey aboard. In July of 1923, the vessel was again stopped and towed into Boston Harbor along with nearly two thousand cases of booze. The captain denied participating with the Bar Harbor rum ring. His ship had alcohol, he conceded, but it was headed for the Caribbean. This time the Coast Guard had overplayed its hand. The men had captured the *Kanduskeag* more than three miles out at sea, in international waters. After a tense few days, the Coast Guard had to release the vessel.

Meanwhile, the cracks in the Bar Harbor rum ring were beginning to show on land, as well. First a load of booze driven to Dr. G. W. Hagerthy in Ellsworth was confiscated as soon as it had been delivered. Men in Ellsworth were being charged and convicted of trying to bribe customs officers.

Then on March 23, 1923, Higgins hit the jackpot. Running one of the largest bootlegging operations in the country, Dan Herlihy was storing liquor all around the island. Among the legitimate Bar Harbor businesses where Herlihy tucked away booze were the Malvern Greenhouses behind the Malvern Hotel and William Pierce's plumbing shop and William Dolliver's garage, both on Main Street. He also stored the stuff in Southwest Harbor at McKay's garage and taxi company. Higgins raided the Malvern Greenhouses and found 210 cases of booze. At Dolliver's garage, he found fifty-two cases of liquor and a keg of rum.

The next week, Sheriff Wescott's man, Deputy Clark, sprang to life. Did Herlihy tip the sheriff off in retaliation for the raid by Higgins? It's not clear, but the see-no-evil Deputy Clark raided a closed-up summer house in Manset and took in fifty-eight kegs of rum and forty assorted bottles of liquor.

Herlihy and nine others were indicted for conspiracy in running the liquor ring on Mount Desert. When the case came to court, Herlihy was named as the kingpin in the racket. Among the men charged with using their boats to run the liquor in from shore, Derby Stanley was charged as the leader. Herlihy would be sentenced to three years in prison in Atlanta, where presumably he couldn't continue running the liquor trade. Stanley received a sizable fine.

George McKay, the garage and taxi owner, received a lighter sentence. The judge didn't impose any serious penalty on John H. Stalford, the Malvern Greenhouses florist, because he deemed the damage to the greenhouses' reputation significant enough punishment. With that, nearly four years of profitable rumrunning came to an end. But the drama of the Bar Harbor rumrunning case was not over.

In October of 1923, Governor Baxter addressed the Women's Christian Temperance Union of Maine. His topic was the state of affairs in Hancock County. With Dan Herlihy and his gang convicted and Herlihy himself in jail, the governor's new target was the sheriff, Ward Wescott. "The Sheriff of Hancock County will be given an opportunity to resign," Baxter declared. "If he does not do so he will be summoned before the Governor and Council on the charge of inefficiency and neglect of duty."

Wescott was hardly the only sheriff in Maine accused by the governor of collaborating with bootleggers. Up and down the state, sheriffs were being run from office as their corruption was exposed. But Ward Wescott chose to fight.

In a spectacular three-day impeachment trial before the Governor's Council, the governor pounded away at Wescott's record of failing to convict any serious liquor cases while an enormous rumrunning gang operated under his nose.

Drivers for Herlihy's operation testified that they were told they had no fear of being stopped in Hancock County because the sheriff didn't care about Prohibition. Others testified that the sheriff's deputy, George Clark, was a regular visitor at Herlihy's club, a reading and card parlor called the Lenox Club. The deputy was seen there, seated with his feet kicked up on the table. The sheriff and the deputy had both received alcohol at the club, the governor charged. And, he said, the sheriff had telephoned Herlihy the day after the governor had demanded he take action against the bootlegger.

Wescott, a stonecutter from Blue Hill, Maine, had served in the Legislature before becoming a popular sheriff. He would testify in his own defense. Yes, he admitted, he had been beaten by Dan Herlihy. He had received no complaints against Herlihy, the sheriff said. Moreover, he believed the bootleggers ran a sophisticated operation, using flashing lights at night to communicate the location of the sheriff's men when they were out looking for booze.

He was under such close surveillance, Wescott said, he was convinced someone watched and reported his movements every time he backed his car out of the driveway. He said he knew Dan Herlihy well enough to say hello to, but that was all. He had never taken liquor from him. He had never visited his club. And he had never called Herlihy on the telephone, which contradicted the information provided by his own deputy. The chief reason he had never arrested Herlihy, Wescott said, was because the bootlegger never sold alcohol himself but hid behind others.

The ruling on the case against Sheriff Wescott wasn't even close. Only the governor and his brother, who served on the Governor's Council, voted to remove the sheriff from office. The other six members of the Council sided with Wescott.

In the aftermath of the case, Dan Herlihy would return to Bar Harbor to live with his wife, a physician. He would open up Dreamwood, a nightclub and ballroom that became a successful venue for boxing matches and concerts. Dreamwood burned to the ground in 1936, four years after Herlihy's death. Having spent forty-five years in Bar Harbor, Herlihy was mourned by many. Among his pallbearers were his old bootlegging co-conspirators, florist John Stalford and taxi-man George MacKay.

For Ward Wescott, the feud with Governor Baxter was only a speed bump in his political career. He had served as sheriff from 1917 to 1925. But he did not seek reelection for one term after the high-profile trial. Then he staged a triumphant return, winning reelection the following year.

Governor Baxter never dropped his grudge against the sheriff, vetoing state budgets if they contained funds for the legal team that defended him at his impeachment trial.

A politician to the end, in 1932 Wescott was in a tight Republican primary for the sheriff's post. He pushed himself too hard during the campaign season. Late on the night of the election, he was told that he had once more won reelection. By the next day he had died of pneumonia.

Howe Higgins, meanwhile, would carry on his frustrating efforts to root out alcohol on Mount Desert Island for nearly ten years, but the destruction of the Herlihy rum ring was the highlight of his career. In 1923 he served a search warrant on the Bar Harbor Bank and Trust, and from its vaults he seized dozens of bottles of liquor owned by summer swells like Joseph Pulitzer and Robert McCormick. But Higgins was chastised in court because he could not prove the liquor hadn't been purchased before Prohibition. However unlikely it might be that a cache of booze would have survived unconsumed for four years on thirsty old Mount Desert, Higgins couldn't prove when it was purchased. He had to return the liquor.

In 1930 Higgins was finally fed up. He handed in his resignation as customs inspector. He noted that he had been warned after one recent liquor seizure that the owners of the booze were too politically connected to be convicted. And the warning was proved right, as it often was.

But Higgins didn't end his pursuit of the rumrunners. In 1930, with the backing of the Women's Christian Temperance Union, Higgins launched a campaign for sheriff. He focused his campaign squarely on the corrupt judiciary, law enforcement, and rumrunners who proliferated in the county. One advertisement read:

On July 10, 1929, Rasmus Hansen a citizen of Manset fell off a dock at Manset and was drowned. The records of his death state "accidental drowning" as the cause. Bootleggers operating without interference from the law, were responsible for the ruin of Hansen's business and were the cause of his death by selling him poison liquor that kept him drunk for days. I will pay $100 reward for evidence sufficient to convict these bootleggers of manslaughter.

Higgins came up short in the election. Among his political weaknesses, he ran as a labor candidate, which smelled of socialism. He would run again and would lose again.

Nevertheless, Howe Higgins would stay active politically his whole life. He ran for Congress as an independent in 1952. Later he was known for his support of universal health care and for his opposition to the Vietnam War. He died in 1974.

Oddities, Misfits, and Miscellaneous Downfalls

You Can't Get Good Help

IN THE SUMMER OF 1889, MRS. ISAAC LAWRENCE VISITED THE SUMMER home of Henry Sedley in Bar Harbor. Mrs. Lawrence discovered her former maid, Rose Wespiser, was working for the Sedleys. "How could you have such a thief in your house?" Mrs. Lawrence said. "I missed many things from my house when she left and am sure that she took them."

Probably assuming that the entire matter was behind her, Mrs. Lawrence visited friends in New York City later that year to celebrate New Year's Eve. It was not a happy New Year. Mrs. Lawrence was served with a lawsuit by her former maid Rose, seeking $10,000 in damages for libeling her. The Sedley family for whom Rose worked was headed by Henry Sedley, a *New York Times* newspaper editor intimately familiar with libel laws.

Rose contended she had left her job with Mrs. Lawrence because she was asked to perform chores that were beneath her station. Such was the fragile state of relations between Mount Desert Island's summer swells and their "help." A maid one moment, a plaintiff the next.

At its peak during the Gilded Age there would be more servants than cottagers soaking up the beauty of Mount Desert in the summer, though the servants had precious little time to soak. The servant class in America had been limited during the first few decades after the American Revolution. Service was considered a British institution and viewed as un-American, which is why the term "help" became standard for American domestic servants.

Yet as the wealth of America's millionaires grew, they clamored for the trappings of the British aristocracy. They often aped the customs of the British country house in which servants tended to the master's every need. In wealthy American households, silver was to be perpetually polished and guest rooms continually cleaned for any eventual visitors.

Accounts of domestic servants are filled with their employers' never-ending demands. The day for a servant was a long one, beginning before a household awoke and ending after the house had gone quiet. Fires needed to be started, meals cooked, commodes and chamber pots emptied, and the house and its animals seen to, cleaned, and maintained.

In America, the servant class lacked the deference that characterized the relationship between British master and British servant that went back for generations. Many, if not most, domestic servants in the United States were immigrants. And America's elite millionaire families chafed at the demands of feeding and clothing an army of servants.

In the earliest days of Bar Harbor's summer resort era, rusticators made use of locals, hired to act as maids and guides at the island hotels. But as the Cottage Era took hold, the need for help far exceeded the supply of local labor. Locals were snapped up as gardeners, caretakers, cooks, and maids. But with as many as 220 mammoth cottages to staff, the families traveling to the island had to import the help from their city homes.

In May and June, the influx of staff would begin as a trickle, setting up the houses for July and August visits. Stables gradually filled with horses, kitchens started to hum, gardens were restored, and the island was readied for the parties to begin. There were certain provisions made for recreation for the servants, athletic leagues and the like, but the fancy accoutrements of the resort were strictly off limits to the help.

Wealthy families at and around the turn of the century would soon face a dilemma of their own making. They constantly complained, "You can't get good help." Yet, by their treatment of their servants these families made factory work, with its regular hours and guaranteed schedules, far more enticing.

Nevertheless, when the summer colony on Mount Desert Island sprang to life each year, it was the disciplined work of the servants that made it happen. But they weren't above creating a little mayhem of their own, from fist fights and illicit assignations to flat-out murder. The summers in the servants' quarters were never dull, as this selection of tales demonstrates.

Fight at Baymeath

In 1895, Joseph and Louise Bowen hired architects to design for them a country cottage at Hulls Cove befitting a wealthy Chicago silk-manufacturer-turned-banker. The Bowens were part of a wave of arrivals who decided to stop renting for their visits to Maine and begin building.

Baymeath was an impressive home. The French Colonial style main house ran to thirty-five rooms. The grounds included formal and practical gardens, swimming pools (both indoor and out), a tea house, greenhouses, cottages for the gardener and butler, plus a stable and coach house. To make it all go, forty servants were required. Footmen, maids, a governess, nurses, grooms, gardeners, cooks, chambermaids, housekeepers, and butlers all inhabited Baymeath in the summer while the Bowens were in residence. Twenty-two horses were brought to the house each summer for the family's use.

With such a large retinue, squabbling and jealousies were probably inevitable. In one instance, the gardener left the family high and dry when he ran off and married the maid from a neighboring estate. In her memoir, *Baymeath*, Louise Bowen noted two instances of labor-related stress. The first involved the family butler, Larson, and his efforts to streamline the laundering of the footmen's pants. With requirements for casual and dress livery, just keeping the staff adequately attired cost a small fortune. Especially troublesome were the pants the staff often wore, which needed care to be kept blindingly white. She recalled:

The only day I ever saw Larson cross was one day when he came in to ask me if he could purchase a stretcher on which to put the white breeches when they had to be washed, which was frequently. He said the stretcher was expensive, it cost $40, but it would save us a good deal of work. I said, "Oh, Larson, that is so expensive! Can't you and the men just put on the breeches and let them dry on you?" He *really was quite annoyed and replied, "I would not take cold even for Mrs. Bowen," so the stretcher was bought, and the breeches were frequently washed.*

Dinners at Baymeath routinely ran to more than thirty guests. But it was the open Sunday teas that truly tested the estate's management, with crowds routinely topping two hundred. All the guests left fed and happy. But on rare occasions the stresses in the servants' quarters boiled over, as Bowen noted in her memoir:

On one occasion, when we were having a smaller entertainment at the house, there was a terrible noise in the pantry and [Joseph] went in at once to see what it was, and found to his utter astonishment that the two butlers had been fighting and they stood each with the others wig in his hand. We did not know they wore wigs. One had a toupee and the other a full wig, and your grandfather was so convulsed by their absolutely bald heads that he just looked at them and said, "Stop fighting!" and walked out.

Other incidents involved Mount Desert's notorious drinking culture.

Freddy Gebhard's Drunken Coachmen

It was the summer of 1895. The first week of September. Frederick Gebhard was summering at Greencourt, the Bar Harbor cottage belonging to Philadelphia socialite Charlotte Pendleton. Phones began ringing at the police station. Two of Freddy Gebhard's coachmen and one of his servants were brawling. The fight spilled from the stables out onto the lawn, and one of the men was badly cut. The men, it turned out, were drunk.

The matter probably would have quickly faded from memory had Freddy Gebhard not climbed on the wagon and stayed there.

By 1895, Frederick Gebhard was known to anyone who followed society news. He was a clubman or a sportsman, which meant he didn't work. He had inherited $5 million from his grandfather (his parents had both died young) and, to the extent he made much of a mark in life, it was in horse racing.

Born in 1860, Freddy had a reputation as a blustery young man who morphed into a Good-Time Charlie. His status as a bon vivant made his life rich fodder for the gossip columns, but he took it all, for the most part, in good humor.

Freddy spent the better part of a decade traipsing around the country following Lillie Langtry, a beautiful British actress. She, too, was a magnet for the press. The affairs of the married Lillie included a romance with the future King of England, Edward VII.

Frederick Gebhard met Lillie Langtry when he was just twenty-two. He toured America with her, portraying himself as her manager. They traveled together in a private rail car and bought his-and-her ranches in California, where they bred race horses.

The press openly speculated that he would marry her as soon as she could obtain a divorce. And they speculated. And they speculated. But Lillie's British husband refused to divorce her, even when she sent legal advisors to him suggesting that there were adequate grounds for such a divorce. He refused even when she offered to pay for it.

When it became clear that Lillie was not getting a divorce anytime soon, she and Freddy broke up. And Freddy took a more sober path, literally.

At one time the words "drunk" and "Freddy Gebhard" mixed as regularly as gin and tonic. But at the urging of his more sensible sister, Freddy had signed up for the Keeley Cure—a month in a sanitarium where people went to stop drinking. As part of the cure, patients were injected with mystery chemicals. Some reported the injections, which included arsenic and strychnine, brought about dramatic transformations in the patient's personalities—and not always for the better.

In 1894, Freddy married a flighty socialite—Lulu Morris—and the couple were regulars at Bar Harbor in the season. In the summer of 1895, Freddy's new anti-alcohol zeal was on full display. Perhaps the Keeley Cure made him irascible or he was just in a bad mood, but when Frederick learned about his drunken fighting servants, he went ballistic.

Frederick had lodged two of his servants with Patrick Herlihy. The Herlihy brothers, Daniel and Patrick, were well known to Bar Harbor police, who struggled to keep the liquor from flowing too freely among the summer colonists.

When police raided a liquor vault in 1894 and impounded the booze, brazen thieves broke into the jail where it was kept and stole it right back. And in 1895, when a police officer tried to confiscate a bottle of liquor from a restaurant downtown, Daniel Herlihy knocked it out of the police officer's hand and smashed the evidence. Patrick testified that the bottle slipped.

The pushing and pulling over liquor was already the talk of the summer colony when Freddy turned the heat up even higher. He stormed to the police station and brought charges against Patrick Herlihy for furnishing his servants with alcohol. He took his coachmen away from the Herlihy lodgings, found others for them, and asked for a bill from Patrick Herlihy.

In a show of cheek, Herlihy prepared the bill and included a $16 charge for sundries. Upon investigation, Freddy learned that the sundries in question were liquor and beer. Patrick Herlihy was eventually convicted of selling liquor to the servants, but not before Freddy Gebhard gave him a tongue lashing in court. Newspapers from Maine to New York reported on the case, which as one paper said, "created no end of talk at Bar Harbor and has been one of the most interesting topics of the present season."

Freddy did not become a fixture in Bar Harbor. He and Lulu divorced in 1901, and she departed with a good portion of his fortune. Freddy then fell for another actress, Marie Wilson, a Florodora Girl. That means she was an actress in *Florodora*, a Broadway musical about six young women and their romantic adventures. Fortunately for Freddy, the Florodora girls were wildly popular with the wealthy men of New York, and Marie had her own fortune. Her money came courtesy of a stock tip from a Wall Street insider she had dated, James Keene.

Marie Wilson and Freddy Gebhard would eventually separate, but she tended to him in his final illness in 1910. Gebhard's sister had repeatedly come to his financial rescue and he departed the earth in "straitened conditions." Today, you can still get a drink made of gin, lime and Chambord in some Manhattan bars called a Florodora. And on Mount Desert alcohol still flows freely.

The Case of the Murderer in the Kitchen

The old expression common to mystery fans, the butler did it, is generally attributed to the novel, *The Door*, and the stage adaptation of the book, *The Butler Did It, Singing*. It was written by the prolific mystery novelist Mary Roberts Rinehart. In her particular case, however, it was the cook who did it—as in, tried to murder her.

Rinehart was born in 1876. She started out her professional life as a nurse. Her husband was a doctor. The couple had three children, and in 1903 they lost much of their savings in the stock market crash. Mary took to writing to recover the family's fortunes, and within the decade she had become a true literary celebrity. In time, Mary became the highest paid author in the United States, and quite possibly the world. Her husband died in 1932, and she began summering in Bar Harbor in 1935, a regular at the parties and socials on the island. By this time, Mary was at the peak of her powers and fame. In 1938, the *Saturday Evening Post* would pay her $65,000 for the rights to serialize her fortieth novel, *The Wall*.

In 1938, Roberts purchased Farview, a cottage in Bar Harbor. She promptly set about renovating, updating, and renaming it Eaglesgate. The property features sweeping ocean views, and today it stands out to visitors for the large bronze moose sculpture that now graces its front lawn.

For Mary, who had suffered two heart attacks, Eaglesgate was a wonderful resting place. And in the summer of 1947, it very nearly became her final resting place.

Rinehart employed Blas Reyes as her cook. His time with the Rineharts went back twenty-five years, but he was temperamental. Reyes ruled the household staff, and if Mary hired a butler, Reyes would make the man's life miserable and run him off. For the summer trip from Washington, DC, to Bar Harbor in 1947, Mary struggled to find a maid willing to accompany her. Eaglesgate was a large house, and maids hesitated to take on the responsibility of a Bar Harbor social season. Out of desperation, Mary hired a butler to join her staff. She explained the situation to Reyes, and in June he submitted notice of his resignation. Mary accepted the notice but did not expect him to actually leave. Reyes had threatened to leave before but never followed through.

On June 21, Mary found one of the household maids, Peggy, crying in the kitchen. Peggy was married to Blas Reyes. Peggy explained that Reyes had told her they were leaving the day before, but she said she refused to accompany him. Just then, Reyes entered the kitchen. As Mary turned, Reyes produced a gun. He aimed it at point blank range at his employer and pulled the trigger. The gun misfired, and Mary ran from the room.

The next few moments were chaos. In the servants' quarters, Ted Falkenstrom, Mary's chauffeur, rushed to her aid. He shoved Reyes to the ground while Mary's personal maid Margaret took the gun from Reyes. Falkenstrom ran outside and threw the gun over a hedge while Mary phoned the police. Back inside, Margaret began screaming as Reyes ran back into the room with two knives. The chauffeur, joined by the gardener, again had to wrestle Reyes to the ground and disarm the cook. The new butler, meanwhile, had run out of the house toward town—afraid he was Reyes's next target.

When the police arrived, Reyes was pinned to the ground under the chauffeur, the gardener, and the maid. Police took Reyes into custody. The cook would never stand trial, because he hanged himself in his jail cell. But the incident would provide still one more challenge for Mary and her household help. In the midst of all the excitement, Mary had encountered a young man in the hallway. He explained he was there to apply for a position as an assistant to the gardener. "You'll have to come back," Mary exclaimed, "there is a man trying to kill me." The young man never returned to inquire about the job.

That year, 1947, would mark the end of Mary Rinehart's problems getting help. That was the year fire swept over the state of Maine, and it was particularly hard on Mount Desert. More than two hundred houses and estates were destroyed along with five grand hotels near downtown Bar Harbor. Mary Rinehart, meanwhile, went on writing for another five years. She died in 1958.

The Butler Actually Did Do It

To wrap up this chapter on servants behaving badly, we turn to an instance where the butler actually did do it.

It was December of 1921 on East Fifty-Seventh Street in Manhattan. A fire broke out at the home of Agnes Carpenter. When firefighters got to her apartments, they found fires burning in three separate locations. That, in itself, was suspicious.

The home had hosted a celebration that evening in the servant's quarters. One of the maids had gotten married. When the festivities died down and the apartment cleaned up, Frederick J. Smith, assistant butler, went for a walk. He returned home around midnight and went to bed. The next thing he remembered was the fire alarm ringing.

Smith dashed down the back stairs to the servants' quarters and found a safe containing the household silver standing open and a fire blazing inside it. Another fire had been kindled in the dining room and a third in the stairway.

Smith's story immediately fell apart. How had he come down the stairway when it was ablaze? When the police inspected Smith's room, they found his bed had not been slept in. When they questioned Agnes's butler, Adams, he told them Smith had asked him to unlock the safe earlier in the evening so he could remove silver for breakfast the next morning. Adams said he had unlocked the safe, but directed Smith to relock it because it contained $190. The only thing that remained of the money in the safe were the charred remnants of the envelope it was in.

But what tipped the scales further against Smith was a tale from the coast of Maine. Agnes Carpenter was a fixture in Bar Harbor's summer community. Each summer, she religiously visited her estate, which overlooked Frenchman Bay, occasionally staying late into the fall.

That year she had stayed into October. Smith had been the butler at Agnes Carpenter's Bar Harbor estate, Hauterive, and the same thing had happened there. A mysterious fire had broken out, and in the confusion, $400 belonging to the chauffeur had gone missing. Police concluded that kind of history rarely repeats itself, and while Smith managed to escape in Bar Harbor, New York police threw him in jail. Presumably he did not get a reference.

Abraham Somes and the Rum

IF WE'RE GOING TO TALK ABOUT LAND SCANDALS ON MOUNT DESERT, we might as well mention the granddaddy of them all—the appropriation of the island from the Wabanaki Indians, who had been using the place for centuries when Europeans first arrived in America.

The trouble started around 1580. Europeans had known of the existence of Mount Desert for roughly fifty years by then, since a Portuguese navigator had brought an English party to the island. He immediately set the tone for future relations by stealing three hundred moose hides from their Indian "trading partners."

Over the next two decades, the Europeans and Indians had minimal interaction. Then, in 1605, five Indians were captured, kidnapped, and taken to England to act as guides for future expeditions.

The local Indians used Mount Desert for hunting and fishing in summer, and they formed a loose association of tribes that traded, and occasionally fought, with one another. Around 1617 an outbreak of disease killed off most of the Indians between Mount Desert and Cape Cod, Massachusetts. Meanwhile, the increasing interest from potential colonizers kicked off 140 years of hostilities (interrupted by occasional treaties) among the French, English, Dutch, and Indians.

When the dust finally cleared, the English claimed victory. Now the Indians had to deal with Sir Francis Bernard, governor of the Massachusetts colony of which Maine was a part. Bernard promised the Indians he had only authorized limited settlement on Indian lands. That included Mount Desert Island, which he reckoned had been abandoned and uninhabited for many years. In a letter to the Passamaquoddy council, Governor Bernard reassured the Indians about the settlers moving into Mount Desert. "It is not their intention to injure the Indians but on the contrary to assist and benefit them."

That the island was considered empty probably surprised the Indians who had been coming there each summer for generations to hunt and fish.

Abraham Somes Arrives

By 1762, an Englishman named Abraham Somes had arrived to begin settling the "empty island." As Somes would explain, Governor Bernard had encouraged him to settle at Mount Desert. Somes and a companion sailed up the coast of Maine from Massachusetts, stopping to investigate harbors along the way. When they arrived at the fjord now called Somes Sound, they liked the look of the place.

Once they landed, Abraham Somes was approached by a group of Indians, one of whom claimed to own all the land around what is now Southwest Harbor. The bargaining began, and Somes was able to buy two islands—Greenings and Sutton—for the price of two jugs of rum. And thus the first permanent English settler had arrived on the island.

There are a few problems with Somes's telling of the story. Historians point out that at the time Somes claims to have peacefully approached the Indians, the Wabanaki and the English colonists were at war. The Massachusetts governor had offered a bounty of $300 per scalp for each Indian killed in Maine. Seems a bit unlikely a friendly interaction was possible given that state of affairs.

Wisely, Somes didn't move permanently to Maine until hostilities ended. Then he came back to Mount Desert and laid out some boundary lines to claim property. Years later, Somes would say he had negotiated the purchase of the land. In swapping the rum to the Indians, he said, he had received a deed from them.

The Deed Is Done

There were a lot of problems with the land deals that British colonists made with Native Americans—language barriers, for one. For another,

Indians did not necessarily view the transactions the way white settlers did. In agreeing to sell lands, the Indians were often agreeing to more of a partnership with the British. The Indians would respect English laws, but the land itself, as they viewed it, remained free for the traditional uses of hunting and fishing. Land ownership, to the British, was viewed the way we do today.

Further, both sides sometimes negotiated in bad faith. The British often got the Indians drunk to persuade them to part with their land. The Indians they did business with often had no actual right to speak for their tribe in disposing of land. If an explorer happened to meet up with an Indian, there was often little care taken to make sure the fellow was in a position to sell anything.

Massachusetts's colonial governors, on the one hand, claimed to respect Indian sovereignty. On the other, they were busy surveying properties, carving out parcels of land and auctioning them to land-hungry settlers.

Throughout New England, problematic land deals were tied up in court for decades. Judges had to sort out who had signed individual deeds and who did and did not have authority to sign over land rights. In the case of Abraham Somes, he had no deed to be contested. Yes, the Indians had given him one, he assured people. But he hadn't bothered to keep it. This also strikes historians as somewhat suspicious.

Most scholars conclude Somes was merely a squatter, albeit authorized by the Massachusetts governor. Somes probably thought he could get away with taking possession of the land regardless. And he was right. With the Indian population greatly depleted, there was little opposition to Somes and the other settlers who began descending on their ancestral hunting grounds.

The remaining Indians gathered at a meeting in 1767 to debate whether they should simply take up arms and slaughter any English settler they could find. The war faction did not carry the day. Violence, for the most part, would be rare, but complaints were not. English settlers groused that Indians were stealing livestock. Indians, meanwhile, objected to the English settling more and more territory that was not theirs to settle.

Over time, as the number of settlers increased, the natural resources of Mount Desert (and elsewhere in Downeast) became scanter. The Indians gradually reduced their hunting. But they did continue seasonal visits to the island right through the 1800s to augment their income selling baskets and other goods to the settlers and then tourists. Eventually they created an encampment at Bar Harbor, providing a concentrated marketplace for their wares, especially baskets. That led to the final push to dispossess the Indians of their summer digs on the island in the late 1800s.

The Final Insult

In the 1860s, the Indians' summer encampment in Bar Harbor was on the east side of what is now Main Street. Though they had long ago lost the run of the island, they had managed to keep a hold on that one spot. By 1881, the camp had been gradually pushed westward to Bar Street. That year, the town relocated them yet again. The Indians had to drag their houses, tents, and wares through town, probably to Albert Meadow, off Main Street.

The Indians offered a wide assortment of products and services each year. In 1884, for instance, more than 250 Indians were on the island in forty tents. They sold baskets, deerskins, pipes, walking sticks, canoes, paddles, snowshoes, lacrosse bats, bows and arrows, moccasins, caps, and toys.

In addition to carrying out their traditional hunting, the Indians offered guide services and rented canoes to visitors. They also set aside some time for fun, such as foot races, canoe races, and other games.

Around 1885, the encampment fell under the watchful eye of the Bar Harbor Village Improvement Association. The association stuck its oar in and opened debate on where the Indians were to be located. Kebo Road? Otter Creek? One of the Porcupines? From 1883 to 1886 the encampment was again nudged westward, to what is now Holland Avenue at West Street. In 1887 it was pushed farther west and inland to Eddy Brook between the ocean and Eden Street. It stayed there through 1889.

In 1889, the Bar Harbor Village Improvement Association, declared a new mission: "[S]ome method of united action is needed in order to preserve the natural beauties of the place, and to encourage artificial improvements, by the ornamentation of the streets and public grounds of the village; by planting and cultivating trees; erecting tasteful buildings, clearing and repairing sidewalks, lighting streets and doing such other acts as shall tend to beautify, adorn and be for the convenience of the village."

If that last catch-all clause about "other acts" struck any of the Indians as ominous, they would have been right to worry. In 1890, the Indian encampment, known to the locals and tourists alike as Squaw Hollow, was moved once again, to Ledgelawn Avenue near the intersection of Cromwell Harbor Road (near where the sewer plant is today).

For the next thirty years the Indian encampment stayed put in what would be its final destination. The Improvement Association at least helped install a water pipe to the area to bring fresh water to the Indians.

Though the association made public health arguments for moving the encampment, there was a strong undercurrent of racism in the way the Indians were viewed. It comes through in this description of the encampment from F. Marion Crawford in his 1896 guide book, *Bar Harbor*:

An element of the picturesque is supplied by an Indian camp, which used for years to be pitched in a marshy field known as Squaw Hollow; but with the advent of a Village Improvement Society certain newfangled and disturbing ideas as to sanitary conditions obtained a hearing, and the Indians were banished to a back road out of the way of sensitive eyes and noses. They claim to be of the Passamaquoddy tribe, speak their own language, and follow the peaceful trades of basket weaving and moccasin-making, and the building of birch-bark canoes. Their little dwellings—some of them tents, some of them shanties covered with tarpaper and strips of bark—are scattered about, and in the shadow of one of them sits a lady of enormous girth, who calls herself their queen, and who wears, perhaps as a badge of sovereignty, a huge fur cap even in the hottest weather. She is not less industrious than other "regular royal" queens, for she sells baskets and tells fortunes even more flattering than the fabled tale of Hope. Some of the young men are fine, swarthy, taciturn creatures, who look as though they knew how to put a knife to other uses than whittling the frame of a canoe; but one does not feel tempted to rush upon Fate for the sake of any of the dumpy and greasy-looking damsels who will soon become like their even dumpier and greasier mothers.

The whole encampment is pungent with the acrid smoke of green wood, and many children—round, good-natured balls of fat in all shades of yellow and brown—roll about in close friendship with queer little dogs, in which the absence of breed produces a family likeness. It is curious to see in the characteristic work of these people the survival of the instinctive taste of semi-savage races, and the total lack of it in everything else. The designs cut on the bark of their canoes, the cunningly blended colors in their basket-work, are thoroughly good in their way; but contact with a higher civilization seems to have affected them as it has the Japanese, turning their attention chiefly to making napkin-rings and collar-boxes, and to a hideous delight in tawdry finery, which is fondly, though distantly, modelled on current American fashions.

Finally, in the 1920s, the encampment began to dwindle. The town had less interest in hosting the Indians, and the Indians had begun seeking more profitable ventures elsewhere. The Indians who still maintained business on the island tended to buy or rent houses and sell their goods in established retail settings.

Jackson Lab's Dr. Jekyll and Mr. Hyde

DR. CLARENCE COOK LITTLE IS A BIT LIKE BAR HARBOR'S ANSWER TO Dr. Jekyll and Mr. Hyde. His work as a doctor led to countless advances in the fight against cancer. But he also caused more cancers than any ten men. Though he was well educated, he embraced some of the philosophies about ethnic cleansing that Adolph Hitler put into tragic action. He stridently criticized other peoples' moral lapses, but he had his own glaring shortcomings.

Little is best known as the founder of the Jackson Laboratory, the highly regarded research institution that has made many contributions to medical science. The laboratory's namesake is Roscoe B. Jackson—a Detroiter and summer resident of Bar Harbor whose father-in-law staked him in the automobile business. The business would become Hudson Motor Cars, and it made Jackson a millionaire.

Jackson and fellow auto magnate Edsel Ford were regulars at Mount Desert, and they both enthusiastically supported Little and his research goals. With their money and his remarkable intellect, Clarence Cook Little created the Jackson Labs that remain an enormous presence in Bar Harbor to this day.

The Rising Star
Clarence Little was born in 1888 in Brookline, Massachusetts. He earned a doctorate of science degree (DSc.) from Harvard University in 1914 studying, among other things, genetics in mice. After a three-year stint in the Signal Corps pushing papers during World War I, Little made his

way to Maine. There the University of Maine hired him as president—a post he would hold from 1922 to 1925.

At just thirty-three, Little was young for the position of president. But his progressive views made him a charismatic and popular leader who stressed physical as well as mental fitness for the students. One of his lasting innovations was the introduction of freshman week—a session, now widely adopted, for incoming freshman to prepare them for their new environment before the start of school.

Things Get Flaky

In 1925, Little departed Maine to become president of the University of Michigan. It was here that his more outlandish enthusiasms came to the fore. In 1928, he chaired the National Conference on Race Betterment at the Battle Creek Sanitarium in Michigan. The sanitarium itself was something of an oddity, a health resort owned by John Harvey Kellogg. Kellogg, who invented cornflakes, held several conferences as part of his Race Betterment Foundation.

Kellogg, Little's benefactor, was a peculiar individual. A surgeon who pioneered and advanced surgical techniques, he was also obsessed with sexual dysfunction and its ties to societal evils. He thought the following problems needed to be reined in:

- women who stayed sexually active after the age of forty-five,
- any excessive sexual activities,
- masturbation of any kind, and
- adultery and the divorces it caused.

These things, Kellogg concluded, were among the causes of crime, disease, and mental feebleness. To weed these undesirable traits out of society, Kellogg supported eugenics.

Eugenics is a broad set of beliefs and practices that encourages improvement of the human race through genetics. Followers of eugenics have fallen across a broad spectrum, with the extreme followers embracing some abhorrent ideas. Radical eugenicists, for example, supported killing people with undesirable traits. Slightly more moderate eugenicists, such as Kellogg and Little, believed people with undesirable traits should be prevented from having children. "I favor legislation that will restrict the production of these poor unhappy people," Little wrote in one paper on the topic. "Treat them kindly, segregate them mercifully, but don't let them be released to go out again into the world and breed more of their kind."

Compulsory sterilization, or negative eugenics, was the practice in which a doctor would identify an individual as having an undesirable inheritable trait. A state board would rule on the case, and if warranted, the person would be sterilized.

Not surprisingly, the targets of these forced sterilizations were disproportionately poor and minorities, who the eugenicists often saw as inferior. Little was far from alone in his beliefs. Thirty-two states have had at one time compulsory sterilization laws on the books. (The eighteen states that can proudly claim to have never approved compulsory sterilization are Arkansas, Alaska, Colorado, Florida, Hawaii, Illinois, Kentucky, Louisiana, Maryland, Massachusetts, Missouri, New Mexico, Ohio, Pennsylvania, Rhode Island, Tennessee, Texas, and Wyoming.)

Among the fans of compulsory sterilization and eugenics was Adolph Hitler, and Nazi eugenics programs were inspired by models in the United States and elsewhere. They began with the mass sterilization of the "genetically diseased" and ended with the Holocaust.

Keeping Order on Campus

Little's views on eugenics and birth control—both voluntary and involuntary—made him something of a lightning rod for criticism. In addition, he forbade students from using alcohol and automobiles. Cars, after all, could be used to visit speakeasies and as places for students to engage in immoral activities.

At the same time, Little was dogged by persistent rumors of adultery. But the sin that ended his career at Michigan was his personality. Though he could be a charming raconteur with his Boston Brahmin accent, he was quick-tempered and obnoxious. In short, he was a lousy academic politician.

Little had been recruited to come to Michigan by the dean of the law school, and he convinced Little to join him in feuding with the law school's wealthiest benefactor. That benefactor, William Cook, was a telegraph company lawyer who had made a fortune in New York.

Cook would eventually build the magnificent buildings that make up the Michigan Law Quadrangle on the Michigan campus. But the prickly Cook kept demanding to control the design. Again and again, he baited the college with promises to build and then backed out.

The impatient Little then jumped into the fray. He informed the board of regents that he proposed to begin fundraising so law school construction could get started. He planned to confront Cook and tell him to either contribute his money quietly or go away. Not surprisingly, the Michigan board of regents didn't like the idea of telling a major donor to go elsewhere.

Moving On from Michigan

In the end, it was Little who went away, and Cook built his Michigan Law monuments at his own pace. As this turmoil played out in Little's career, his home life got even rockier.

In 1929, Little divorced his wife of eighteen years and, within a month of the divorce becoming final, married Beatrice Johnson, eleven years his junior. Johnson was an executive assistant at the American Birth Control League, which Little formed with Margaret Sanger and Lothrop Stoddard.

Sanger was an outspoken proponent of birth control, but she permanently damaged her reputation by joining the eugenicists. She called for forced sterilization to weed out inferior traits and produce genetically superior people. Stoddard was a Klansman, a journalist, and a favorite of Adolph Hitler.

The philosophical stew that bubbled around the issues of racial cleansing and birth control was a murky one, and leaders of the birth control movement often found themselves slipping into indefensible ethical positions. They conveniently dropped those viewpoints after Hitler's atrocities became well-known.

In 1931, Little advocated for giving the state the power to euthanize people suffering from incurable disease or mental illness. While he was not outspoken on issues of race or poverty, he was an active member of the Galton Society—a blatantly racist organization. It aimed to prevent poor people and minorities from reproducing in order to create a Nordic master race.

The Galton Society was surprisingly unscientific for a man like Little to endorse. When their experiments disproved their theory that the rich were smarter than the poor, they simply concluded the test was flawed, not the assumption.

The history of Beatrice Johnson and Clarence Cook Little is a little cloudy, as well. For a time, Beatrice lived with Little and his first wife as their servant. He brought her to Michigan with him and hired her to run the university's Office of the Dean of Women. Other sources identify her as a laboratory assistant. Exactly when she morphed from maid to secretary to lab assistant to lover is left to the reader to ponder.

There's no record of what Little's friend Kellogg made of this turn of events, though he had published his general thoughts on the matter: "The Bible rule for divorce, laid down by the Great Teacher, is little regarded in these degenerate days," Kellogg wrote. "There can be no doubt that this shameless trifling with a divine institution is regarded by High Heaven as the vilest abomination. Our divorce laws virtually offer a premium for unchastity."

And while he and Little spoke out about many types of people who shouldn't be allowed to reproduce, they apparently never concluded that divorce was an inherited trait that warranted forced sterilization.

Smoke Gets in Your Eyes

Newly remarried, Little moved to Bar Harbor full-time. With the backing of his wealthy friends, he increased his research work, establishing the Jackson research laboratory. Here he bred strains of mice with genetic makeups ideal for cancer research. His goal was to expand upon his ideas that genetics plays a major role in developing cancer. In addition to conducting his own research, there was steady demand for Little's test mice from other researchers, as well.

The final chapter in Little's life was perhaps his most ignominious. For sixteen years, Little had been managing director of the American

Cancer Society. As a scientist, Little believed the causes of cancer were genetic, even as evidence was mounting that environmental factors played an important role in the disease. As he fell out with his fellow scientists, Little quit the American Cancer Society in 1945.

Then in 1952, *Readers Digest* magazine published the article, "Cancer by the Carton." The article converted scientific findings into lay terms and exposed the links between cancer and cigarette smoking, America's popular pastime.

American tobacco companies scrambled to find a rebuttal to the growing pile of evidence that smoking cigarettes led to lung cancer. The companies established a research institute to promote junk science to muddy the picture and slow the public's awareness of smoking risks. And to head their new institute, they hired Clarence Cook Little.

Little's credibility as a preeminent cancer researcher was above reproach. He had founded one of the most important cancer research institutions in the world and run the leading anticancer organization in the United States. His name was not for sale—or at least you might think not.

But Little agreed to serve as head of the Tobacco Industry Research Committee, becoming the public face for Big Tobacco. He refuted study after study linking tobacco and cancer. From 1954 to 1969, he regularly testified before Congress and in other forums that tobacco did not cause cancer—or at least it wasn't proved to.

Little died in 1971, leaving a remarkable legacy. Through his genetics research, which developed mice that are widely used in cancer research to this day, he did as much to cure cancer as any single person. At the same time, his work for the Tobacco Industry Research Committee lent the organization the credibility to keep tobacco popular and legal for decades, doing as much to cause cancer as anyone on Earth.

The Many, Many Mad, Mad Hoyts

JUST BEFORE HENRY MARTYN HOYT DIED SUDDENLY IN 1910, EACH OF his five children seemed to be headed for a brilliant future. One of his daughters was a German countess, the other a high-society matron who lived in a Washington, DC, showplace. His oldest son had captured the critics' notice as a talented artist after graduating from Yale just after his twentieth birthday.

His two youngest children, separated by eleven years from the older ones, seemed set on the same golden path. They lived in a Washington, DC, mansion, attended exclusive private schools, and traveled to Europe. Son Morton was expected to graduate from Yale and perhaps go into law, and Nancy would marry after coming out in Washington's elite social circles. They all spent idyllic summers in Bar Harbor.

For fifty-six years the Hoyts summered on Mount Desert, most years at the Yellow House connected to the Rock End Hotel near Gilpatricks Cove in Northeast Harbor. (The house was the winter home of the Savage family, who rented it out in summer months.)

In 1910, few could have predicted each of Henry Hoyt's five children would make international news for the next three decades, and for all the wrong reasons: divorces and affairs, flamboyant drunken escapades, erratic behavior, and suicides.

Newspapers called them the Mad Hoyts.

But their madness also carried with it a measure of genius and a flair for celebrity. Henry's oldest daughter would achieve lasting literary fame as the poet and novelist Elinor Wylie. His youngest, Nancy, would write best-selling books and witty *New Yorker* articles. Even his wastrel young-est son would manage to befriend F. Scott Fitzgerald and marry Tallulah Bankhead's sister—three, maybe four, times.

Henry and Anne—the Parents

Henry Martyn Hoyt, often described as a government lawyer, was much more than that. The son of a Pennsylvania governor, Henry Hoyt had arrived in Washington from Philadelphia in 1897 as an assistant attor-ney general. Later, as solicitor general of the United States, he broke up J. P. Morgan's Northern Securities railroad cartel, establishing Theodore Roosevelt's reputation as a trust buster. He also prosecuted the famous contempt of court case against Chattanooga, Tennessee, sheriff Joseph Shipp, who had allowed a mob to lynch a black man accused of rape.

His legal accomplishments made him a favorite of Teddy Roosevelt and a potential candidate for the US Supreme Court.

Philander Knox, his boss in the Justice and State departments, called Henry Hoyt one of the best and ablest public men he'd ever known. "Gentleness, forbearance and sympathy were his chief human qualities," said Knox.

His family saw another side of the gentle father. He had an inor-dinate love of rye whiskey, and his moods swung dangerously. Twice he suffered bouts of nervous collapse and exhaustion that required him to be sent away, first to New Mexico, then to Canada.

When Philander Knox became US secretary of state, he quickly brought Henry Hoyt over to the State Department as special counsel. Hoyt was negotiating a treaty with Canada in the fall of 1910 when he suddenly fell ill. He was sent home and diagnosed with a perforated ulcer that developed into peritonitis. On November 20, 1910, Henry Martyn Hoyt died in his bed.

His death left Anne McMichael Hoyt a widow with five children. She was not temperamentally suited to her new role. She was the granddaughter of a Philadelphia mayor and daughter of the president of the city's leading bank. Where shy Henry downplayed his consid-erable accomplishments, Anne cared deeply for social status and pres-tige. Where Henry was gentle and thoughtful, Anne was domineering, manipulative, and unusually touchy. A granddaughter described her as a bitter and cynical old lady. She made Henry miserable.

When the Hoyts' oldest daughter, Elinor, was seven, Anne Hoyt suffered a heart attack and typhoid fever. With a hypochondriac's love of attention, she spent days at a time in her upstairs bedroom, regularly demanding doses of restoratives and cordials. During most of her older children's formative years, she played the invalid.

When hypochondria didn't work, Mrs. Hoyt tried histrionics. She once left a suicide note for her children to find, but their unconcerned response discouraged her from trying it again.

When Henry died, his biggest secret came to light. He had been taking solace from his awful marriage with a mistress, a secret he kept hidden almost to the end of his life. She was possibly an employee of the Justice Department, and her back garden was said to border the Hoyts' backyard on Rhode Island Avenue. Henry was undoubtedly with her during his long absences from home.

As Henry lay dying, his mistress emerged from the shadows. She had tried to enter the house to see her lover one last time, but Mrs. Hoyt wouldn't let her in. Henry Hoyt's death inspired his daughter Elinor to commit the first documented case of Hoyt madness: She ran away from her husband and their three-year-old son with a married man sixteen years older than she.

Her elopement would be the signature event of her life and launch the Mad Hoyts into national notoriety for decades to come.

Elinor Wylie—the Writer

Elinor Hoyt was born in Somerville, New Jersey, on September 7, 1885, a child of privilege if not great wealth. She had an Irish governess who taught her old Celtic ballads, which she put into her poetry. As a child she wrote imaginative short stories and fairy tales. One friend said she could lie like a trooper.

When Elinor was two, the Hoyts moved to Rosemont, Pennsylvania, on Philadelphia's Main Line, and they lived there for the next ten years. When she was four, her family spent the summer on Mount Desert Island and would do so for more than five decades.

That first year the Hoyts stayed in Captain Rodick's Birch Tree Inn. Then they returned to Northeast Harbor and stayed in a number of rooms in one of the hotels. Mrs. Hoyt, a child or grandchild in tow, came back every year. She would rent a large cottage, often the Yellow House in the Field or the Whitmore Cottage on Manchester Road in Northeast Harbor.

Elinor spent her summers on Mount Desert reading the books she loved, painting, sailing, rowing, and swimming. Her sister Nancy said she usually carried a book or painting things and sought out her favorite trails and mountain tops. She wrote one of her first poems at Asticou: "The sun had sunken in the West / The lights of the day had fled / The moon upon the quiet sky / Her peaceful beams had shed. / Slowly the silver crescent rose / O'er meadow, hill & dale, / It lit the ocean's broad expanse / And shone upon a sail."

In 1903, Anne Hoyt sent her two eldest daughters, seventeen-year-old Elinor and her rival younger sister Connie, to Europe with their grand-father, Morton McMichael. They shopped in Paris, visited the theater in London, and met *Dracula* author Bram Stoker. He was so impressed with their beauty and elegance he dedicated his novel *The Jewel of Seven Stars* to them.

Elinor wanted desperately to enter Bryn Mawr on her return from Europe, but Mrs. Hoyt thought college undesirable, even improper, for a girl of Elinor's social status. And so she began to groom her eldest daughter for her debut in high society.

The Henry Hoyts didn't have nearly as much money as the fabu-lously wealthy Thomas Walshes, who threw a lavish ball and dinners for their only daughter Evalyn during the 1903 social season. But Elinor's aloof elegance, matched by her razor wit, made her the reigning beauty of her set.

"She was as crisp and fresh as a crocus; her hair was spring-like and hyacinthine," wrote Nancy. "Her complexion was apple-blossom, and her nature so annoyingly aloof as to make her practically useless."

Even acid-tongued Alice Roosevelt Longworth called Elinor "lumi-nous and radiant" that year. She dutifully made the rounds of teas and dinners at embassies, social clubs, and luxury hotels, even a dance at the White House, all under the watchful eyes of the debutantes' mothers.

Elinor faced fierce pressure to marry, and a disastrous romance was followed by a disastrous marriage. She first fell in love with a tall, fair-haired suitor. The fragile romance, according to Nancy, was "conducted on technically classic lines from the rowboat above the cool emerald eel-grass at Northeast Harbor, to the actual conservatory with pink and white striped curtains in Washington, DC."

Then, two years after her debut, the young man dumped Elinor. Embittered and on the rebound, she suddenly agreed to marry Philip Hichborn, a twenty-four-year-old lawyer she barely knew. She had met him in Bar Harbor one summer, and he had chased her unsuccessfully for a year.

Philip was charming, handsome and bright, educated at Harvard, with wit enough to be accepted at the Hasty Pudding Club and to edit the *Lampoon*. His father was a rear admiral with a powerful position in the Navy.

What Elinor didn't know was that Philip Hichborn had once been hospitalized for mental illness. A doctor at Johns Hopkins identified his problem as dementia praecox, a catch-all phrase at the time. Today Philip would probably be diagnosed as bipolar.

On December 13, 1906, Elinor Hoyt gave her mother the wedding she always wanted. President Theodore Roosevelt attended and the Episcopal bishop officiated.

Elinor and Philip

It wasn't long before Elinor came to believe she had married a madman. She didn't understand her husband's mood swings, his black depressions, or his exuberant high spirits. She felt suffocated by his possessiveness, then frightened by his declarations of hatred for her and his threats of suicide.

The couple moved into a beautiful mansion in an exclusive Washington neighborhood. Ten months after they wed, Elinor gave birth to Philip Hichborn, Jr., a healthy baby. He may even have been happy for a little while.

On the surface, everything seemed fine. Mrs. Hoyt counseled Elinor to keep it that way and to be patient with Philip.

But Elinor began to suffer from high blood pressure and migraine headaches. She decided she wanted a divorce. Her father agreed with her. He hated Philip Hichborn, saw little merit in him, and he knew the Hichborn family didn't have a problem with divorce. Weeks after Elinor and Philip were married, Philip's sister Martha had ended her marriage to Jimmie Blaine, the ne'er-do-well son of the late secretary of state, James G. Blaine.

When a wealthy lawyer began a bold campaign to court Elinor, both in Washington and on Mount Desert Island, she welcomed his attention.

Horace Wylie

Horace Wylie, wrote a biographer, "suffered from an intemperate weakness for beautiful women all his life." And Horace Wylie thought Elinor the most beautiful person he had ever seen. He claimed he almost gasped the first time he laid eyes on her.

At forty-two, Horace Wylie was still trim and athletic, a clubman and a dandy who wore European suits and flaring, upturned moustaches. He also had the college education that Elinor lacked, and he would guide and encourage her interest in literature. But truth be told, his family found him a bit of a bore.

One day, he called on Elinor at her home in Washington, claiming he needed to check the references of a furnace repairman. Elinor's mother-in-law was in the next room, but that didn't stop Wylie. He asked Elinor loud questions about the boiler in between whispered praise of her hair and her wrists. They began to have secret luncheons in Washington. Then one day he kissed her in his car in the middle of Rock Creek Park.

By the spring of 1910, Elinor's infatuation with Horace Wylie made her want a divorce more than ever. So did her sister Connie's spectacular marriage to a quiet and intelligent German diplomat, Baron Ferdinand von Stumm. Connie, a happy new countess, her mother's favorite, must have presented a painful contrast to Elinor as she endured her miserable marriage.

Henry Hoyt died nine months after Connie's wedding. Elinor felt she had no one to turn to. And finding out about her father's infidelity made her realize that he had chosen to escape an unhappy marriage.

Her friend Rebecca West recalled that Elinor "always expected me to take it for granted that when you found out that your father had been in love with someone not your mother, why, of course, you left your own husband; you just had to, you were so upset. Quite beyond argument."

Years later Elinor told another friend how stifled she felt. "I was desperate, and I ran away with Horace," she said. "He was twenty years older than I, and father as well as husband to me."

Elinor on the Run

About a month after her father died, Elinor and Horace disappeared. They told no one of their plans. Mrs. Hoyt found a note from her daughter. "Don't let this kill you," Elinor wrote. "I have run away."

Mrs. Hoyt fainted.

The *Washington Post* called it the "scandal that shocked two continents." Even President Taft vowed he would order his diplomatic corps to bring home the runaway bride if anyone found her.

At first, Mrs. Hoyt and the Hichborns tried to deny the elopement, to no avail. They hired investigators to track down the fleeing couple, who traveled under assumed names. Eventually they found them. Elinor and Horace had simply driven out of Washington to a rural train station, boarded a train to Canada and then a ship from Montreal. They were somewhere in Europe.

"When Washington learned that in reality they had become lovers and, what is more, had actually run away together, there was a general sitting-up and gasping in sheer astonishment," reported the *Boston Daily Globe*.

Mrs. Hoyt went to work. She contacted Elinor and persuaded her to meet her in Paris. She had already planned a trip to Germany, where Connie was expected to deliver her first child in February 1911.

When Elinor agreed to see her mother, Mrs. Hoyt hit on a plan to lure her back to her family: She would bring Elinor's son, Philip, Jr. So she sailed to France with her three unmarried children and her grandson.

Elinor, years later, said the one bad thing she regretted doing was abandoning her child. But in Paris, in 1911, she did not seem impressed or moved by the sight of her three-year-old son.

Mrs. Hoyt took Philip with her to Stuttgart, where Connie soon delivered a baby boy.

Elinor and Horace spent the next five years roaming Europe in exile under assumed names. If they saw someone they recognized, they moved on.

There was one strange interlude, however. Three months after the rendezvous in Paris, Horace and Elinor returned to the United States for an experiment: They would return to their spouses for five months and try to make their marriages work.

But Henry couldn't live without Elinor, and the Hichborns refused to let Philip have anything to do with his wife. Furious, Katharine Wylie and Philip Hichborn refused to divorce their spouses.

Philip wrote the next shocking chapter in Elinor's life story. On January 8, 1912, Philip Hichborn filed for divorce, charging his wife with misconduct with Horace Wylie. Two months later, he blew his brains out at his sister's home with a revolver. His suicide note read, "I am not to blame for this. I think I have lost my mind."

Horace Wylie's estranged wife, Katharine, told the news by telephone, fainted dead away when she heard it.

The suicide made front-page news across the country. The *Boston Globe* reported he killed himself "from despondency and humiliation over the elopement more than a year ago of his wife."

"Capital Again Shocked," screamed the headline. "Tragic End to Bitter Story."

But it was far from the end of the Mad Hoyt story.

Though she had abandoned her son, Elinor desperately wanted to have a child with Horace. In December 1914, she delivered a stillborn baby. So great was her sorrow she went blind temporarily.

World War I
The approach of World War I forced Elinor and Horace to leave England in 1915. It also kept Connie in Europe.

She was alone in Belgium with her young son, her husband having left for his diplomatic duties. She sided strongly with Germany, filling her letters home with screeds against France, England, and the rest of the Allies.

Mrs. Hoyt took her youngest two, Nancy and Morton, to visit Connie in Europe but left as soon as Germany declared war. She wanted to take Connie home with her, but she couldn't. Americans were rabidly anti-German and would not have welcomed Connie.

Elinor and Horace sailed to Boston, traveled the South, and then retreated to Somesville in the summer of 1916.

Elinor rhapsodized about the island's charms: "The ridiculous, mature beauty of the spot, paralleled only by Como, Maggiore, Capri or Tahoe, with the purple-blue mountains rising straight out of the blue sea, has a classic precision," she wrote.

In the fall of 1916, Katharine Wylie finally agreed to divorce Horace. Washington gossips whispered why: She consented to the divorce as a gift to her daughter for her debut season.

When Elinor and Horace finally married in the fall of 1916, they were stunned to find it did nothing to erase the stigma of their elopement. Elinor's brother Henry warned her to stay away from the family in Washington over the Christmas holidays. Horace had lost all his club memberships, so Elinor and Horace rented a little apartment above a grocery store in Bar Harbor through December.

But in Bar Harbor, the townspeople rejected them as well, turning away from them in the street. Shopkeepers wouldn't trade with Elinor, whom they viewed as the mother who abandoned her little son for a life of sin. She had trouble buying enough food to put a meal on the table.

Back to Washington they went, and for the next five years, Elinor and Horace shuttled back and forth along the East Coast, spending summers on Mount Desert Island. They moved frequently to ever-shabbier surroundings as their financial difficulties deepened. Horace had settled much of his wealth on his wife and children in 1911, and five years of travel had lightened his wallet. Back in Washington, his disgrace prevented him from practicing law.

By 1919 they had to rent a cottage on Mount Desert Island for the winter to save money.

For Elinor, it was a period of creative ferment as well as of physical and emotional strain. As Elinor Wylie she began to write the poems that established her reputation as one of the foremost poets of her generation. As Mrs. Horace Wylie, she tried to have a second child, but suffered several miscarriages and delivered a baby who lived only a week.

Unable to have a second child, Elinor tried to reconcile with the first. Philip, age eleven, came to visit her at their rented cottage on Mount Desert Island in the summer. Since his father's suicide, Philip had lived with his Grandmother Hichborn. He was a disruptive child, and during his visit with his mother he dislocated a water pump and nearly ruined the car. Elinor believed he had been brought up to hate her and only saw him a few more times before she died.

Philip III inherited his father's brains and charm. He, too, graduated from Harvard, where he edited the *Lampoon*; and he, too, married a beautiful debutante. But Philip inherited his father's demons as well. His marriage soon ended in divorce, and he moved to California where he died a few days after a drunken fall. Like his father, he had not yet turned twenty-nine.

His lawyer said Philip Hichborn, Jr.'s life was the saddest life he had ever known.

Henry and Martin Go to War

The horrors of the European battlefield in World War I are well known, and it's possible they exacerbated the mental instability of Elinor's oldest brother, Henry. He had inherited his father's temperament, brilliant, shy, mercurial. He entered Yale at sixteen, graduated, and embarked on a promising career as an artist. When the United States entered the war, he had a wife and two children.

Henry joined the Air Service and flew missions in France and Italy, came down with trench fever, and was honorably discharged at the end of the war. When he returned home, his moods see-sawed between buoyant spirits and deep depression.

The youngest Hoyt son, Morton, also enlisted, but in the Tank Corps. He had dropped out of Yale to go to war and moved home after the armistice. Morton had no gainful employment except as his mother's chauffeur. He frittered away his days, sitting on a park bench in Dupont Circle talking about literature with a moonstruck teenager who would become the wealthy philanthropist Brooke Astor.

"Morton was slouchy and always had a cigarette hanging from his mouth, which I found appealing," Astor wrote. "He seemed so much older than the other boys I knew, and I felt that through him I was stepping into grown-up life." Astor couldn't have been more wrong. Morton never really grew up at all.

In the spring of 1920, Morton Hoyt attended a show at Keith's Review in Washington, DC. He saw a beautiful girl in the audience and fell for her immediately.

The seventeen-year-old girl was Eugenia Bankhead, the older sister of the actress Tallulah Bankhead and the daughter of Alabama congressman William Bankhead, later Speaker of the House of Representatives. Known as "Baby" or "Gene," she had a steadying influence on her self-destructive, attention-seeking sister Tallulah. That is, until she got mixed up with Morton Hoyt.

For the next three Mondays, Morton managed to sit next to Eugenia at Keith's. Finally, in June he told her he was tired of waiting and introduced himself. That day they took a drive to Rockville, Maryland, and got married.

Morton and Eugenia returned from their wedding to her home, where Congressman Bankhead kicked Morton out. He had no problem getting an annulment because Eugenia was underage. That didn't discourage the young lovers, as they hit Washington's party circuit hard, often dancing their flamboyant tango until dawn.

By the time Morton began his serial marriages to Eugenia, his older brother Henry's wife had left him. Henry was tormented by her desertion and by his pushy mother, who tried to enlist him in her campaign to restore Elinor's reputation.

As their youngest sister Nancy's coming-out party approached, Henry ordered Elinor to stay away from the festivities. Her presence, stinking of scandal, might damage Nancy's marriage prospects.

In 1920 Henry moved into a studio on West Tenth Street in New York with his old friend Bill Benet. Benet moved in Bohemian literary circles; both he and his more famous younger brother, Stephen Vincent Benet, would win the Pulitzer Prize for poetry.

At first, Henry rode a creative wave while living with Bill Benet. But then he said he couldn't seem to work because he had too many things on his mind. He spent little time painting and more time writing poetry, then tearing up his words. In July, he briefly entered a sanitarium.

By the third week in August of 1920, Henry was well enough to go to Northeast Harbor for his brother Morton's second marriage to Eugenia Bankhead. All his siblings came to the wedding at his mother's cottage, the Yellow House in the Field. Connie brought her two children. Morton got drunk and ate the bridesmaids' gardenias. After the wedding, Morton and Eugenia went to New York, renting an apartment next to their friends Scott and Zelda Fitzgerald.

One week after Morton's wedding, Henry received a letter saying the literary journal *The Bookman* had accepted one of his poems. The good news didn't lift his spirits. That night Bill Benet heard the phone ring as he walked up the stairs to their flat. He tried to open the door, but it was locked. He got the key from the landlord and opened the door to find Henry's dead body spread-eagled on the floor. A rubber tube attached to the gaslight made it immediately clear what happened.

The next day Morton read about his brother's suicide in the newspaper.

Sisters

After Henry's death, Bill Benet and Elinor started collecting his poems to publish as a memorial. Meanwhile, Bill helped Elinor publish her own poems. By then Elinor had gotten tired of Horace Wylie.

Well before she ended her second marriage, Elinor announced her intention to marry Bill Benet. She went to Rhode Island, at the time the divorce capital of the East, to get a divorce. She swore under oath that she had lived in Bristol, Rhode Island, for three years, a year longer than the state's divorce law required. Later, two witnesses who swore Elinor had been living in Bristol turned out to be mythical—but she had already married Bill Benet.

Living in Greenwich Village with Bill Benet, she was no longer the social pariah known as the runaway bride. For two years she held a day job as *Vanity Fair*'s literary editor. At night she drank cocktails into the wee hours with her friends from the Algonquin Round Table.

Over the next eight years, Elinor Wylie published four critically acclaimed volumes of poetry. Since poetry didn't pay the bills, she wrote four best-selling novels to make money. When her first novel, *Jennifer Lorn*, was published, her friends gave her a torchlight parade.

Elinor paved the way for Nancy, seventeen years younger, to pursue a literary career. Nancy wrote middlebrow romance novels, backed up Dorothy Parker as the *New Yorker*'s book reviewer, and wrote satirical pieces like *Confessions of a Man-Eating Debutante*.

Nancy, the last of the Mad Hoyts, shared her brother Morton's high spirits and love of alcohol. Critic Edmund Wilson called Nancy "Elinor Wylie's idiot sister." In 1923, she made a splash on the society pages by creating her own matrimonial sensation.

In early 1921, the HMS *Raleigh Admiral Grants* was anchored off the Washington Navy Yard. Young British officers, including Lt. Frederick Wiseman-Clarke, joined Nancy's smart set at society dances and dinners. That summer, Mrs. Hoyt took Nancy to stay at The Yellow House, and the wealthy young naval lieutenant turned up on their front doorstep. Local gossips whispered Fred and Nancy were engaged.

Mrs. Hoyt planned another big society wedding, this time for May of 1923. Family and friends came to Washington all the way from Europe and Mexico City. Expensive wedding gifts were sent, the church was decorated. On the day before her wedding, Nancy had lunch with her affianced and everything seemed to go smoothly.

Unfortunately for Fred, Nancy didn't want to get married, or at least she didn't want to marry him. That night, Elinor asked her why she was getting married if she didn't want to. And she reminded Nancy she didn't have to stay celibate just because she didn't have a husband, something Nancy already knew.

Nancy called off the wedding without giving the heartbroken naval lieutenant—or any of the wedding guests—a reason why.

"It's a damn rotten show all around," Lt. Frederick Wiseman-Clarke told the *Boston Globe* as he boarded an ocean liner bound for home.

Nancy's aborted wedding was followed by still another Hoyt family tragedy. On August 3, 1923, the *New York Times* published a brief item stating that Baroness von Stumm had died suddenly in Murnaw, Bavaria. Connie, too, had inherited her father's madness, though her symptoms had apparently gone unnoticed. Rumors flew about her suicide. According to one, she drowned in Holland, devastated by an unhappy love affair. According to another, she shot herself at dinner before the soup was served.

One day in 1926, Dorothy Parker came to Elinor's Greenwich Village apartment, distraught and threatening suicide. Elinor and Bill Benet talked her out of killing herself, but as Elinor wrote to her mother, "We were very queer ones for her to come to in a way. I suppose she thinks we are experts on the subject."

Final Days

Elinor continued to suffer hypertension and migraines, and her drinking didn't help. While downing cocktails she often recited her doctor's warnings against alcohol, and she once wrote she could live on scotch and aspirin. One New Year's Eve, she and Bill attended a party at a New York speakeasy for twenty-four couples. The party moved to their house afterward to drink bootleg liquor. Novelist Ford Madox Ford was among the guests.

"I have never seen and hardly imagined such a scene as there was at Elinor's before I left," Ford wrote to a friend. "The floors of three rooms being entirely covered with reclining couples shoulder to shoulder so that stepping out was like leaving a battlefield."

In the summer of 1928, Elinor visited England while Bill Benet stayed behind. She fell briefly but madly in love with the husband of a friend, Clifford Woodhouse. But in June, she fell down a flight of stairs and injured her back. *The New York Post* infuriated her with the suggestion she had thrown herself down the steps.

Elinor had actually suffered the first of three strokes that would kill her. She sailed back to New York in December and returned home to the apartment she still shared with Bill Benet. On the evening of December 16, she called to him and asked for a drink of water. Then she stood, took a few steps, and uttered her final words: "Is that all there is?" She fell dead, only forty-three years old.

Morton and Eugenia

By the time Elinor died, Eugenia and Morton had been married eight years and were bored with each other. They decided to divorce.

Morton then went on a bender in Paris. According to one story, he took a hot poker at a party and branded himself with it. According to another, he chopped up a whisk broom and ate it with cream and sugar as if it were breakfast cereal.

Morton then made news on the voyage home by jumping over the railing of the ocean liner *Rochambeau*. He was lucky the crew fished him out of the Atlantic. The angry captain locked him in sick bay until they reached land, and he brushed by the newspaper reporters waiting for him at the dock. His mother had to make amends with a substantial contribution to a seaman's charity.

Certainly, alcohol played a role in Morton's adventure. When Eugenia read about it in the newspapers, she decided he needed her after all. They quickly remarried and moved to an apartment in Miami. Tallulah drily noted that they had a runabout car and were probably having fun, but the marriage wouldn't last. Eugenia was flighty, she told a friend, and Morton was unstable.

Tallulah nailed it. The third Hoyt-Bankhead marriage lasted less than a year. Morton stayed in a Reno, Nevada, bungalow to establish residency. The future Mrs. Brooke Astor, in town for the same reason, was delighted to find her old flame right next door.

Nine days after her divorce from Morton Hoyt, Eugenia married again. This time she pledged her eternal love to Wilfred Lawson Butt, a former college football player. Unfortunately, Wilfred already had a wife. The marriage lasted three weeks.

It's unclear exactly how many more times Eugenia got married. In March of 1932 she said she was going to France to remarry Morton Hoyt, the only man she ever truly loved. According to one news report, albeit a questionable one, they did tie the knot a fourth time. But if they did, it didn't last long. By September 1933, Eugenie was calling off an engagement to the son of a Scottish coal baron. She told the press she wasn't terribly disappointed.

Morton occasionally wrote for *Vanity Fair*, no doubt helped by Elinor, but he never settled down to any serious employment. He next appeared in the news in June of 1944, when the *Bar Harbor Times* reported he returned from Compiegne Prison Camp in France. He had presumably been rounded up in Paris and taken to the camp when the United States entered World War II. As an American expatriate, he was probably treated fairly well.

Morton, an alcoholic ruin, went back home to live out the remaining few years of his life with his mother in her Rhode Island Avenue home.

Nancy, Last of the Mad Hoyts

Nancy would bring the family's saga full circle, ending the Mad Hoyts' romp through the society pages and scandal sheets the way it began: with an elopement.

Three years after Nancy jilted Frederick Wiseman-Clarke at the altar, she married one of his friends in England. Her marriage to writer Gerald Wynn-Wynne lasted four months. Nancy returned home to her mother, telling reporters they had "temperamental differences." Within a year she announced her engagement to Edward D. Curtis, described as "a Boston man connected with the Paris branch of the Guaranty Trust Co."

That marriage foundered as well. Elinor, in a letter to Nancy, supplied the reason: "You've married a chorus girl and now you must sit and admire her legs."

The marriage did produce a child, Edwina, in 1928. She spent most of her childhood with Mrs. Hoyt, after testifying against her mother in a custody case. Nancy spent summers on Mount Desert with them in Mrs. Hoyt's rented cottages.

Nancy never married again, but not for want of trying. A gushing romance with the Marquis of Donegal culminated in an anonymously published book of their love letters, called *Promise Not to Tell*.

In 1932, tobacco heir Smith Reynolds was murdered mysteriously at his home after a friend's twenty-first birthday party. Amid the sensational news coverage of the killing appeared Nancy's claim that she had planned to marry Smith Reynolds.

Five years later, the last of the Mad Hoyts stunned Bar Harbor one final time. Nancy in 1937 ran off with a taxi driver she'd known for ten days.

"Nancy Hoyt Curtis is the madcap, novel-writing daughter of a respectable, socialite family," reported *Life* magazine. "Veteran of many a romantic escapade, Nancy this time startled Bar Harbor by running off with a local taxi driver. The elopement ended at the Canadian border where police turned them back."

The *Washington Herald* noted the taxi driver was "hustled to the lockup" while she "sought surcease at a cocktail lounge." *United Press International* reported he was slightly shorter and considerably younger than Nancy.

"I have given birth to a generation of vipers," her mother once snapped. Mrs. Hoyt predicted she would outlive all her children, and she very nearly did. In the summer of 1949, Morton joined Nancy and Mrs. Hoyt at Whitmore Cottage on Manchester Road in Northeast Harbor. On August 6, Anne McMichael Hoyt died at MDI Hospital at the age of eighty-eight.

When she was buried at Forest Hills Cemetery in Northeast Harbor, Morton was too sick to act as his mother's pallbearer. He died fifteen days later.

Nancy and Morton each received just $1,000 from their mother's bequest. Mrs. Hoyt left her granddaughter Edwina the bulk of her estate, which she frittered away. Nancy lived another five years, sick and alcoholic but creating no more matrimonial sensations.

She died in 1954, the last of the Mad Hoyts.

They Came, They Summered, They Mystified

IN THE HISTORY OF ACADIA, THERE ARE STORIES OF GREAT FAILURES and frauds, and then there are the quirky events that sort of defy categorization. They generate lots of talk, speculation, and finally shrugs as they pass into history. Here is a selection of three.

The Strange Disappearance of Raymond Robins
On September 3, 1932, word reached Margaret Dreier Robins in Southwest Harbor that her husband was missing. Raymond and Margaret Robins were on Mount Desert visiting Margaret's sister Mary at the home she shared with her companion.

Raymond and Margaret were both figures in the progressive movement. Margaret was an organizer for women's rights, and Raymond was a sometime politician and political advisor. He had traveled to Russia on behalf of President Woodrow Wilson and urged official recognition of the newly formed Soviet Union. He went on to be active in the Settlement House movement, promoting better conditions for women.

By 1932 Raymond Robins was mainly known as a top advisor to President Herbert Hoover. The president relied on Robins to lead his campaign to retain Prohibition, which was rapidly losing popular support and would be repealed the next year.

Raymond had been engaged in a futile, months-long speaking tour to drum up support for Prohibition. Exhausted, he had visited Maine. He left for New York and then planned to go on to Washington for a visit with President Hoover. Only he never made it. Raymond was last seen in New York having lunch with a friend.

The news that the president's confidante was missing swept across the country. A friend reported that Robins had been seen in Chicago. Federal agents searched that city for signs that he had been there.

Soon, Margaret received a ransom demand from kidnappers claiming that they would release Robins in return for $50,000. The note was mailed from Pennsylvania, and investigators began looking there for clues.

Margaret, meanwhile, had her own fears. Over the years Raymond had received vague threats from bootleggers. "My husband has come through so many battles safely and I have such faith in his resourcefulness and persuasiveness that unless they have killed him without giving him a chance I feel he will come out of this in some way," Margaret said from Southwest Harbor.

Raymond had indeed been resourceful in the past. As a young man he had founded a phosphate mining company. Later he struck gold in the Yukon, securing resources that, coupled with Margaret's substantial inheritance, allowed him to pursue his interests unencumbered by any need for employment. He was a close friend of both Teddy Roosevelt and Hoover.

Margaret issued a statement that no reward would be paid for Raymond's return, and she continued to put forward the theory that rum-runners had attacked him.

Friends suggested he might be undertaking a secret mission of some sort against bootleggers. Or perhaps he was wrapped up in some international political intrigue. Quietly, however, another theory began surfacing: a mental breakdown.

Mental illness was hiding out in Raymond's family tree, and he had suffered breakdowns in the past.

Police investigating a fraud ring uncovered another gruesome rumor that might have explained Raymond's disappearance. According to the story, bootleggers had kidnapped him, put him on a New Jersey rumrunner's boat, taken him out to sea, trussed him up, weighted him down, and dumped him in the ocean.

It was a thirteen-year-old boy from Whittier, North Carolina, who finally solved the mystery, however. The truth turned out to be stranger than the theories that had been floated. The youngster saw a photo of Robins in the local paper and brought it to his father.

"Did the man look familiar?" asked the boy. Yes, his father concurred, it was Reynolds Rogers, a man who had recently moved to town claiming he was a mining engineer. Acting on the boy's tip, federal agents arrived in North Carolina and confronted Rogers/Robins.

Reynolds Rogers at first maintained he was not Raymond Robins. A number of townspeople owned up that they had suspected Rogers and Robins were one and the same. Though he was generally polite and agreeable, the man had odd habits. He spent most of his time hiking and praying at an altar topped with a cross he had constructed in the woods.

But his story that he knew nothing of Raymond Robins didn't wash. In his pockets investigators found newspaper clippings about his disappearance. Robins was taken to a nearby hospital and reunited with his wife. From there the couple departed for their winter home in Florida. Amnesia was the official diagnosis, though many people noted that amnesia could be a convenient excuse for someone who simply didn't want to explain his odd behavior.

Margaret passed away in 1935 of heart disease. That same year Raymond fell from a ladder while pruning some trees and broke his back; the accident left him paralyzed from the waist down. He died in 1954.

Thomas Lawson Disappears from Southwest Harbor
In October of 1922 headlines around the world blared the news: Thomas W. Lawson had gone missing from his sister's home in Southwest Harbor. For decades Lawson's exploits had made for good reading, and this final chapter in his career was to be no different. Was he suicidal? Was it a stunt to shock Wall Street? Was it pure publicity seeking? The world waited for answers.

Thomas Lawson is the classic rags-to-riches-to-rags story. The son of immigrants from Canada, he went to work at age twelve when his father died. After a string of odd jobs, he landed at a bank. There he saw the inner workings of the banks' financing of railroads.

The process was simple: Pump up stock prices with phony claims and then sell shares to unschooled investors. Once the bank sold all the shares, it would shut off the public relations spigot and let the stock collapse in price. After the collapse, the banks would repurchase the stock, rename the railroad, and start the process all over again.

By sixteen, Lawson had plunged in on an Ohio railroad whose stock the bank had let collapse. As the price soared, the teenager found he had $60,000—an unimaginable sum for a boy to possess in 1873. But Lawson lost the money just as quickly. He tried to plunge into another stock manipulation scheme, this one involving Boston Water and Power, and badly misread the signs.

But the experience had Lawson hooked. Inside knowledge, he realized, was how fortunes were made in the stock markets. The uninformed investor was just a sheep being led to the shearing. By mediating a feud over the ownership of gas companies in Boston, Lawson ingratiated himself with the most influential financiers of the day: the Henry Rogers and William Rockefeller ring that ran Standard Oil.

Lawson brought a new idea to Standard—consolidate the copper industry, corner the market, and sell the copper companies at a wild profit. It was a rocky path, but ultimately Lawson's plan worked—sort of. The group never did corner the copper market, but under the name Amalgamated Copper they did manage to fleece investors out of millions of dollars.

Lawson and his confederates pushed the prices of copper stocks up and down to suit their needs, bankrupting western copper interests. One furious copper mine owner in Arizona threatened to come to Boston and shoot Lawson.

Lawson profitably pursued his schemes until the early 1900s. Along the way he spent lavishly. He outbid other millionaires to buy a new hybrid carnation flower and named it for his wife. He invented a baseball card game that became wildly popular. He bred dogs by the hundreds and built a formidable racing stable.

He accumulated master artworks, sculptures, and exotic animals and plants. To house them all he built a $6 million mansion in Scituate, Massachusetts, called Dreamworld. He commissioned a yacht to contend for the America's Cup at a cost of almost $200,000. When he failed to meet the rules for entry, he had it scrapped.

In 1900 he built *The Dreamer*, billed as the most luxurious yacht of its day, and cruised it from Maine to the Carolinas. In Southwest Harbor he bought a house for his sister and visited among the posh cottagers.

Lawson bought a string of islands off Isle au Haut and pledged to make them into a Venice-like city. But as his fortune grew—reaching an estimated $50 million at its peak—Lawson began believing he alone created it. His ego led to a falling out with the Standard Oil money that made his schemes viable.

Furious, Lawson decided that a tell-all would be his revenge. He published a series of books and magazine articles exposing the frauds of Wall Street. His books mixed fact with fantasy, but they exposed how stock manipulators fleeced the investors. Of course, no one had been better at ripping off investors than Lawson himself.

Lawson became a household name—a hero to many Americans disgusted by Wall Street chicanery. But then Lawson's spending began outpacing his resources.

Students of the great Age of Sail will remember there was only one seven-masted schooner ever built in modern times: the *Thomas W. Lawson*. It was named for its owner, and like many of his grandiose ideas it ultimately went bust.

The *Thomas W. Lawson* was built to compete with more modern steamships. The ship could carry enormous cargoes, but it was too big for many ports. It was difficult to sail and unstable in bad weather. Time and again, the *Thomas W. Lawson* was refitted in efforts to make it financially viable. Finally, it sank in 1907 off England's Isles of Scilly, killing eighteen of its twenty crew members.

In 1916, Lawson made headlines again. When he collaborated with the Rockefeller machine, he was accustomed to learning of important news from Washington well in advance of the public. Such information as court decisions and presidential orders could all be used profitably to make investment decisions before the rest of the market knew what was coming.

In December of 1916, President Wilson ordered a telegram sent to the European powers then fighting in World War I. The missive outlined his plans to keep the United States out of the war. The so-called "peace note" had a profound effect on the markets when it became public. But Lawson charged that advance notice of the note had made substantial profits for politically connected investors.

In the firestorm that followed, Congress did its usual best to not find out the truth. The controversy died out, tarring only a handful of people. But the incident further alienated Lawson from his former colleagues.

By 1922, Lawson was nearing the end of his life. His wife had died in 1906, a blow from which he never completely recovered. At Dreamworld, he set a place at dinner for his wife every night for sixteen years after her death. The sprawling complex had grown to include riding stables, a gymnasium, barns for horses and sheep, and kennels for his dogs. He had an enormous library.

Several times Lawson dabbled in the stock markets, but his old enemies bested him. In 1922, he and his partner sold their seat on the Boston Stock Exchange to a firm where Lawson could speculate in stocks less visibly. In May of 1922, the firm went bankrupt and its president committed suicide. Now with dwindling funds, the reclusive Lawson put his Dreamworld and all its contents up for sale in an October auction.

Gold and silver pieces, master artworks, sumptuous furnishings, plus the 210-acre grounds and buildings were all to be sold off. Unable to face the humiliation, Lawson fled to Southwest Harbor to stay with his sister. Then he disappeared. The disappearance was a last stroke of publicity for Lawson, and it kept the auction of his property in the headlines in the days before the sale.

Thanks to the ballyhoo over his "disappearance," the sale cleared all of Lawson's debts and left him comfortably well off. He resurfaced in a more modest home in Boston's Fenway and vowed he would conquer Wall Street once more, but it would never happen. At the auction of Dreamworld, Lawson's friends purchased a small cottage and grounds known as The Nest. It was where Lawson and his wife had retired when they wanted to be alone, and it contained the mausoleum where she was buried.

In 1925, Thomas Lawson died. His remains were buried in the tomb at The Nest where his wife lay.

S. Weir Mitchell: The Quack with the Midas Touch

Dr. Silas Weir Mitchell's strange ideas about women's health and his bizarre treatments for their nerves actually helped propel him to the pinnacle of Mount Desert society.

As a doctor, Silas Weir Mitchell made a wonderful novelist, and he spent his long summers in Bar Harbor writing fiction. He had connections in both literary and scientific circles, as well as in Philadelphia society, which allowed him to bring interesting and important people to the island. Almost as soon as he came to Bar Harbor in 1891, he became the leader of the so-called "walking and talking" set, the backbone of island society in that era.

Among the many pioneering medical theories that Mitchell espoused: Women who engaged in "over brainwork" would develop stunted bodies and contracted pelvises. Further, too much study quite probably led women to produce babies with large heads.

Mitchell and a group of colleagues contributed these thoughts to an essay on the coeducation of women in 1889. Mitchell didn't discourage women from obtaining advanced education but simply suggested they should be educated in womanly arts, such as homemaking, lest they find themselves married and unable to function. Women, he thought, shouldn't fill their heads with useless facts about science while their husbands went hungry for lack of a proper meal.

These days S. Weir Mitchell's reputation has been rehabilitated somewhat by defenders who say he was overly maligned by exaggerations of his methods. But still, he doesn't exactly have a strong professional following. The best that can be said for him is that he was a product of his times and not out to harm anyone.

Mitchell was born in Philadelphia in 1829, the son of prominent physician John Kearsley Mitchell. After fumbling about for a profession, he followed in his father's footsteps and became a doctor. He specialized in nervous disorders and, during the Civil War, devoted much of his practice to treating soldiers with nerve injuries. After the war, he cultivated a wealthy class of patients, many of them women, who suffered from various neuroses such as depression, anxiety, obsessive behavior, and hypochondria. To help his patients recover, he developed what was known as the "rest cure."

The cure involved isolating the patients—even preventing them from reading and writing in extreme cases. Mitchell confined them to bed for six weeks to two months and force-fed (rectally, if necessary) a diet heavy in fat and milk, with added doses of strychnine and arsenic. His patients were also subjected to massages and electro stimulation to keep their muscles from atrophying and icepacks to stimulate blood flow. Otherwise, they were to be kept completely quiet and alone.

Mitchell pioneered the treatment on soldiers to heal wounded nerves so painful the victims couldn't focus on anything else. He expanded it to otherwise healthy women when demand developed for the cure. The treatment was just the course of action for a pouty or sullen wife.

The cure had a moral as well as a medical component. It was designed to adjust the attitude of the patient. Mitchell concluded that certain women enjoyed lying abed and sewing, reveling in sympathy while keeping life interesting by occasionally entertaining friends and family at bedside.

The rest cure, by contrast, created an aversion to lying in bed to disrupt "the whole daily drama of the sick-room, with its little selfishnesses and its craving for sympathy and indulgence," he wrote in his book, *Fat and Blood*.

Part of Mitchell's philosophy held that the physician must be forceful and authoritarian in giving treatment. He had no use for hypochondriacs and once boasted of setting one patient's bed on fire to get her up. He threatened to rape another if she didn't get out of bed. And in at least one instance he managed to kill a patient. Convinced she was exaggerating her physical ailments, he had her force-fed his fat-milk diet until she died.

Charlotte Perkins Gilman wrote the short story *The Yellow Wallpaper* in 1890 about Mitchell's rest cure. It nearly drove her insane as she stared at the yellow wallpaper in her room while undergoing the treatment.

Some of his more vocal critics charged that Mitchell's goal was to create a more subservient woman—something Mitchell's own words seemed to support.

"The woman's desire to be on a level of competition with man and to assume his duties is, I am sure, making mischief," Mitchell wrote in his book *Doctor and Patient*.

For men he offered a rest cure that encouraged mental stimulation. And for those who needed it, he created a "West Cure," which involved the overstressed man traveling west and engaging in physical activity such as calf roping, horse riding, and hunting. The goal was for the man to return refreshed and ready for the rigors of the business world.

Still, some women as well as men commended Mitchell for his treatment. The well-to-do and the socially prominent lined up for it. Teddy Roosevelt, Walt Whitman, Jane Addams (Mitchell's summer neighbor in Bar Harbor), and Virginia Woolf all jumped at the chance—voluntarily—to take the cure.

When Mitchell wasn't curing people, he was busy writing. Though he wrote many books (often featuring hysterical women) his masterpiece was *Hugh Wynne, Free Quaker*, a historical novel set in Philadelphia during the American Revolution.

Mitchell mainly did his writing during his long summer vacations. He had been a regular at Newport up until 1891, when he grew tired of its nouveau riche residents. That year, he visited Bar Harbor for the first time. He had obtained New York Bishop William Doane's blessing, and he quickly became the doyen of Bar Harbor's emerging elite.

Each year Mitchell would set a course for Bar Harbor from Philadelphia trailed by a gaggle of society ladies who couldn't bear to be separated from him and his healing arts. One such visitor was Anna Livingston-Reade Street Morton, wife of the US vice president, Levi Morton. Mrs. Morton, a repeat patient for the rest cure, was just the right sort of person Mitchell encouraged in Bar Harbor society.

When Mitchell wasn't curing his patients or writing or walking and talking, he took a leading role in improving Bar Harbor to make it more to his and his friends' liking. The whole island needed a brushup to conform to the standards of the incoming flock of visitors. Though automobiles were acceptable for cities, they needed to be prohibited on Mount Desert. Though alcohol flowed freely in the homes of the wealthy summer visitors, the Maine laws on prohibition needed to be maintained.

S. Weir Mitchell joined the Village Improvement Association along with George Vanderbilt and John Stewart Kennedy. The association worked to eliminate some of the sites that the summer residents considered eyesores. They leafleted children with instructions on proper behavior and warnings against littering.

The Village Improvement Association held special contempt for the American Indians who had been frequenting Bar Harbor and Acadia for centuries. The Association ousted the Indians from their downtown location off to a small corner of town.

Right up through 1914, Mitchell cranked out his books by the dozen and, in later years, handed off the duties at his Philadelphia clinic to his son. He had one brush with financial disaster when a bank he directed fell to ruin under bad management, and he had to tap his savings to prop it up. But at the time of his death, Mitchell's fortunes were still strong and his books still selling. It would be a few more years before his rest cure theories were dismissed as quackery.

Sources

A book of this kind finds its inspiration in countless sources accumulated over many years, and any effort at providing an exhaustive list of them is bound to be a flawed effort. To those reporters and authors we have overlooked in this acknowledgment, please accept our apologies.

In addition to the list of print sources listed below, we would like to acknowledge several web resources that were invaluable sources of inspiration and information:

The Downeast Dilettante

The New York Social Diary

The Friends of Island History

Below you'll find a list of resources that contributed to each of the chapters included in this book.

It's a Rich Man's World
The Man Who Stole Cadillac Mountain
The Man Who Found the Money: John Stewart Kennedy and the Financing of the Western Railroads by Saul Engelbourg and Leonard Bushkoff
James J. Hill: Empire Builder of the Northwest by Michael P. Malone
The Story of Acadia by George B. Dorr

The Fabulous McLeans and Their Hoodoo Diamond
Father Struck It Rich by Evalyn Walsh McLean
Acadia: The Complete Guide by James Kaiser
New York Daily News (Newspaper)
Boston Globe (Newspaper)

Joseph Pulitzer and His Tower of Silence
Kids on Strike! by Susan Campbell Bartoletti

The Stotesburys Send the Better People Packing
Whitemarsh Hall: The Estate of Edward T. Stotesbury by Charles G. Zwicker and Edward C. Zwicker

Pearson's Magazine
Rothstein: The Life, Times, and Murder of the Criminal Genius Who Fixed the 1919 World Series by David Pietrusza

LOVE, MARRIAGE, AND MISERY
J. P. Morgan Can't Fool Anyone
Morgan: American Financier by Jean Strouse
Town Topics (Newspaper)
The Last Resorts by Cleveland Amory

The Alimony King and His Alimony Queen
Bethesda Magazine

Breaking Up Is Hard to Do–Vanderbilt Style
The First Tycoon: The Epic Life of Cornelius Vanderbilt by T. J. Stiles
A Voice from Old New York: A Memoir of My Youth by Louis Auchincloss
Gossip about the Vanderbilts: Some Stories of the Sons That Are True Enough to Be Interesting, Commercial Gazette, Scrapbook, William H. Vanderbilt New York City and Brooklyn Papers, Vol. 2, Shelburne Farms Archives
Fortune's Children: The Fall of the House of Vanderbilt by Arthur T. Vanderbilt
The Vanderbilt Women: Dynasty of Wealth, Glamour and Tragedy by Clarice Stasz
Alva Vanderbilt Belmont: Unlikely Champion of Women's Rights by Sylvia D. Hoffert

The Many, Many, Many Loves of Cornelia Baxter
Bar Harbor Times (Newspaper)
Bar Harbor Record (Newspaper)
Bar Harbor Mount Desert Herald (Newspaper)
San Francisco Chronicle (Newspaper)
Brooklyn Daily Eagle (Newspaper)

The Wealthy Teenage Widow Who Wanted to Be Alone
Gilded Lives, Fatal Voyage: The Titanic's First-Class Passengers and Their World by High Brewster
Titanic: Women and Children First by Judith B. Geller
Canton Daily News (Newspaper)
New York Times (Newspaper)

POLITICAL BAD BOYS
Daddies Dearest
The Indiana State Sentinel (Newspaper)
Terre Haute Sentinel (Newspaper)
Life of James G. Blaine: "The Plumed Knight," by Willis Fletcher Johnson
Continental Liar from the State of Maine: James G. Blaine by Neil Rolde

No Dynasty for Jimmie
Continental Liar from the State of Maine: James G. Blaine by Neil Rolde
Brooklyn Eagle (Newspaper)
New York Times (Newspaper)
San Francisco Chronicle (Newspaper)

The Duchess of Dix Island
Brooklyn Eagle (Newspaper)
New York Times (Newspaper)
Congressional Record
Philadelphia Inquirer (Newspaper)
Bar Harbor Times (Newspaper)
Bar Harbor Record (Newspaper)
Bar Harbor Mount Desert Herald (Newspaper)

The Louisiana Lottery King Builds a Seaside Mansion
New York Times (Newspaper)
Hulls Cove Residence, Sand Beach Residence, and Lunt House Acadia National Park, National Register Determination of Eligibility
New York Journal (Newspaper)
New York Sun (Newspaper)

Mount Desert Welcomes the KKK
Chebacco, Magazine of the Mount Desert Island Historical Society
Bar Harbor Times (Newspaper)
Bar Harbor Record (Newspaper)
Bar Harbor Mount Desert Herald (Newspaper)

Nelson Rockefeller Lands on the Rocks
Time magazine
New York Times (Newspaper)
On His Own Terms: A Life of Nelson Rockefeller by Richard Norton Smith

CRIMES AND MISDEMEANORS
A Royal Mess: The Harry Oakes Murder
Bar Harbor Times (Newspaper)
Bar Harbor Record (Newspaper)
Bar Harbor Mount Desert Herald (Newspaper)
The Life and Death of Sir Harry Oakes by Geoffrey Bocca
A Conspiracy of Crowns by Alfred De Marigny with Mickey Herskowitz

A Serial Killer Is Born
San Francisco Chronicle (Newspaper)
Chicago Tribune (Newspaper)
It Gave Everybody Something to Do by Louise Thoresen

The Flatiron Murder
Bar Harbor Times (Newspaper)
Bar Harbor Record (Newspaper)
Bar Harbor Mount Desert Herald (Newspaper)
Ellsworth American (Newspaper)

Prohibition Follies: Three for the Road
Bar Harbor in the Roaring Twenties: From Village Life to the High Life on Mount Desert Island by Luann Yette
Chebacco, Magazine of the Mount Desert Island Historical Society
Bar Harbor Times (Newspaper)
Bar Harbor Record (Newspaper)
Bar Harbor Mount Desert Herald (Newspaper)
Bangor Daily News (Newspaper)
Kennebec Journal (Newspaper)
Portland Press Herald (Newspaper)

ODDITIES, MISFITS AND MISCELLANEOUS DOWNFALLS
You Can't Get Good Help
Baymeath by Louise Bowen
Bar Harbor Times (Newspaper)
Bar Harbor Record (Newspaper)
Bar Harbor Mount Desert Herald (Newspaper)

Abraham Somes and the Rum
The Story of Mount Desert Island, Maine by Samuel Eliot Morrison
Indians in Eden by Bunny McBride

Jackson Lab's Dr. Jekyll and Mr. Hyde
Giving It All Away: The Story of William W. Cook and His Michigan Law Quadrangle by Margaret A. Leary
Bar Harbor Times (Newspaper)
Bar Harbor Record (Newspaper)
Bar Harbor Mount Desert Herald (Newspaper)
Congressional Record

The Many, Many Mad, Mad Hoyts
Elinor Wylie, A Life Apart: A Biography by Stanley Olson
The Last Mrs. Astor: A New York Story by Frances Kiernan
A Private Madness: The Genius of Elinor Wylie by Evelyn Helmick Hively
William Brockman Bankhead by Paul Goodridge
Flawed Light: American Women Poets and Alcohol by Brett Candlish Millier
Ford Madox Ford: A Dual Life: Volume II: The After-War World by Max Saunders
Boston Daily Globe (Newspaper)

Bernardsville News (Newspaper)
Ames Daily Tribune (Newspaper)
Washington Post (Newspaper)

They Came, They Summered, They Mystified
Bar Harbor Times (Newspaper)
Bar Harbor Record (Newspaper)
Bar Harbor Mount Desert Herald (Newspaper)
New York Times (Newspaper)

INDEX

ABOUT THE AUTHORS

Dan and Leslie Landrigan are the writers behind the *New England Historical Society* blog. Since its inception in 2014, the blog—dedicated to the exploration and promotion of New England history—has hosted more than three million visitors. With backgrounds in journalism and publishing, they now live on the coast in Stonington, Maine, where they pursue their passionate interest in history.